GOD AND AMERICA'S LEADERS

Brad O'Leary
GOD AND
AMERICA'S
LEADERS

*A Collection of Quotations by America's Presidents
and Founding Fathers on God and Religion*

WND Books

God & America's Leaders

WND Books

Published by WorldNetDaily

Washington, D.C.

Copyright © 2010
Brad O'Leary

Jacket design by Linda Daly
Interior design by Neuwirth & Associates, Inc.

WND Books are distributed to the trade by:
Midpoint Trade Books
27 West 20th Street, Suite 1102
New York, NY 10011

WND Books are available at special discounts for bulk purchases. WND Books, Inc. also publishes books in electronic formats. For more information call (541) 474-1776 or visit www.wndbooks.com.

First Edition

ISBN 13 Digit: 978-1-935071-26-6

Library of Congress information available

Printed in the United States of America

10 9 8 7 6 5 4 3 2 1

TABLE OF CONTENTS

PREFACE

The quotations contained in this book on God by our Founding Fathers and our country's leaders underscore the principles that were the foundation of this country. Even though a 2007 Gallup Poll shows that nine out of ten Americans believe in God, strangely enough there are those who are convinced that the bedrock of the creation of the United States of America is based solely on secular principles rather than religious ones.

There is a reason why the Ten Commandments, Scripture quotations, and beautiful artwork depicting biblical scenes are in this country's Capitol, the Supreme Court, and other federal buildings. Our early U.S. presidents were strong believers in God. For instance, president John Quincy Adams became one of the presidents of the American Bible Society. He wrote, in an address to the Bible Society, "The Bible carries with it the history of the creation, the fall and redemption of man, and discloses to him, in the infant born at Bethlehem, the legislator and savior of the world."

Our Declaration of Independence was, undoubtedly, a political document. But it also emerged in a time when the Bible was the principal literary record. The Bible had a powerful influence on the thoughts contained in the Declaration, and this fact shouldn't be ignored. While the words in the Declaration did not come directly from the Bible, the sentiment that was underneath what was expressed came from the one book that was read throughout the colonies—the Bible.

It has been said that human government needs God and faith to survive; I couldn't agree more. The Declaration pointedly says what will provide success: "With a prayer of reliance on divine providence." George Washington noted that "religion and morality are indispensable supports . . . let us with caution indulge the supposition that morality can be maintained without religion." Early on, the Bible came with settlers to Jamestown and Plymouth. The colonists brought their Bibles as they immigrated to a new land. When the Revolution came, the influence of the Bible was deep and profound. The signers of the Declaration of Independence knew their Bible well.

A shortage of Bibles was created when the War for Independence raged because there was no trade with England, from which most Bibles came. The newly constituted Continental Congress had a committee that reported "the use of the Bible is so universal and its importance so great that . . . the committee recommends that Congress will order the Committee of Commerce to import 20,000 Bibles." The Bibles were to come from Holland, Scotland, and elsewhere "into the parts of the States of the Union." And the Congress gave such an order on September 11, 1777. The president of the Continental Congress was Elias Boudinot, who also was the chief founder of the American Bible Society and its first president.

None of this is to suggest that America was founded as a theocracy or that religion should direct national policy. However, people who believe in God can make a powerful witness to equality, fairness, decency, and charity. The authors of the United States of America believed in God and in religious liberty. Faith and the Bible are not to be banished from the public square if we are to honor the power of faith to change lives for the better and to create a society where all are created equal and can be part of the "pursuit of happiness."

It was James Madison who said, "We have staked the future of all of our political institutions upon the capacity of mankind for self-government . . . according to the Ten Commandments of God." Abraham Lincoln was clear about his beliefs, saying, "We have been the recipients of the choicest bounties of heaven. . . . But we have forgotten God. We have vainly imagined that all these blessings were produced by some superior wisdom and virtue of our own."

We should remember a tradition started by George Washington. Our first president was sworn into office with his hand on an open Bible. At the conclusion of his oath, he closed his eyes and said, in a prayerful voice, "So help me God." As he uttered those words, he kissed the Bible.

Even the Liberty Bell has a biblical tie. These words are inscribed on the bell: "Proclaim Liberty through all the land to all the inhabitants thereof . . ." (Lev. 25:10).

The Bible has, indeed, played an essential role in the creation of the United States, and it continues to provide the moral compass for our nation. As Andrew Jackson was dying, he looked at the family Bible and said to his doctor, "That book, sir, is the rock on which our Republic rests."

—Brad O'Leary

GOD AND AMERICA'S LEADERS

THE 1st AMENDMENT

Religious references in the constitutions of
the thirteen original colonies:

· CONNECTICUT CONSTITUTION ·

Preamble.

The People of Connecticut acknowledging with gratitude, the good providence of God, in having permitted them to enjoy a free government; do, in order more effectually to define, secure, and perpetuate the liberties, rights and privileges which they have derived from their ancestors; hereby, after a careful consideration and revision, ordain and establish the following constitution and form of civil government.

RELIGION CLAUSES

Article I, section 3.

The exercise and enjoyment of religious profession and worship, without discrimination, shall forever be free to all persons in the state; provided, that the right hereby declared and established, shall not be so construed as to excuse acts of licentiousness, or to justify practices inconsistent with the peace and safety of the state.

Article I, section 20.
No person shall be denied the equal protection of the law nor be subjected to segregation or discrimination in the exercise or enjoyment of his or her civil or political rights because of religion, race, color, ancestry, national origin, sex or physical or mental disability.

Article VI, section 7.
The general assembly may provide by law for voting in the choice of any officer to be elected or upon any question to be voted on at an election by qualified voters of the state who are unable to appear at the polling place on the day of election because of absence from the city or town of which they are inhabitants or because of sickness or physical disability or because the tenets of their religion forbid secular activity.

Article VII.
It being the right of all men to worship the Supreme Being, the Great Creator and Preserver of the Universe, and to render that worship in a mode consistent with the dictates of their consciences, no person shall by law be compelled to join or support, nor be classed or associated with, any congregation, church or religious association. No preference shall be given by law to any religious society or denomination in the state. Each shall have and enjoy the same and equal powers, rights and privileges, and may support and maintain the ministers or teachers of its society or denomination, and may build and repair houses for public worship.

Article XI, section 1.
Members of the general assembly, and all officers, executive and judicial, shall, before they enter on the duties of their respective offices, take the following oath or affirmation, to wit:

You do solemnly swear (or affirm, as the case may be) that you will support the constitution of the United States, and the constitution of the state of Connecticut, so long as you continue a citizen thereof; and that you will faithfully discharge, according to law, the duties of the office of . . . to the best of your abilities. So help you God.

· DELAWARE CONSTITUTION ·

Preamble.

Through Divine goodness, all people have by nature the rights of worshiping and serving their Creator according to the dictates of their consciences, of enjoying and defending life and liberty, of acquiring and protecting reputation and property, and in general of obtaining objects suitable to their condition, without injury by one to another; and as these rights are essential to their welfare, for due exercise thereof, power is inherent in them; and therefore all just authority in the institutions of political society is derived from the people, and established with their consent, to advance their happiness; and they may for this end, as circumstances require, from time to time, alter their Constitution of government.

RELIGION CLAUSES

Article 1, section 1.

Although it is the duty of all persons frequently to assemble together for the public worship of Almighty God; and piety and morality, on which the prosperity of communities depends, are hereby promoted; yet no person shall or ought to be compelled to attend any religious worship, to contribute to the erection or support of any place of worship, or to the maintenance of any ministry, against his or her own free will and consent; and no power shall or ought to be vested in or assumed by any magistrate that shall in any case interfere with, or in any manner control the rights of conscience, in the free exercise of religious worship, nor a preference given by law to any religious societies, denominations, or modes of worship.

Article I, section 2.
No religious test shall be required as a qualification to any office, or public trust, under this State.

The rights, privileges, immunities and estates of religious societies and corporate bodies, except as herein otherwise provided, shall remain as if the Constitution of this State had not been altered.

· GEORGIA CONSTITUTION ·

Preamble.
To perpetuate the principles of free government, insure justice to all, preserve peace, promote the interest and happiness of the citizen and of the family, and transmit to posterity the enjoyment of liberty, we the people of Georgia, relying upon the protection and guidance of Almighty God, do ordain and establish this Constitution.

RELIGION CLAUSES

Article I, section 1, paragraph 3.
Each person has the natural and inalienable right to worship God, each according to the dictates of that person's own

conscience; and no human authority should, in any case, control or interfere with such right of conscience.

Article I, section 1, paragraph 4.
No inhabitant of this state shall be molested in person or property or be prohibited from holding any public office or trust on account of religious opinions; but the right of freedom of religion shall not be so construed as to excuse acts of licentiousness or justify practices inconsistent with the peace and safety of the state.

Article I, section 2, paragraph 7.
No money shall ever be taken from the public treasury, directly or indirectly, in aid of any church, sect, cult, or religious denomination or of any sectarian institution.

· MARYLAND CONSTITUTION ·

Preamble.
We, the People of the State of Maryland, grateful to Almighty God for our civil and religious liberty, and taking into our serious consideration the best means of establishing a good Constitution in this State for the sure foundation and more permanent security thereof, declare. . . .

RELIGION CLAUSES

Article 36.
That as it is the duty of every man to worship God in such manner as he thinks most acceptable to him, all persons are equally entitled to protection in their religious liberty; wherefore,

no person ought by any law to be molested in his person or estate, on account of his religious persuasion, or profession, or for his religious practice, unless, under the color of religion, he shall disturb the good order, peace or safety of the State, or shall infringe the laws of morality, or injure others in their natural, civil or religious rights; nor ought any person to be compelled to frequent, or maintain, or contribute, unless on contract, to maintain, any place of worship, or any ministry; nor shall any person, otherwise competent, be deemed incompetent as a witness, or juror, on account of his religious belief; provided, he believes in the existence of God, and that under his dispensation such person will be held morally accountable for his acts, and be rewarded or punished therefor either in this world or in the world to come.

Nothing shall prohibit or require the making reference to belief in, reliance upon, or invoking the aid of God or a Supreme Being in any governmental or public document, proceeding, activity, ceremony, school, institution, or place.

Article 37.

That no religious test ought ever to be required as a qualification for any office of profit or trust in this State, other than a declaration of belief in the existence of God; nor shall the Legislature prescribe any other oath of office than the oath prescribed by this Constitution.

Article 39.

That the manner of administering an oath or affirmation to any person, ought to be such as those of the religious persuasion, profession, or denomination, of which he is a member, generally esteem the most effectual confirmation by the attestation of the Divine Being.

· MASSACHUSETTS CONSTITUTION ·

Preamble.

We, therefore, the people of Massachusetts, acknowledging, with grateful hearts, the goodness of the great Legislator of the universe, in affording us, in the course of his providence, an opportunity, deliberately and peaceably, without fraud, violence or surprise, of entering into an original, explicit, and solemn compact with each other; and of forming a new constitution of civil government, for ourselves and posterity; and devoutly imploring his direction in so interesting a design, do agree upon, ordain and establish the following Declaration of Rights, and Frame of Government, as the Constitution of the Commonwealth of Massachusetts.

RELIGION CLAUSES

Article II.

It is the right as well as the duty of all men in society, publicly, and at stated seasons to worship the Supreme Being, the great Creator and Preserver of the universe. And no subject shall be hurt, molested, or restrained, in his person, liberty, or estate, for worshiping God in the manner and season most agreeable to the dictates of his own conscience; or for his religious profession or sentiments; provided he doth not disturb the public peace, or obstruct others in their religious worship.

Article VI, Amendment.

Instead of the oath of allegiance prescribed by the constitution, the following oath shall be taken and subscribed by every person chosen or appointed to any office, civil or military under the government of this commonwealth, before he shall enter on the duties of his office, to wit:

> "I, A. B., do solemnly swear, that I will bear true faith and allegiance to the Commonwealth of Massachusetts, and will support the constitution thereof. So help me God."

Provided, That when any person shall be of the denomination called Quakers, and shall decline taking said oath, he shall make his affirmation in the foregoing form, omitting the word "swear" and inserting instead thereof the word "affirm;" and omitting the words "So help me God," and subjoining, instead thereof, the words "This I do under the pains and penalties of perjury."

Article XI, Amendment.
Instead of the third article of the bill of rights, the following modification and amendment thereof is substituted.

> "As the public worship of God and instructions in piety, religion and morality, promote the happiness and prosperity of a people and the security of a republican government;—therefore, the several religious societies of this commonwealth, whether corporate or unincorporate, at any meeting legally warned and holden for that purpose, shall ever have the right to elect their pastors or religious teachers. To contract with them for their support. To raise money for erecting and repairing houses for public worship, for the maintenance of religious instruction, and for the payment of necessary expenses: and all persons belonging to any religious society shall be taken and held to be members, until they shall file with the clerk of such society, a written notice, declaring the dissolution of their membership, and thenceforth shall not be liable for any grant

or contract which may be thereafter made, or entered into by such society: —and all religious sects and denominations, demeaning themselves peaceably, and as good citizens of the commonwealth, shall be equally under the protection of the law; and no subordination of any one sect or denomination to another shall ever be established by law."

· New Hampshire Constitution ·

RELIGION CLAUSES

Part First, article 5.
Every individual has a natural and unalienable right to worship God according to the dictates of his own conscience, and reason; and no subject shall be hurt, molested, or restrained, in his person, liberty, or estate, for worshiping God in the manner and season most agreeable to the dictates of his own conscience; or for his religious profession, sentiments, or persuasion; provided he doth not disturb the public peace or disturb others in their religious worship.

Part First, article 6.
As morality and piety, rightly grounded on high principles, will give the best and greatest security to government, and will lay, in the hearts of men, the strongest obligations to due subjection; and as the knowledge of these is most likely to be propagated through a society, therefore, the several parishes, bodies, corporate, or religious societies shall at all times have the right of electing their own teachers, and of contracting with them for their support or maintenance, or both. But no person shall ever be compelled to pay towards the support of the schools of any sect or denomination. And every person, denomination or

sect shall be equally under the protection of the law; and no subordination of any one sect, denomination or persuasion to another shall ever be established.

• NEW JERSEY CONSTITUTION •

No person shall be deprived of the inestimable privilege of worshiping Almighty God in a manner agreeable to the dictates of his own conscience; nor under any pretense whatever be compelled to attend any place of worship contrary to his faith and judgment; nor shall any person be obliged to pay tithes, taxes, or other rates for building or repairing any church or churches, place or places of worship, or for the maintenance of any minister or ministry, contrary to what he believes to be right or has deliberately and voluntarily engaged to perform.

There shall be no establishment of one religious sect in preference to another; no religious or racial test shall be required as a qualification for any office or public trust.

No person shall be denied the enjoyment of any civil or military right, nor be discriminated against in the exercise of any civil or military right, nor be segregated in the militia or in the public schools, because of religious principles, race, color, ancestry or national origin.

• NEW YORK CONSTITUTION •

Preamble.
We the people of the State of New York, grateful to Almighty God for our Freedom, in order to secure its blessings, do establish this constitution.

RELIGION CLAUSES

Article I, section 3.

The free exercise and enjoyment of religious profession and worship, without discrimination or preference, shall forever be allowed in this state to all humankind; and no person shall be rendered incompetent to be a witness on account of his or her opinions on matters of religious belief; but the liberty of conscience hereby secured shall not be so construed as to excuse acts of licentiousness, or justify practices inconsistent with the peace or safety of this state.

Article I, section 11.

No person shall be denied the equal protection of the laws of this state or any subdivision thereof. No person shall, because of race, color, creed or religion, be subjected to any discrimination in his or her civil rights by any other person or by any firm, corporation, or institution, or by the state or any agency or subdivision of the state.

Article XIII, section 1.

Members of the legislature, and all officers, executive and judicial, except such inferior officers as shall be by law exempted, shall, before they enter on the duties of their respective offices, take and subscribe the following oath or affirmation: "I do solemnly swear (or affirm) that I will support the constitution of the United States, and the constitution of the State of New York, and that I will faithfully discharge the duties of the office of . . . , according to the best of my ability;" and no other oath, declaration or test shall be required as a qualification for any office of public trust, except that any committee of a political party may, by rule, provide for equal representation of the sexes on any such committee, and a state convention of a political party, at which candidates for public office are nominated, may, by rule, provide for equal representation of the sexes on any committee of such party.

· NORTH CAROLINA CONSTITUTION ·

Preamble.
We, the people of the State of North Carolina, grateful to Almighty God, the Sovereign Ruler of Nations, for the preservation of the American Union and the existence of our civil, political and religious liberties, and acknowledging our dependence upon him for the continuance of those blessings to us and our posterity, do, for the more certain security thereof and for the better government of this State, ordain and establish this Constitution.

RELIGION CLAUSES

Article I, section 1.
We hold it to be self-evident that all persons are created equal; that they are endowed by their Creator with certain inalienable rights; that among these are life, liberty, the enjoyment of the fruits of their own labor, and the pursuit of happiness.

Article I, section 13.
All persons have a natural and inalienable right to worship Almighty God according to the dictates of their own consciences, and no human authority shall, in any case whatever, control or interfere with the rights of conscience.

· PENNSYLVANIA CONSTITUTION ·

Preamble.

We, the people of the Commonwealth of Pennsylvania, grateful to Almighty God for the blessings of civil and religious liberty, and humbly invoking his guidance, do ordain and establish this Constitution.

RELIGION CLAUSES

Article I, section 3.

All men have a natural and indefeasible right to worship Almighty God according to the dictates of their own consciences; no man can of right be compelled to attend, erect or support any place of worship or to maintain any ministry against his consent; no human authority can, in any case whatever, control or interfere with the rights of conscience, and no preference shall ever be given by law to any religious establishments or modes of worship.

Article I, section 4.

No person who acknowledges the being of a God and a future state of rewards and punishments shall, on account of his religious sentiments, be disqualified to hold any office or place of trust or profit under this Commonwealth.

· RHODE ISLAND CONSTITUTION ·

Preamble.

We, the people of the State of Rhode Island and Providence Plantations, grateful to Almighty God for the civil and religious liberty which he hath so long permitted us to enjoy, and looking to him for a blessing upon our endeavors to secure and to transmit the same, unimpaired, to succeeding generations, do ordain and establish this Constitution of government.

RELIGION CLAUSES

Article I, section 3.

Whereas Almighty God hath created the mind free; and all attempts to influence it by temporal punishments or burdens, or by civil incapacitations, tend to beget habits of hypocrisy and meanness; and whereas a principal object of our venerable ancestors, in their migration to this country and their settlement of this state, was, as they expressed it, to hold forth a lively experiment that a flourishing civil state may stand and be best maintained with full liberty in religious concernments; we, therefore, declare that no person shall be compelled to frequent or to support any religious worship, place, or ministry whatever, except in fulfillment of such person's voluntary contract; nor enforced, restrained, molested, or burdened in body or goods; nor disqualified from holding any office; nor otherwise suffer on account of such person's religious belief; and that every person shall be free to worship God according to the dictates of such person's conscience, and to profess and by argument to maintain such person's opinion in matters of religion; and that the same shall in no wise diminish, enlarge, or affect the civil capacity of any person.

· South Carolina Constitution ·

RELIGION CLAUSES

Article I, section 2.

The General Assembly shall make no law respecting an establishment of religion or prohibiting the free exercise thereof, or abridging the freedom of speech or of the press; or the right of the people peaceably to assemble and to petition the government or any department thereof for a redress of grievances.

Article III, section 26.

Members of the General Assembly, and all officers, before they enter upon the duties of their respective offices, and all members of the bar, before they enter upon the practice of their profession, shall take and subscribe the following oath: "I do solemnly swear (or affirm) that I am duly qualified, according to the Constitution of this State, to exercise the duties of the office to which I have been elected, (or appointed), and that I will, to the best of my ability, discharge the duties thereof, and preserve, protect and defend the Constitution of this State and of the United States. So help me God."

Article VI, section 5.

Members of the General Assembly, and all officers, before they enter upon the duties of their respective offices, and all members of the bar, before they enter upon the practice of their profession, shall take and subscribe the following oath: "I do solemnly swear (or affirm) that I am duly qualified, according to the Constitution of this State, to exercise the duties of the office to which I have been elected, (or appointed), and that I will, to the best of my ability, discharge the duties thereof, and preserve, protect, and defend the Constitution of this State and of the United States. So help me God."

Article XIII, section 1.
The militia of this State shall consist of all able-bodied male citizens of the State between the ages of eighteen and forty-five years, except such persons as are now or may be exempted by the laws of the United States or this State, or who from religious scruples may be adverse to bearing arms, and shall be organized, officered, armed, equipped and disciplined as the General Assembly may by law direct.

· VIRGINIA CONSTITUTION ·

RELIGION CLAUSES

Article I, section 16.
That religion or the duty which we owe to our Creator, and the manner of discharging it, can be directed only by reason and conviction, not by force or violence; and, therefore, all men are equally entitled to the free exercise of religion, according to the dictates of conscience; and that it is the mutual duty of all to practice Christian forbearance, love, and charity towards each other. No man shall be compelled to frequent or support any religious worship, place, or ministry whatsoever, nor shall be enforced, restrained, molested, or burthened in his body or goods, nor shall otherwise suffer on account of his religious opinions or belief; but all men shall be free to profess and by argument to maintain their opinions in matters of religion, and the same shall in nowise diminish, enlarge, or affect their civil capacities. And the General Assembly shall not prescribe any religious test whatever, or confer any peculiar privileges or

advantages on any sect or denomination, or pass any law requiring or authorizing any religious society, or the people of any district within this Commonwealth, to levy on themselves or others, any tax for the erection or repair of any house of public worship, or for the support of any church or ministry; but it shall be left free to every person to select his religious instructor, and to make for his support such private contract as he shall please.

Article II, section 7.
All officers elected or appointed under or pursuant to this Constitution shall, before they enter on the performance of their public duties, severally take and subscribe the following oath or affirmation: "I do solemnly swear (or affirm) that I will support the Constitution of the United States, and the Constitution of the Commonwealth of Virginia, and that I will faithfully and impartially discharge all the duties incumbent upon me as . . . , according to the best of my ability (so help me God)."

Article IV, section 16.
The General Assembly shall not make any appropriation of public funds, personal property, or real estate to any church or sectarian society, or any association or institution of any kind whatever which is entirely or partly, directly or indirectly, controlled by any church or sectarian society. Nor shall the General Assembly make any like appropriation to any charitable institution which is not owned or controlled by the Commonwealth; the General Assembly may, however, make appropriations to nonsectarian institutions for the reform of youthful criminals and may also authorize counties, cities, or towns to make such appropriations to any charitable institution or association.

THE BIBLE & SCRIPTURES

Thus my beloved friends, hath God in his condescending grace appointed us to become his humble instruments in opening the eyes of the blind; in cheering the abodes of primeval darkness with the joyful sounds of redeeming love; in fulfilling the encouraging prophecy of the angel flying through the midst of heaven, having the everlasting Gospel in his hands, to preach to all nations, languages, tongues, and people on the earth.

—ELIAS BOUDINOT, president of the Continental Congress, 1782–1783; congressman from New Jersey, 1790–1795; and president of the American Bible Society (ABS), May 5, 1817.
W. P. Strickland, *History of the American Bible Society* (New York: 1849), pp. 349-350.

It is impossible to rightly govern the world without God and the Bible.

—GEORGE WASHINGTON, 1st U.S. president.
Henry Halley's Bible Handbook,
(Grand Rapids, MI: Zondervan, 1927, 1965), p. 18.

We now see Christians, in different countries, and of different denominations, spontaneously and cordially engaged in conveying the Scriptures, and the knowledge of salvation, to the heathen inhabitants of different regions. . . . From the nature, the tendency, and the results of these recent and singular changes, events, and institutions; from their coincidence, and admirable adjustment, as means for making known the holy Scriptures, and inculcating the will of the Divine and merciful Author, throughout the world; and from the devotedness with which they are carrying into operation, there is reason to conclude that they have been produced by him in whose hand are the hearts of all men. . . . They who march under the banners of Emmanuel have God with them; and consequently have nothing to fear.

> —JOHN JAY, president of the Continental Congress, 1778-1779;
> and 1st chief justice of the U.S. Supreme Court, 1789-1795.
> Letter to the American Bible Society, May 8, 1823.
> Johnston, *Correspondence of Jay*, pp. 4489-4492.

The Bible contains the most profound Philosophy, the most perfect Morality, and the most refined Policy, that ever was conceived upon earth. It is the most Republican Book in the World, and therefore I will still revere it.

> —JOHN ADAMS, 2nd U.S. president.
> Letter to Benjamin Rush, February 2, 1807.
> *Old Family Letters*, pp. 127-128.

I have examined all religions, as well as my narrow sphere, my straightened means, and my busy life, would allow; and the result is that the Bible is the best book in the World. It contains more of my little Philosophy than all the Libraries I have seen: and such Parts of it as I cannot reconcile to my little Phylosophy I postpone for further Investigation.

> —JOHN ADAMS, 2nd U.S. president.

Letter to Thomas Jefferson, December 25, 1813.
Cappon, *Adams-Jefferson Letters*, vol. 2, p. 412.

What suspicions of interpolation, and indeed of fabrication, might not be confuted if we had the originals! In an age or in ages when fraud, forgery, and perjury were considered as lawful means of propagating truth by philosophers, legislators, and theologians, what may not be suspected?

JOHN ADAMS, 2nd U.S. president.
Marginal note in John Disney's *Memoirs* (1785)
of Arthur Sykes. Haraszti, *Prophets of Progress*, p. 296.

Must a man possess a Library equal to that mentioned by St. Luke which he says the whole world would not contain and live to the age of Methusalah before he could read half of it before he can work out his salvation with fear and trembling? I find in the Old Testament and especially the new internal evidence of a philosophy a morality and a Polity which my head and heart embraces for its equity humanity and benevolence. This is my religion.

—JOHN ADAMS, 2nd U.S. president.
To Adrian van der Kemp, January 23, 1813. Adams Papers
(microfilm), reel 121, Library of Congress.

He who made all men hath made the truths necessary to human happiness obvious to all. . . . Our forefathers opened the Bible to all.

—SAMUEL ADAMS, Massachusetts delegate to the Continental Congress, 1775-1781. "American Independence," August 1, 1776. Speech delivered at the State House in Philadelphia.

In forming and settling my Belief relative to the Doctrines of Christianity, I adopted no Articles from Creeds, but such only as on careful Examination I found to be confirmed by the Bible.

—JOHN JAY, president of the Continental Congress, 1778-1779; and 1st chief justice of the U.S. Supreme Court, 1789-1795. Letter to Samuel Miller, February 18, 1822. Jay Papers (online edition), Columbia University Library.

Why, then, should not the Bible regain the place it once held as a school-book? Its morals are pure, its examples captivating and noble. The reverence for the sacred book, that is thus early impressed, lasts long, and probably, if not impressed in infancy, never takes firm hold of the mind.

—FISHER AMES, member of Congress from Massachusetts, 1789-1797. *The Christian Life and Character of the Civil Institutions of the United States*, 1864.

That precious book divine, by inspiration given, is the sun of the moral firmament, and will continue to be the life, the light, and the joy of men "till heavenly gloried break upon the view, in brighter worlds above."

—ENOCH L. FANCHER, ABS president and New York Supreme Court justice. To messengers A.D.F. Randolph, William H. Crosby, and Hiriam Forrester, December 14, 1885. Corresponding Secretary Files, American Bible Society (ABS) Archives.

When we reflect that the doctrines of the Bible brought to those shores our pilgrim fathers; that we owe to the Bible our glorious country; that our civil, religious, and social institutions are the legitimate offspring of the principles of the Bible; and that rational liberty can only be maintained by the dissemination of a religion that aims to fit men to govern themselves—the cause of the American Bible Society must commend itself to the sympathy and approbation of all.

—ABBOT LAWRENCE, ABS vice president
and U.S. congressman. To the ABS, May 5, 1819.
Corresponding Secretary Files, ABS Archives.

While spending a few days in New York, ... I took occasion to look in at the great exhibition of Mr. Edison's wonderful telephonic and phonographic instruments and experiments. I heard messages and music and voices from far distant places. ... It was all marvellous and seemed almost miraculous. ... I cannot help thinking, however, here to-day, as I look around on the volumes with which our shelves are crowded, how far more marvellous, how really miraculous, have been the preservation and transmission, through so many centuries, of the voices and messages and music which the Bible holds ever ready within its sacred covers, to communicate with all who have eyes to read or ears to hear. These priceless contents of the Old and New Testaments, with so much of the most ancient history, so much of the divinest poetry, so much of the sublimest prophecy and imagery, and with all their revelations of God and of Christ, have been preserved and transmitted from generation to generation, through so many ages, by no mere human ingenuity or instrumentality. To no earthly telephones or phonographs, but primarily, as Gladstone has recently written, to "pens and tongues commissioned from on high," is the world indebted for the story of creation and of the cross.

—ROBERT C. WINTHROP, ABS vice president, U.S. senator
and U.S. congressman. Address at the annual meeting of the
Massachusetts Bible Society, May 26, 1890. *Massachusetts Bible
Society Annual Report*, 1890, ABS Archives, p. 8.

We deal with one book,—if we may not rather call it a whole library of books. We certainly do not forget that there are fifty or sixty productions, and even more, written by forty or fifty different authors, in the single volume which is called the Bible. One book, notwithstanding, it still is, and ever will be—one in spirit, one in authority, one in its appeal to the acceptance, affection, and reverence of mankind.

> —ROBERT C. WINTHROP, ABS vice president, U.S. senator and U.S. congressman. In an address at the eighty-third annual meeting of the Massachusetts Bible Society, March 21, 1892. Massachusetts Bible Society Annual Report, 1892, ABS Archives, p. 7.

I will hazard the assertion that no man ever did, or ever will, become truly eloquent without being a constant reader of the Bible, and an admirer of the purity and sublimity of its language.

> —FISHER AMES, member of Congress from Massachusetts, 1789-1797. "Tribute to the Hon. Fisher Ames," *The Panoplist, and Missionary Magazine United*, Farrand, Mallary, and Co., vol. 1, June 1, 1809, p. 94.

Who of us does not feel assured that the volume, for whose unceasing publication and circulation we are organized to take part in providing, is destined still and ever to be counted as the Book of Books; the choicest of all possessions to those who have it, the most needed by those who have it not; the book which has
• inspired, and is inspiring, and will never fail to inspire, whatever is worthiest and most exalted in human thought, word, and act; affording at once the wisest counsels for the present, and the surest and only hopes and promises for the future!

> —ROBERT C. WINTHROP, ABS vice president, U.S. senator and U.S. congressman. Address at the annual meeting of the

Massachusetts Bible Society, May 28, 1883. *Massachusetts Bible Society Annual Report*, 1883, ABS Archives, p. 9.

Diffuse the knowledge of the Bible and the hungry will be fed, and the naked clothed. Diffuse the knowledge of the Bible and the stranger will be sheltered, the prisoner visited, and the sick ministered unto. Diffuse the knowledge of the Bible and Temperance will rest upon a surer basis than any mere private pledge or public statute.

—ROBERT C. WINTHROP, ABS vice president, U.S. senator and U.S. congressman. Address delivered at the annual meeting of the Massachusetts Bible Society in Boston, May 28, 1849. Robert Charles Winthrop, *Addresses and Speeches on Various occasions*, Little Brown & Co., 1852.

There is no subject on which people are readier to form rash opinions than religion. The Bible is the best corrective to these. A man should sit down to it with the determination of taking his lesson just as he finds it—of founding his creed upon the principle of "Thus saith the Lord," and deriving his every idea and his every impression of religious truth from the authentic record of God's will.

—HANNA [presumably MARK (MARCUS ALONZO)], American businessman and politician. Quoted in the *Bible Society Record*, vol. XXVIII, no. 3, March 15, 1883, p. 44.

The great translations of the Bible into the common tongue have appeared in stirring times; whether as cause, or consequence, or concomitant of these, it is not easy to say. But the Bible in the hands of the people has been associated with movement, and never with stagnation. I do not mean to assert that its influence is revolutionary. As a revelation of God's will and saving grace to man, it was doubtless a complete revolution for systems of ethics and religion, and also for thought and life. But as a social force, as revealing man to himself in his duties and rights, his capacity and destiny, it has been conservative and gradual in its effects. Its process has been by evolution rather than revolution.

—JOSHUA L. CHAMBERLAIN, ABS vice president and governor of Maine, at Wycliffe Semi-Millennial Commemoration, December 2, 1880. Reported in the *Bible Society Record*, vol. XXV, no. 12, December 1880, p. 179.

The highest historical probability can be adduced in support of the proposition, that, if it were possible to annihilate the Bible, and with it all its influences, we should destroy with it the whole spiritual system of the moral world, all our great moral ideas, refinement of manners, constitutional government, equitable administration and security of property, our schools, hospitals and benevolent associations, the press, the fine arts, the equality of the sexes, and the blessings of the fireside; in a word, all that distinguishes Europe and America from Turkey and hindosta.

—EDWARD EVERETT, American statesman and scholar. Quoted in the *Bible Society Record*, vol. XVII, no. 10, October 17, 1872, p. 156.

The whole hope of human progress is suspended on the ever growing influence of the Bible.

—WILLIAM H. SEWARD, American statesman. William Henry Seward. *The Life of William H. Seward with Selections from His Works*, (Redfield, 1855), p. 210.

I have always said, and always will say, that the studious perusal of the Sacred Volume will make better citizens, better fathers, and better husbands.

—THOMAS JEFFERSON, 2nd U.S. president. To Daniel Webster. Cambridge in the "*Centennial*" *Proceedings*, July 3, 1875, in celebration of the centennial anniversary of Washington's taking command of the Continental Army in Cambridge. Cammai, City Council, 1875, p. 106.

From the time that, at my mother's feet, or on my father's knee, I first learned to lisp verses from the Sacred Writings, they have been my daily study and vigilant contemplation. If there be anything in my style or thoughts to be commended, the credit is due to my kind parents in instilling into my mind an early love of the Scriptures.

Ah, my friend, the poetry of Isaiah, and Job, and habakkuk is beautiful indeed, but when you reach your sixty-ninth year, you will give more for the fourteenth or seventeenth chapter of John's Gospel, or for one of the Epistles, than for all the poetry of the Bible.

—DANIEL WEBSTER, American orator, lawyer, and statesman. Joseph Banvard, *The American Statesman: Or Illustrations of the Life and Character of Daniel Webster*, 1856, p. 294.

Never, perhaps, in the history of man, has the Bible, with its heavenly teachings, its consolations, and its hopes, appeared so adapted and so essential to the wellbeing of individuals and of nations, as at the present moment, when human passions are so rampant; radicalism, in its worst forms, so rife; when long established principles and ancient institutions are overturned; and when so much that is human seems tending to disintegration and ruin. But whether, in the agitations of nations, or the individual conflicts of life, the Bible is equally adapted and essential. It is everywhere especially needed in the present crisis of our own country. On the tented field and in the ship of war, where patriotic duty puts in constant jeopardy the life of the soldier and the sailor, is this blessed volume particularly needed. Greatly needed, too, are all its consolations and support among the mutilated, the sick, and the dying, in the hospitals. In the lone home, too, of the widow and the fatherless. . . are the healing and sustaining influences and gracious promises of the Bible especially needed. But above all, to the conscience-stricken soul, agonized under a deep sense of sin, and looking in vain elsewhere for relief, is the Bible indeed precious; for there alone is revealed the great truth, that in the infinite mercy of God through the merits of a crucified Saviour, can he find pardon and peace.

—LUTHER BRADISH, ABS president.
Address of the president at the ABS annual meeting,
May 14, 1863. Anniversary Addresses, ABS Archives.

Philosophy may boast of its influence in elevating the mind; yet nothing but the Bible can reach the ills of our fallen nature, and give the sufficient remedy.

—THEODORE FRELINGHUYSEN, U.S. senator and ABS
president. Address of the president at the ABS annual meeting,
May 10, 1860. Anniversary Addresses, ABS Archives.

The Bible has taken away the reproach that the Christian religion could not benefit a people until civilization had prepared the way. The truth is, there can be no sound and enduring civilization without it. Wherever the word of God has found favour, it has given wisdom and peace, and all that is excellent, and of good report.

—THEODORE FRELINGHUYSEN, U.S. senator and ABS president.
Ibid.

While there is much to alarm and afflict us in the political agitations of our country, one thing is of special comfort: in the cause of the Bible Society, we are still one—bound together by the bands of Christian kindness, animated by like hopes, earnest in like purposes, and cheered by the same sympathies. The Bible can harmonize discordant elements. It is of power to unite extremes, to reconcile differences and compose to peace. It subdues by weapons of light and love, that are mighty through God to the pulling down of strongholds and bringing every thought into captivity to the obedience of Christ. Nothing can withstand such influence.

—THEODORE FRELINGHUYSEN, U.S. senator and ABS
president. Address of the president at the ABS annual meeting,
May 9, 1861. Anniversary Addresses, ABS Archives.

There is a wonderful property in the *memory* which enables it, in old age, to recover the knowledge it had acquired in early life, after it had been apparently forgotten for forty or fifty years. Of how much consequence, then, must it be to fill the mind with that species of knowledge, in childhood and youth, which, when *recalled* in the decline of life, will support the soul under the infirmities of age, and smooth the avenues of approaching death! The Bible is the only book which is capable of affording this support to old age; and it is for this reason that we find it resorted to with so much diligence and pleasure by such old people as have read it in early life. I can recollect many instances of this kind, in persons who discovered no attachment to the

Bible in the meridian of their lives, who have, notwithstanding, spent the evening of them in reading no other book.

> —BENJAMIN RUSH, member of the Continental Congress, 1776-1777. *Essays, Literary, Moral and Philosophical,* Thomas and William Bradford, 1806, p. 97.

It is the truth of God, of the inspiration of his own Spirit. Its history, its doctrines, and all its principles are true. They can never deceive, nor mislead, nor disappoint us. Every promise is sure, every direction safe, and every requirement just, befitting, and seasonable. The Bible claims all this and abundantly sustains it. It has stood the test of scrutiny and of time. It has met the assaults of all its adversaries from ingenious infidelity to malignant mockery, and it stands to-day in its majesty, with heaven and earth confirming it, as the unshakable and incontestable word of the God of truth. Art and science, reason and philosophy, harmonize and concur in bearing witness to its absolute verity.

> —THEODORE FRELINGHUYSEN, U.S. senator and ABS president. Address of the president at the ABS annual meeting, May 12, 1859. Anniversary Addresses, ABS Archives.

Suppose a nation in some distant region should take the Bible for their only law book, and every member should regulate his conduct by the precepts there exhibited! Every member would be obliged in conscience, to temperance, frugality, and industry; to justice, kindness, and charity towards his fellow men; and to piety, love and reverence toward Almighty God. . . . What a Eutopia, what a Paradise would this region be.

> —JOHN ADAMS, 2nd U.S. president. In a diary entry February 22, 1756 L.H. Butterfield, ed., *Diary and Autobiography of John Adams.*

You ask me what Bible I take as the standard of my faith—the Hebrew, the Samaritan, the Old English translation, or what? I answer, the Bible containing the Sermon on the Mount—any Bible that I can . . . understand. The New Testament I have repeatedly read in the original Greek, in the Latin, in the Geneva Protestant, in Sacy's Catholic French translations, in Luther's German translations, in the common English Protestant, and in the Douay Catholic translations. I take any one of them for my standard of faith. . . .

—JOHN QUINCY ADAMS, 6th U.S. president and diplomat. In writing from London to Boston, after negotiating the Treaty of Ghent. Worthington Chauncey Ford, *Writings of John Quincy Adams* (New York: Macmillan, 1916), vol. 6, pp. 135-136.

The deluded heathen mother, as she offers her child to an unknown God against all the pleadings of the heart, witnesses to the sad necessity of the Bible. Human nature, in its griefs as well as in its joys and thankfulness, thirsts for an object on which to lean its dependence for relief and sympathy.

—THEODORE FRELINGHUYSEN, U.S. senator and ABS president. Address of the president at the ABS annual meeting, May 13, 1858. Anniversary Addresses, ABS Archives.

If the Bible did no other service, its clear revelations of man's immortal destiny would be beyond all price. That anxious and heretofore unresolved question is brought to light here, and stands out, clear and full, like the sun at noonday. But far more than this we owe to it. Its teaching reconciles God to man. It repairs the ruin of the great transgression. It assures of pardon by atonement, and remission of sin by the shedding of blood. And when the conscience sinks in despondency under the weight of its felt guilt, and fearfully asks how can man be just with God, it comes near to him with an infinite ransom.

—THEODORE FRELINGHUYSEN, U.S. senator and ABS president. Address of the president at the ABS annual meeting, May 14, 1857. Anniversary Addresses, ABS Archives.

The Bible will be an open volume whenever the rights of man, as a rational and accountable being, are asserted and enjoyed. Let him come to feel, with an enlightened conviction, that he must answer for himself in the judgment of the great day, and he will search the Scriptures with deep and anxious earnestness, and all the more resolvedly should any question his privilege or attempt to interrupt its exercise.

—THEODORE FRELINGHUYSEN, U.S. senator and ABS president. Ibid., p. 95.

Men are beginning to feel that to chain the Bible, or in any degree to restrain the free and full use of it as an open volume, is not only a reproach to human reason but an abridgment of human rights, at war alike with the laws of God and the inalienable privileges of an immortal and accountable creature.

—THEODORE FRELINGHUYSEN, U.S. senator and ABS president. Address of the president at the ABS annual meeting, May 10, 1849. Annual Report, 1849, ABS Archives, p. 96.

Every plea that can rouse the conscience, and every hope that can cheer and elevate the soul, has a record in the Bible.

—THEODORE FRELINGHUYSEN, U.S. senator and ABS president. Ibid., p. 87.

Let us ponder well and faithfully cherish the sentiment, that to protect and preserve our national and social privileges, we must have *a Bible influence*—the dominion and sway of sound principles that are of mighty energy, reaching the heart and deciding the issues of life. The code of ethics, to move us, must come to us on the authority of God and hold us to the responsibilities of the judgment; and this can be taught only from the Bible. All other schemes of reformation and improvement that are of human device, partake of human frailty. They are defective in the motives which bow the will and bind the conscience. But when God speaks in his word, men will hear, and multitudes heed to good purpose.

—THEODORE FRELINGHUYSEN, U.S. senator and
ABS president. Address of the president at the annual meeting,
May 14, 1846. *ABS Annual Report*, 1846, ABS Archives, p. 87.

Indeed all, it is believed, who have escaped from the bondage of a degrading superstition, and are now conscious of their deliverance, will, when addressed with fraternal kindness, cheerfully receive the Scriptures of Truth; while all who are not ashamed of their Puritan or their English descent, can scarcely fail to appreciate that holy Book, to whose benign influence may be attributed alike our national aggrandizement, our individual prosperity, and our hope of future blessedness.

—JOHN COTTON SMITH, Connecticut governor, member of
Congress and ABS president. Letter to the delegates at the
semi-annual meeting of the ABS, November 1, 1843.
Corresponding Secretary Files, ABS Archives.

If the discovery by Martin Luther of a Bible which lay neglected and covered with dust in a monastery, a book which, though a monk and a priest, he had never before seen, much less perused, if this heaven-directed discovery became both the incipient and final cause of what is emphatically called the Reformation, may we not confidently trust that the universal circulation of the same blessed book through the facilities of the press and the prayers of God's people, will eventually render that reformation EQUALLY UNIVERSAL?

—JOHN COTTON SMITH, Connecticut governor, member of Congress and ABS president. Ibid.

That book is indeed the best gift which God has ever given to man.

—ABRAHAM LINCOLN, 16th U.S. president. To a delegation of African Americans at Baltimore who presented him a Bible. David DeCamp Thompson, *Abraham Lincoln, The First American* (Eaton & Mains, 1894), p. 104.

One cannot study the story of the rise and development of the men and women who have been and continue to be pathfinders and benefactors of our people, and not recognize the outstanding place the Bible has occupied as the guide and inspiration of their thought and practice.

—FRANKLIN D. ROOSEVELT, 32nd U.S. president. Statement on the four hundredth anniversary of the printing of the English Bible, October 6, 1935.

I am profitably engaged in reading the Bible. Take all of this Book upon reason that you can, and the balance upon faith, and you will live and die a better man.

—ABRAHAM LINCOLN, 16th U.S. president. Baron Godfrey Rathbone and Benson Charnwood, *Abraham Lincoln* (H. Holt and Co., 1917), p. 440.

My custom is to read four or five chapters of the Bible every morning immediately after rising.... It seems to me the most suitable manner of beginning the day.... (It is an invaluable and inexhaustible mine of knowledge and virtue.)

—JOHN QUINCY ADAMS, 6th U.S. president and diplomat.
(J.M. Alden, 1850) *Letters of John Quincy Adams to His Son on The Bible and Its Teachings*, pp. 11, 12, 20.

That book, Sir, is the Rock upon which our republic rests.

—ANDREW JACKSON, 7th U.S. president.
Henry Halley, *Halley's Bible Handbook*
(Grand Rapids, MI: Zondervan, 1927, 1965), p. 18.

Sir, I am in the hands of a merciful God. I have full confidence in his goodness and mercy.... The Bible is true. I have tried to conform to its spirit as near as possible. Upon that sacred volume I rest my hope for eternal salvation, through the merits and blood of our blessed Lord and Saviour, Jesus Christ.

—ANDREW JACKSON, 7th U.S. president.
May 29, 1845, a few weeks before his death. Robert V. Remini,
Andrew Jackson and the Course of American Freedom, 1822-1832
(New York: Harper & Row, 1981), p. 519.

Our forebears were a people who read one book. Happily for them and for us that book was the Bible. From earliest childhood through all the years to advanced age it was for them the source of an amazing fortitude, the fountain of peaceful and lasting spiritual energy.

> —HARRY TRUMAN, 33rd U.S. president.
> ABS Archives, Presidential Autograph Collection.

To my mind the colporteurs, the agents of the Bible Society, tramping through countrysides or traveling by every sort of conveyance in every sort of land, carrying with them little cargoes of books containing the Word of God, and spreading them, seem like the shuttles in a great loom that is weaving the spirits of men together.

> —WOODROW WILSON, 28th U.S. president.
> Address at a celebration of the one hundredth
> anniversary of the founding of the ABS,
> Washington, May 7, 1916.

Every thinking man, when he thinks, realizes what a very large number of people tend to forget that the teachings of the Bible are so interwoven and entwined with our whole civic and social life that it would be literally—I do not mean figuratively, I mean literally—impossible for us to figure to ourselves what that life would be if these teachings were removed. We would lose almost all the standards by which we now judge both public and private morals. . . . Almost every man who has based his life-work added to the sum of human achievement of which the race is proud . . . has based his life-work largely upon the teachings of the Bible. Sometimes it was done unconsciously, more often consciously; and among the very greatest men a disproportionately large number have been diligent and close students of the Bible at first hand.

—THEODORE ROOSEVELT, 26th U.S. president.
Address to the Long Island Bible Society,
June 11, 1901. Ferdinand Cowle Inglehart,
"Theodore Roosevelt: The Man As I Knew Him,"
The Christian Herald, 1919, pp. 307 308.

The immense moral influence of the Bible, though of course infinitely the most important, is not the only power it has for good. In addition there is the unceasing influence it exerts on the side of good taste, of good literature, of proper sense of proportion, of simple and straightforward writing and thinking.

This is not a small matter in an age when there is a tendency to read much that even if not actually harmful on moral grounds is yet injurious, because it represents slip shod, slov enly thought and work; not the kind of serious thought, of serious expression, which we like to see in anything that goes into the fiber of our character.

—THEODORE ROOSEVELT, 26th U.S. president. Ibid., p. 312.

The Bible does not teach us to shirk difficulties, but to overcome them. That is a lesson that each one of us who has children is bound in honor to teach these children if he or she expects to see them become fitted to play the part of men and women in our world.

—THEODORE ROOSEVELT, 26th U.S. president. Ibid.

If we read the Bible aright, we read a book which teaches us to go forth and do the work of the Lord; to do the work of the Lord in the world as we find it; to try to make things better in this world, even if only a little better, because we have lived in it.

—THEODORE ROOSEVELT, 26th U.S. president. Ibid.

Where we have been truest and most consistent in obeying its precepts, we have attained the greatest measure of contentment and prosperity. . . . I commend its thoughtful and reverent reading to all our people.

—FRANKLIN D. ROOSEVELT, 32nd U.S. president.
Statement on the four hundredth anniversary of the
printing of the English Bible, October 6, 1935.

Hold fast to the Bible as the sheet anchor of your liberties; write its precepts on your hearts and *practice them in your lives.* To the influence of this book we are indebted for the progress made in true civilization, and to this we must look as our guide in the future.

—ULYSSES S. GRANT, 18th U.S. president and American general.
Emma Elizabeth Brown, *Life of Ulysses Simpson Grant,*
(D. Lothrope & Co., 1885), p. 335.

It is fitting that Universal Bible Sunday be observed annually on a day selected for that purpose by the American Bible Society. I congratulate the Society for sponsoring such a universal observance. Everyone of us must gain satisfaction and strength through the practical application of the teachings of Christianity, for they affect the individual lives of men and women everywhere. I am confirmed in my deep belief that God is marching on.

—FRANKLIN D. ROOSEVELT, 32nd U.S. president.
Letter to Mr. George William Brown at Bible House,
dated November 4, 1933. ABS Archives,
Presidential Autograph Collection.

The ministry of the Bible to individuals and to humanity holds a significant place, unique to the foundation of our country's history and foremost as a factor contributing to its greatness and success. We may well stress the value of lessons to be gained from its study.

—W.T. GARDINER, governor of Maine.
November 12, 1929. News Release on Universal Bible Sunday.

Humanity desperately needs today a moral and spiritual rebirth, a revitalization of religion. There is no sure way to this supreme goal save through adherence to the teaching of the Bible.

—CORDELL HULL, U.S. secretary of state.
The Jewish Spectator, Jewish Publishing Co., 1936, p. 4.

So great is my veneration for the Bible, that the earlier my children begin to read it the more confident will be my hope that they will prove useful citizens of their country and respectable members of society.

—JOHN QUINCY ADAMS, 6th U.S. president and diplomat.
Letters of John Quincy Adams to His Son, on the Bible and Its Teachings, John Quincy Adams, (J.M. Alden, 1850) p. 9.

We know that a great proportion of mankind are ignorant of the revealed will of God, and that they have strong claims to the sympathy and compassion which we, who are favored with it, feel and are manifesting for them. . . . By conveying the Bible to people thus circumstanced, we certainly do them a most interesting act of kindness.

—JOHN JAY, president of the Continental Congress, 1778-1779;
and 1st chief justice of the U.S. Supreme Court, 1789-1795.
Address at the ABS annual meeting,
May 13, 1824. John Jay's Papers, Manuscript collection,
ABS Archives.

You may look through the Bible from cover to cover and nowhere will you find a line that can be construed into an apology for the man of brains who sins against the light. On the contrary, in the Bible, taking that as a guide, you will find that because much has been given to you much will be expected from you; and a heavier condemnation is to be visited upon the able man who goes wrong than upon his weaker brother who cannot do the harm that the other does, because it is not in him to do it.

—THEODORE ROOSEVELT, 26th U.S. president.
Inglehart, Ferdinand Cowle, "Theodore Roosevelt: The Man As I Knew Him", *The Christian Herald*, 1919, p. 310.

Parties are reformed and governments are corrected by the impulses coming out of the hearts of those who never exercised authority and never organized parties. Those are the sources of strength, and I pray God that these sources may never cease to be spiritualized by immortal subjections of these words of inspiration of the Bible. If any statesman, sunk in the practices which debase a nation, will but read this single book he will go to his prayers abashed.

—WOODROW WILSON, 28th U.S. president.
Woodrow Wilson, *The Politics of Woodrow Wilson:*
Selections from His Speeches and Writings,
(Ayer Publishing, 1970), pp. 105-106.

The Bible is the Word of Life. I beg that you will read it and find this out for yourselves. When you have read it you will know that it is the Word of God, because you will have found the key to your own heart, your own happiness and your own duty.

—WOODROW WILSON, 28th U.S. president.
December 9, 1928. News Release on Universal Bible Sunday.

This American Bible Society has done a great work and a great good by circulating the Bible so as to be in the reach of all.

—HON. CHAMP CLARK, speaker of the U.S. House of
Representatives. Excerpt from Address at the ABS Centennial
Celebration in Washington, D.C., *Bible Society Record*, vol. 61, no.
6, June 1916, p. 122.

No greater agency for good has ever come to humanity than the agency through which this greatest of all books is distributed. This book appeals alike to the old and the young, the rich and the poor, the learned and the ignorant, the high and the low.

—WESLEY L. JONES, U.S. senator. Excerpt from Address
at the ABS Centennial Celebration
in Washington, D.C., *Bible Society Record*, vol. 61, no. 6,
June 1916, p. 124.

I wish it [the Bible] might fall into the hands of every thought-ful man in America.

—T.R. MARSHALL, U.S. vice president.
"Centennial History of the ABS,"
by Rev. Henry Otis Dwight, LL.D. Quoted in the
Bible Society Record, vol. 61, no. 9, September 1916, p. 182.

I know not how long a republican government can flourish among a great people who have not the Bible. But this I do know, that the existing government of this country could never have had existence but for the Bible. And, further, I do in my conscience believe, that if at every decade of years a copy of the Bible could be found in every family of the land, its republican institutions would be perpetual.

—WILLIAM H. SEWARD, U.S. secretary of state.
Frederick W. Seward, *William H. Seward: An Autobiography from 1801 to 1834*. (Derby and Miller, 1891), p. 407.

The whole of the inspiration of our civilization springs from the teachings of Christ and the lessons of the Prophets. To read the Bible for these fundamentals is a necessity of American life.

—HERBERT HOOVER, 31st U.S. president.
ABS Record, December 1964.

Menaced by collectivist trends, we must seek revival of our strength in the spiritual foundations which are the bedrock of our republic. Democracy is the outgrowth of the religious conviction of the sacredness of every human life. On the religious side, its highest embodiment is The Bible; on the political side, the Constitution.

—HERBERT HOOVER, 31st U.S. president.
"Our Christian Heritage," *Letter from Plymouth Rock*
(Marlborough, NH: The Plymouth Rock Foundation , 1954), p. 7.

It is good to know that the Bible is still the world's best-selling Book; it should also be the best read.

—CHIEF JUSTICE EARL WARREN, 14th U.S. chief justice.
Bible Society Record, February 1964, p. 22.

Those of us who believe in the democratic way of life therefore take heart and courage from the fact that the Bible, after centuries of circulation, still holds its place as the world's best seller.

—FRANKLIN D. ROOSEVELT, 32nd U.S. president.
To Rev. Francis C. Stifler, editorial secretary of ABS,
November 13, 1939. Presidential Autograph Collection,
ABS Archives.

The words from the Bible that have just been read to us carry a great message. It is one that influenced our fathers deeply, and guided them when they shaped our way of life. As a country, we have long understood that to help the suffering is to serve God. Through our communities and our governments as well as through out charities we have sought to carry out this Divine command to aid the hungry, the needy, and the sick. Today, however, the words of the parable of the Last Judgment have fresh meaning for us.

—HARRY S. TRUMAN, 33rd U.S. president. Radio address as part of Interdenominational Program, "One Great Hour," March 26, 1949.

The spirit and the purpose which your Society represents are older than America itself. For we can truly be said to have founded our country on the principles of this Book. The holy Bible was the most important possession that our forebears placed aboard their ships as they embarked for the New World.

—LYNDON B. JOHNSON, 36th U.S. president.
Remarks at a ceremony marking 1966 as the "Year of the Bible,"
January 19, 1966.

We can truly be said to have founded our country on the principles of this Book.

—LYNDON B. JOHNSON, 36th U.S. president.
March 18, 1966, News Release, accepting the 750 millionth
copy of Scripture distributed by ABS.

For as each of us pauses to reflect on the meaning of the Bible in our lives, we surely have some special instance for which to express our thanks to God for strengthening our faith through holy Writ.

—RICHARD NIXON, 37th U.S. president.
Statement about National Bible Week, October 22, 1969.

Speaking as Billy Graham might, I can say that the Bible tells us that when we look at the strength of the two sexes, that God made man out of the soft earth, but he made women out of a hard rib. The woman is the stronger of the two.

—RICHARD NIXON, 37th U.S. president.
Remarks at ceremonies honoring Billy Graham in
Charlotte, North Carolina, October 15, 1971.

Today's generation of Americans must face those challenges as our parents and as our grandparents met theirs—with courage, with sacrifice, with determination, but always with love of our country and our God.

—GERALD FORD, 38th U.S. president.
Remarks in Birmingham, Alabama, May 3, 1976.

In this Bicentennial year, we will often reflect on the events of 200 years ago. As we recall the crises of those early days, let us also reflect on the profound faith in God which inspired the founding fathers.

—GERALD FORD, 38th U.S. president.
Proclamation 4422—National Day of Prayer, March 16, 1976.

I believe it is no accident of history, no coincidence, that this Nation, which declared its dependence on God even while declaring its independence from foreign domination, has become the greatest nation in the history of the world. We are taught in the Psalms, that blessed is the nation whose God is the Lord. I believe that very, very deeply, and I know you believe it, too.

GERALD FORD, 38th U.S. president.
Remarks at the Combined Convention of the
National Religious Broadcasters and the
National Association of Evangelicals, February 22, 1976.

Here before me is the Bible used in the inauguration of our first President, in 1789, and I have just taken the oath of office on the Bible my mother gave me a few years ago, opened to a timeless admonition from the ancient prophet Micah: "He hath showed thee, O man, what is good; and what doth the Lord require of thee, but to do justly, and to love mercy, and to walk humbly with thy God." (Micah 6:8)

—JIMMY CARTER, 39th U.S. president.
Inaugural Address of Jimmy Carter, January 20, 1977.

We learned from the Bible about the fallibilities even of people who were given great responsibility. I remember the story of the escape of the Israelites from Egypt, when Moses was a man anointed by God to lead. And when the Israelites were in a battle, God told Moses, "hold up your arm." And as long as Moses held up his arms, the Israelites won. But after an hour or two or three, his arm got weary and it began to sink, and the Israelites began to lose. And his brother, Aaron, went and propped up his arm for a while. And later on Hut propped up Moses' arm for a while, and the Israelites won.

Well, I don't under any circumstances equate myself with Moses. But I would like to remind you of this: You elected me to be President. You gave me a job to do. As long as I'm in the White house, I'm going to try to do a good job, because you have confidence in me.

—JIMMY CARTER, 39th U.S. president.
Atlanta, Georgia. Remarks at the Southern Salute to the
President Dinner, January 20, 1978.

So, our faith in God, no matter what form it may have taken in our own individual lives, can be a basis for repairing the damage that has been done to the human spirit and should be a constant reminder that we have an equivalent responsibility to care for the environment, the ecology, the place where we live. We have a responsibility for stewardship.

The Bible says that the body is a temple of God and that we should care for our own bodies and for those around us.

—JIMMY CARTER, 39th U.S. president. Denver, Colorado. Remarks at the governor's Annual Prayer Breakfast, May 4, 1978.

We're blessed to have its words of strength, comfort, and truth. I'm accused of being simplistic at times with some of the problems that confront us. But I've often wondered: Within the covers of that single Book are all the answers to all the problems that face us today, if we'd only look there. "The grass withereth, the flower fadeth, but the word of our God shall stand forever." I hope Americans will read and study the Bible in 1983. It's my firm belief that the enduring values, as I say, presented in its pages have a great meaning for each of us and for our nation. The Bible can touch our hearts, order our minds, refresh our souls.

—RONALD REAGAN, 40th U.S. president. Remarks at the annual convention of the National Religious Broadcasters, January 31, 1983.

Can we resolve to reach, learn, and try to heed the greatest message ever written—God's word and the holy Bible. Inside its pages lie all the answers to all the problems that man has ever known.

—RONALD REAGAN, 40th U.S. president. Remarks at the Annual National Prayer Breakfast, February 3, 1983.

The Bible says: "If my people who are called by my name humble themselves and pray and seek my face and turn from their wicked ways, then I will hear from heaven and forgive their sins and heal their land." Many, many years ago, my mother had underlined that particular passage in the Bible. And I had her

Bible that I could place my hand on when I took the oath of office in 1980. And I had it opened to that passage that she had underlined. Today more and more Americans are seeking his face. And, yes, he has begun to heal our land.

> —RONALD REAGAN, 40th U.S. president.
> Remarks to the Student Congress on Evangelism, July 28, 1988.

I came here because I needed to hear the sermon. I came here because your church stands for what our country ought to be and where it ought to go. I came here because the Bible says that good Christians are also supposed to be good citizens. And I ask you this whole week to pray for me and pray for the members of Congress; ask us not to turn away from our ministry.

> —WILLIAM CLINTON, 42nd U.S. president.
> Remarks by the president during church services, Full Gospel
> AME Zion Church, Maryland, August 14, 1994.

Ephesians says we should speak the truth with our neighbors, for we are members, one of another. I believe that. I think that is the single most important political insight, or social insight, in the Bible. And I think it is what should drive us as we behave together.

> —WILLIAM CLINTON, 42nd U.S. president.
> Remarks by the president from the Metropolitan
> Baptist Church, December 7, 1997.

We're honored to be in the midst of a social entrepreneur whose guidebook for entrepreneurship to help others is the Bible.

> —GEORGE W. BUSH, 43rd U.S. president.
> President Bush honors Martin Luther King, Junior,
> in church service, January 20, 2003.

For near a half century, have I anxiously and critically studied that invaluable treasure; and I still scarcely ever take it up, that I do not find something new—that I do not receive some valuable addition to my stock of knowledge; or perceive some instructive fact, never observed before. In short, were you to ask me to recommend the most valuable book in the world, I should fix on the Bible as the most instructive, both to the wise and ignorant. Were you to ask me for one, affording the most rational and pleasing entertainment to the inquiring mind, I should repeat, it is the Bible; and should you renew the inquiry, for the best philosophy, or the most interesting history, I should still urge you to look into your Bible. I would make it, in short, the Alpha and Omega of knowledge.

—ELIAS BOUDINOT, president of the
Continental Congress, 1782-1783, and ABS president.
The Age of Revelation (Philadelphia: Asbury Dickins, 1801), p. xv.

I was born into a Christian family, nurtured as a Southern Baptist, and have been involved in weekly Bible lessons all my life, first as a student and then, from early manhood, as a teacher.

—JIMMY CARTER, 39th U.S. president.
Our Endangered Values. (New York: Simon & Schuster, 2005), p. 16.

It seems obvious to me that, in its totality, the Bible presented God's spiritual message, but that the ancient authors of the holy Scriptures were not experts on geology, biology, or cosmology, and were not blessed with the use of electron microscopes, carbon-dating techniques, or the hubble telescope.

—JIMMY CARTER, 39th U.S. president. Ibid., p. 48

Hold fast to the Bible as the sheet anchor of your liberties. Write its precepts in your hearts, and practice them in your lives. To the influence of this book are we indebted for all the progress made in true civilizations, and to this we must look as our guide in the future.

—ULYSSES S. GRANT, 18th U.S. president.
In a letter to the editor, *Sunday School Times*,
Philadelphia, June 6, 1876.

The holy Scriptures are able to make us wise unto Salvation, through Faith which is in Jesus Christ. All Scripture given by Inspiration of God is profitable for Doctrine, for Reproof, for Correction, for Instruction in Righteousness that the Man of God may be perfect, thoroughly furnished unto all good Works. The Scriptures give a full and ample testimony to all the principal Doctrines of the Christian Faith; and therefore no divine or inward Communication at this Day, however necessary, do or can contradict that testimony. They are the most excellent Writings in the world; therefore, very heavenly Writings and the use of them very conformable and necessary to the Church and We are bound to give Praise to God, for his wonderful Providence in preserving these Writings so pure and uncorrupted as We have them, to testify of his Truth even against those whom he made instrumental in preserving them.

—JOHN DICKINSON, member of the First Continental
Congress. "Religious Instruction for Youth," undated.
R. R. Logan Papers, Historical Society of Pennsylvania.

To qualify the apostles for their important task, they were blessed with the direction and guidance of the holy Spirit, and by him were enabled to preach the Gospel with concordant accuracy, and in divers languages: they were also endued with power to prove the truth of their doctrine, and of their authority to preach it, by wonderful and supernatural signs and miracles. A merciful Providence also provided that some of these inspired men should commit to writing such accounts of the Gospel, and of their acts and proceedings in preaching it, as *would* constitute and establish a *standard* whereby future preachers and generations might ascertain what they ought to believe and to do; and be thereby secured against the danger of being misled by mistakes and corruptions incident to tradition. The Bible contains these writings, and exhibits such a connected series of the Divine revelations and dispensations respecting the present and future state of mankind, and so amply attested by internal and external evidence, that we have no reason to desire or expect that further miracles will be wrought to confirm the belief and confidence which they invite and require.

—JOHN JAY, president of the Continental Congress;
1778-1779; and 1st chief justice of the U.S. Supreme Court,
1789-1795. To the ABS, May 12, 1825. Johnston,
Correspondence of Jay, vol. 4, pp. 503-504.

In regard to this Great Book, I have but to say, it is the best gift God has given to man. All the good the Savior gave to the world was communicated through this book. But for it we could not know right from wrong.

—ABRAHAM LINCOLN, 16th U.S. president.
Reply to Loyal Colored People of Baltimore upon presentation
of a Bible, September 7, 1864. *Collected Works of
Abraham Lincoln*, vol. VII, p. 542.

The more profoundly we study this wonderful Book, and the more closely we observe its divine precepts, the better citizens we will become and the higher will be our destiny as a nation.

—WILLIAM MCKINLEY, 25th U.S. president.
Gary DeMar, *America's Christian History: The Untold Story*
(Atlanta, GA: American Vision Publishers, Inc., 1993), p. 60.

We cannot read the history of our rise and development as a nation, without reckoning with the place the Bible has occupied in shaping the advances of the Republic. . . . [W]here we have been the truest and most consistent in obeying its precepts, we have attained the greatest measure of contentment and prosperity.

—FRANKLIN D. ROOSEVELT, 32nd U.S. president. In a radio
broadcast, 1935. Gabriel Sivan, *The Bible and Civilization* (New
York: Quadrangle/The New York Times Book Co., 1973), p. 178.

You see the heroism and the goodness of man and know in a special way that we are all God's children. We all have souls, and we all have the same problems. I'm convinced more than ever that man finds liberation only when he binds himself to God and commits himself to his fellow man. We'll never find every answer, solve every problem, or heal every wound, but we can do a lot if we walk together down that one path that we know provides real hope. I'm so thankful that there will always be one day in the year when people all over our land can sit down as neighbors and friends and remind ourselves of what our real task is. The task was spelled out in the Old and New Testaments.

—RONALD REAGAN, 40th U.S. president.
Kenger, *God and Ronald Reagan: A Spiritual Life*,
(Harper Collins, 2004), p. 278.

In like manner we daily read chapters in the Bible rich with divine truths without perceiving them. The next generation will probably perceive them and wonder at our blindness in not finding them out. "Each verse in the Bible," says Luther, "is a bush with a bird in it. But the bird will not fly from it till the bush is well beaten." I have been astonished to find how much justice there is in this observation. I never read a chapter in the Bible without seeing something in it I never saw before.

—BENJAMIN RUSH, member of the Continental Congress, 1776-1777. Butterfield, *Letters of Rush*, vol. 1, p. 484.

By renouncing the Bible, philosophers swing from their moorings upon all moral subjects. Our Saviour in speaking of it calls it the "Truth" in the abstract. It is the only correct map of the human heart that ever has been published. It contains a faithful representation of all its follies, vices, and crimes. All systems of religion, morals, and government not founded upon it must perish, and how consoling the thought—it will not only survive the wreck of these systems but the world itself. "The Gates of hell shall not prevail against it."

—BENJAMIN RUSH, member of the Continental Congress, 1776-1777. Ibid., vol. 2, p. 936.

The Bible is a book of faith, and a book of doctrine, and a book of morals, and a book of religion, of especial revelation from God; but it is also a book which teaches man his own individual responsibility, his own dignity, and his equality with his fellow-man.

—DANIEL WEBSTER, American orator, lawyer, and statesman. In an address of the Bunker Hill Monument, June 17, 1843.

[The Bible is] a book which reveals men unto themselves, not as creatures in bondage, not as men under human authority, not as those bidden to take counsel and command of any human source. It reveals every man to himself as a distinct moral agent, responsible not to men, not even to those men whom he has put over him in authority, but responsible through his own conscience to his Lord and Maker. Whenever a man sees this vision he stands up a free man, whatever may be the government under which he lives, if he sees beyond the circumstances of his own life.

—WOODROW WILSON, 28th U.S. president. Speech on the tercentenary of the King James Bible, Denver, May 7, 1911.

There is no other book so various as the Bible, nor one so full of concentrated wisdom. Whether it be of law, business, morals, or that vision which leads the imagination in the creation of constructive enterprises for the happiness of mankind, he who seeks for guidance in any of these things may look inside its covers and find illumination. The study of this Book in your Bible classes is a postgraduate course in the richest library of human experience.

—HERBERT HOOVER, 31st U.S. president. Message to the Federation of Men's Bible Classes, May 5, 1929.

When you have read the Bible you will know it is the Word of God.

—WOODROW WILSON, 28th U.S. president. Letter to the Soldiers and Sailors of the United States, August 1917.

Did not the writers of the Gospels testify, by their whole conduct, that they were men of integrity, impartiality and virtue? Did they not teach and inculcate the most pure and strict morality ever taught to man, and that on pain of the utmost displeasure of

Almighty God? Some of these disciples who afterwards wrote the Gospels, were personally acquainted with Jesus Christ, attended him during his life, and were actually concerned in many of the events they relate. They were intimately acquainted with Joseph and Mary; and one of them took Mary to his own house after the crucifixion, at the request of his dying Lord, and she dwelt with him for fifteen years. The brothers and sisters of Jesus Christ after the flesh, were among his disciples, and several of them sealed their faith with their blood. If these circumstances did not constitute the Apostles the most proper historians to record the life, actions and doctrines of their master, and do not operate as a strong confirmation of the facts they relate, I know not what human testimony can amount to proof; neither can I see, what reason there can be, for giving credit to the most approved histories either of nations or individuals. . . . These historians have given us the account of the birth of their Lord and master, not only as they received it from Joseph and Mary; but as they had it from him in his life time, as well as from the influence and direction of the holy spirit, with which they were so openly and publicly filled, in presence of so many witnesses. Besides it is acknowledged, that the morality they inculcate, is of the most pure and benevolent kind: and that to mislead their adherents and followers, by publishing untruths to ruin and deceive them, would have been contrary to every principle of morality and benevolence. If you look through their whole history, every part of it bears the mark of truth and credibility. They urge in all their teachings, the strictest attention to truth, and threaten the severest displeasure of Almighty God against falsehood, dissimulation and hypocrisy.

—ELIAS BOUDINOT, president of the Continental Congress, 1782-1783, and ABS president. *The Age of Revelation* (Philadelphia: Asbury Dickins, 1801), pp. 56-60.

It is to be regretted but so I believe the fact to be, that except the Bible there is not a true history in the world.

—JOHN JAY, president of the Continental Congress, 1778-1779;
and 1st chief justice of the U.S. Supreme Court, 1789-1795.
Letter to Jedidiah Morse, February 28, 1797. Johnston,
Correspondence of Jay, vol. 4, p. 225.

Read the bible then, as you would read Livy or Tacitus. . . . For example in the book of Joshua we are told the sun stood still for several hours. Were we to read that fact in Livy or Tacitus we should class it with their showers of blood, speaking of statues, beasts &c., but it is said that the writer of that book was inspired. Examine therefore candidly what evidence there is of his having been inspired. The pretension is entitled to your enquiry, because millions believe it. On the other hand you are Astronomer enough to know how contrary it is to the law of nature that a body revolving on its axis, as the earth does, should have stopped, should not by that sudden stoppage have prostrated animals, trees, buildings, and should after a certain time have resumed its revolution, and that without a second general prostration. Is this arrest of the earth's motion, or the evidence which affirms it, most within the law of probabilities?

—THOMAS JEFFERSON, 2nd U.S. president.
Letter to Peter Carr, August 10, 1787.
Boyd, *Papers of Thomas Jefferson*, vol. 12, pp. 15-16.

Nor did the question ever occur to me before. Where get we the ten commandments? The book indeed gives them to us verbatim. But where did it get them? For itself tells us they were written by the finger of God on tables of stone, which were destroyed by Moses: it specifies those on the 2d. set of tables in different form and substance, but still without saying how the others were recovered. But the whole history of these books is so defective and doubtful that it seems vain to attempt minute enquiry into it: and such tricks have been plaid with their text, and with the texts of other books relating to them, that we have a right, from that cause, to entertain much doubt what parts of them are genuine. In the New testament there is internal evidence that parts of it have proceeded from an extraordinary man; and that other parts are the fabric of very inferior minds. It is as easy to separate those parts, as to pick out diamonds from dunghills. The matter of the first was such as would be preserved in the memory of the hearers, and handed on by tradition for a long time; the latter such stuff as might be gathered up, for imbedding it, any where, and at any time.

—THOMAS JEFFERSON, 2nd U.S. president.
Letter to John Adams, January 24, 1814. Ibid., vol. 2, p. 421.

And what has not been misunderstood or misrepresented? The spirit of God could not or would not dictate words that could not be misunderstood or perverted. Misinterpretations of the Scriptures of the old and new Testaments have founded Mosques and Cathedrals, have made saints Cardinals and Popes, Tyrants and Despots without Number, and deluged three quarters of the Globe I mean all Christian and Mahometan Countries at times in blood.

—JOHN ADAMS, 2nd U.S. president.
Letter to Benjamin Rush, March 23, 1809. *Old Family Letters*, p. 226.

I perfectly agree with you in the sentiment that our Business is to do our Duty and leave Events to him, without whose appointment and permission nothing comes to pass. That Duty however appears to me to call particularly on all ministers of the Gospel to look more to the Author and Finisher of our Faith than to the Expositors of it; and disregarding the doubtful and mysterious doctrines by which the latter have divided Christians from Christians, to unite in defending the plain and intelligible faith delivered to us by our Redeemer and his apostles.

—JOHN JAY, president of the Continental Congress, 1778-1779; and 1st chief justice of the U.S. Supreme Court, 1789-1795. Letter to John Lathrop, March 3, 1801. Jay Papers (online edition), Columbia University Library.

The greatest men of every age and nation since, whether Jews, Christians or heathens, unite their testimony in favour of Moses being the writer of these books, as the word of God, and coming down from him; our Lord Jesus Christ and his apostles add their attestation. The religious jealousy, the known accuracy, indefatigable care, and curious precision of the Jews as a people, not to mention the separation of the ten tribes by which a violent and lasting opposition and hatred arose between them, so that they became a watch over each other, give peculiar and demonstrative weight to the evidence, as far as it relates to these books having been preserved and handed down to us without important alterations: and the experience of every serious and attentive believer, in addition to the continued fulfilment of the predictions contained in them even at this day; leaves no reasonable doubt on their minds, with regard to their truth and inspiration. It is almost four thousand years since they have been written; and never have they been denied to be the work of Moses, as the word of God, till modern times. It is true, as has been already observed, Aben Ezra, a Jew of considerable note, about the year 1200, first supposed that these books had

been written in the time of the kings; but then he considered
them as inspired writings, let who would be the author of them,
and received them as absolute verity. It never entered into his
head, to disbelieve the facts recorded in them, or to doubt their
being the word or commandments of God.

> —ELIAS BOUDINOT, president of the Continental Congress,
> 1782-1783, and ABS president. *The Age of Revelation*
> (Philadelphia: Asbury Dickins, 1801), p. 322.

The Scriptures of the Two Testaments speak in a familiar and
consonant manner of the one true God, of the Messiah and of
the holy Spirit. The authorities being equal, we ought in constru-
ing them, preserve that harmony and not raise up such a meta-
physical civil war between them, that men of common understanding and improvements may be so perplexed, as not to know,
whether they ought to take side with the Old Testament or with
the New Testament, and at last from the doubtfulness of their
Titles, fall into an indifference and contempt for both of them.

> —JOHN DICKINSON, member of the First Continental
> Congress. Undated notes on religion. R. R. Logan Collection,
> Historical Society of Pennsylvania.

. . . you say you have never seen executed, a comparison of the
morality of the old testament with that of the new. And yet no
two things were ever more unlike.

> —THOMAS JEFFERSON, 2nd U.S. president. Letter to John Adams,
> August 22, 1813. Cappon, *Adams-Jefferson Letters*, vol. 2, p. 368.

We are told, that there are many passages in the old testament,
that are improper to be read by children, and that the greatest

part of it is no way interesting to mankind under the present dispensation of the gospel. There are I grant, several chapters, and many verses in the old testament, which in their present unfortunate translation, should be passed over by children. But I deny that any of the books of the old testament are not interesting to mankind, under the gospel dispensation. Most of the characters, events, and ceremonies, mentioned in them, are personal, providential, or instituted types of the Messiah: All of which have been, or remain yet to be, fulfilled by him. It is from an ignorance or neglect of these types, that we have so many deists in christendom; for so irrefragably do they prove the truth of christianity, that I am sure a young man who had been regularly instructed in their meaning, could never doubt afterwards of the truth of any of its principles. If any obscurity appears in these principles, it is only (to use the words of the poet) *because they are dark, with excessive bright.*

—BENJAMIN RUSH, member of the Continental Congress, 1776-1777. *Essays: Literary, Moral, and Philosophical,* pp. 60-61.

The late bereaving stroke of divine Providence in our family is very afflicting to me. . . . It is my earnest prayer that this Providence may be suitably regarded by me and all the family and especially the surviving children of our family and his child, that they may be excited to be always in an actual readiness for death. Our children have all been brought up under the bond of the covenant of baptism, but those of them who are come to years of discretion should consider that it is indispensably necessary for them to give their cordial consent to the covenant of grace and that it is their duty to make a public profession of religion and attend all the ordinances of the gospel and in order to understand how this should be done in a proper manner they should search the scripture and attend all the public preaching. The sermon that I agreed with Ms. Moses to print will give much light on that subject.

—ROGER SHERMAN, member of the Continental Congress.
To Rebecca Sherman, January 29, 1789. *Sherman Papers*,
Yale University Library.

I am delighted to send warm greetings to all those celebrating the 175th anniversary of the American Bible Society. . . .

Since 1816, your society has helped to spread the Word of God to people throughout the Nation and the world. In so doing, you have brought them inspiration and enlightenment. I commend your dedication to such a worthy cause, and especially your efforts to distribute the Bible to those who might not be able to buy one for themselves.

—GEORGE H.W. BUSH, 41st U.S. president.
In a letter from the White House to the ABS, March 22, 1991.
Presidential Autograph Collection, ABS Archives.

As one Nation under God, we Americans are deeply mindful of both our dependence on the Almighty and our obligations as a people he has richly blessed. From our first days as a Republic, we have relied on God's strength and guidance; entrusted with the gifts of freedom and prosperity, we in turn have a responsibility to serve as a beacon to the world.

The holy Scriptures offer us guidance as we seek to fulfill that responsibility, striving—as individuals and as a Nation—to be a force for good in the world. As the Psalm says, "Thy Word is a light unto my path and a lamp unto my feet."

—GEORGE H.W. BUSH, 41st U.S. president. Ibid.

I think that no soldier could wish you anything but the most complete success in your purpose of holding a Universal Bible Sunday. The longer one lives close to the turmoil and sacrifice and suffering of the battlefield, the more he becomes conscious of the eternal worth of the spiritual values inherent in the Christian religion. Moreover, because this war constitutes a direct conflict between the forces of evil and those of Christian principles of human rights and dignity, every movement which increases general familiarization with those principles has a direct uplifting effect upon the soldiery and citizens of the United Nations.

—DWIGHT D. EISENHOWER, 34th U.S. president.
In a letter from the office of the commander in chief to Stifler,
editorial secretary, ABS, October 28, 1943. ABS Archives.

The custom of reading the Bible together has brought strength to many families. United in a vital faith, parents and children can accomplish great things for good.

—DWIGHT D. EISENHOWER, 34th U.S. president.
In a letter from the White House to the ABS, 1957.
Presidential Autograph Collection, ABS Archives.

Please accept my best wishes for the greatest possible success for this year's Worldwide Bible Reading Campaign, to take place between Thanksgiving and Christmas. In this period between the two holidays, when Americans give thanks for their blessings and renew their hopes for a just and lasting peace in the world, all of us, of whatever religious belief, may well turn to the *Bible* for guidance and inspiration for the tasks which lie ahead. I hope that many individuals and many families will do so, and that they will continue this practice in the

New Year, joined by men and women of faith and good will in other lands.

> — DWIGHT D. EISENHOWER, 34th U.S. president.
> Letter to the ABS, August 22, 1955.
> Presidential Autograph Collection, ABS Archives.

Like stored wisdom, the lessons of the Bible are useless unless they are lifted out and employed. A faithful reading of Scripture provides the courage and strength required for the living of our time.

> —DWIGHT D. EISENHOWER, 34th U.S. president.
> In a letter from the White House to the ABS,
> November 4, 1958. Presidential Autograph Collection,
> ABS Archives.

Mrs. Eisenhower and I want to thank you again for bringing to the White house yesterday seventy-seven Bibles, each in a different language. The Bibles have been permanently placed in the White house library, and will be used in appropriate fashion whenever we have visitors from foreign lands.

> —DWIGHT D. EISENHOWER, 34th U.S. president.
> Letter from the White House to the ABS,
> November 5, 1953. Presidential Autograph Collection,
> ABS Archives.

The Bible is endorsed by the ages. Our civilization is built upon its words.

In no other book is there such a collection of inspired wisdom, reality, and hope. It describes the condition of man and the promise of man with such power that, through many eras and

generations, it has made the mighty humble and has strengthened the weak.

—DWIGHT D. EISENHOWER, 34th U.S. president.
Letter from the White House to the ABS,
August 21, 1956. Presidential Autograph Collection,
ABS Archives.

We are grateful to your great voluntary society for distributing
the Bible over the past one hundred forty years, without comment or interpretation, throughout the breadth of our land
and across the seven seas. You have written The Word upon the
doorposts of the world.

—DWIGHT D. EISENHOWER, 34th U.S. president.
In a letter from the White House to the ABS,
August 21, 1956. Presidential Autograph Collection,
ABS Archives.

... the purpose of a devout and united people was set forth in
the pages of the Bible: Moses led his people out of slavery
toward the Promised Land. Their purpose was threefold:

(1) to live in freedom,

(2) to work in a prosperous land "flowing with milk and
honey," and

(3) to obey the commandments of God—within their own
country and in their dealings with other nations.

This Biblical story of the Promised Land inspired the founders of America. It continues to inspire us, and we are privileged
to hand it down, bright and strong, to every generation.

—DWIGHT D. EISENHOWER, 34th U.S. president.
In a letter from the White House to the ABS,

September 28, 1960. Presidential Autograph Collection,
ABS Archives.

Our forefathers were inspired by the Bible and its message of human liberation. Throughout American history, the Bible has nurtured the American heart, mind and spirit.

The Bible provides a new inspiration to new generations. The Word of God continues to ennoble our thoughts and deeds and enlarge our vision.

—GERALD FORD, 38th U.S. president.
In a letter from the White House to the ABS,
November 1976. ABS Archives.

I appreciate very highly the unmerited honor conferred on me by the Board of Managers of the American Bible Society. . . . Believing however the American Bible Society is engaged in a great and good work—a work universally meriting of encouragement and aid, I gratefully accept the place assigned to me.

—RUTHERFORD B. HAYES, 19th U.S. president and ABS vice president 1880 until his death in 1893. In a letter from the Executive Mansion, Washington, D.C., July 20, 1880.

Whatever mutations may come in the affairs of men and of human society, the Bible remains the Book of Books, winning constantly wider acceptance among men wherever they live, as the inspired vehicle of the greatest truths that have been revealed to the world.

—WARREN G. HARDING, 29th U.S. president. In a letter from the White House to Mr. Haven, ABS, May 2, 1923. ABS Archives.

... the Book of Books, from the pages of which have come those ideals that root our government and our national life firmly in the consciences of men and women.

—HERBERT HOOVER, 31st U.S. president.
In a letter from the White House to Mr. George William Brown,
general secretary, ABS, October 25, 1929.
ABS Archives.

The moral precepts and phrases of the Bible are woven into the fabric of our national life. Its wisdom has traveled with our people because it helped them to live creatively, helpfully and victoriously. It will travel with mankind in all his new adventures.

—JOHN F. KENNEDY, 35th U.S. president.
In a letter from the White House to Mr. Nettinga,
Secretary, ABS, July 19, 1961. ABS Archives.

The American Bible Society has, since 1816, engaged in the distribution of scriptures in nearly all of the languages of mankind. It is not enough, however, that the Bible be translated, published and distributed; it must also be read.

Therefore, I urge people everywhere to read the Bible in whatever version or translation they choose.

—JOHN F. KENNEDY, 35th U.S. president.
In a letter from the White House to Mr. Smith,
president, ABS, September 20, 1962. ABS Archives.

I have read your obliging letter of the 20th June with the copy of the Bible which the Board of Managers of the American Bible Society have done me the honor to present in this a handsome edition, and the work does credit to those who performed it.

Be pleased to communicate my thanks for it to the Board and assure them that if my health was equal to my inclinations to render *active* services to the Society, I should manifest it by better evidence than professions.

> —JOHN JAY, president of the Continental Congress, 1778-1779;
> and 1st chief justice of the U.S. Supreme Court, 1789-1795.
> In a letter from the White House to Rev. M. James Milner,
> secretary to the managers, ABS, July 26, 1819, ABS Archives

The Bible is a binding and abiding force in a world too often gripped by hatred and prejudice. Men of every country, creed, and calling turn to its pages for solace and for strength. It is a Divine Book. And it is a human book. It is a spiritual as well as a material staff of life. Its message is couched in simple, human accounts which have for centuries gladdened men's hearts and uplifted despairing spirits. Those who perpetuate the cherished tradition of National Bible Week perform a good that can never be accurately measured or adequately praised. And those who participate in this observance, enrich their own lives with a nobler purpose and a firmer faith as brothers in the Fatherhood of God.

> —LYNDON B. JOHNSON, 36th U.S. president.
> In a letter from the White House to the ABS,
> October 4, 1967. ABS Archives.

I am glad to accept your invitation to be honorary chairman of the 21st Annual Worldwide Bible Reading. . . .

That you are able to furnish the Scriptures in the language of the people of so many countries is indeed impressive. The Bible in any language enriches and stabilizes it and makes it a more potent instrument of literary and cultural expression. Of more significance, however, is the fact that it gives to conscience and social concern in these countries a common vocabulary of moral expression furnishing a standard of conduct by which tyranny can be brought to judgment, and gives to the weary, the oppressed, and the heavy laden an articulation of rights which they can plead before the bar of world conscience.

—LYNDON B. JOHNSON, 36th U.S. president.
In a letter from the White House to Mr. Everett Smith,
president, ABS, May 15, 1964. ABS Archives.

It was a common saying among the Puritan fathers of this land that brown bread and the Gospel are good fare.

Architects of progress, we often forget that the brown bread of those intrepid pilgrims was the leaven of our present prosperity.

Members of a materialistic-minded society, we often neglect the Gospel that nourishes the spirit which still sustains us all.

So as the American Bible Society observes this sesquicentennial of its founding, it invokes a tradition as sacred as this native soil on which it thrives.

As your members set out to perpetuate and enhance a legacy so dynamic and so dear, I know that Americans everywhere are with you in spirit. And your president solemnly joins the task you are in.

—LYNDON B. JOHNSON, 36th U.S. president.
In a letter from the White House to Mr. Everett Smith,
president, ABS, November 3, 1966. ABS Archives.

The Bible comes with many covers, on varying grades of paper and in multiple languages. But its purpose is unchanged: man's firm instructions and wonderful promises from God. It holds our answers and hopes. It is life's greatest truth.

While this mighty book traces our history and projects into tomorrow, it remains the best possible guidepost for today's living.

> —LYNDON B. JOHNSON, 36th U.S. president.
> In a letter from the White House to the ABS,
> August 12, 1968, ABS Archives

In this decade when we are more than ever called upon to turn our hands and hearts to assisting those in our country for whom our general prosperity is still a distant dream, it is well that we refresh our spirits and fortify our resolves by reading the holy Scripture.

> —RICHARD NIXON, 37th U.S. president.
> In a letter from the White House to the ABS,
> November 1970. ABS Archives.

In our own country the hand of every president has rested on the Bible as he has taken the oath of office; and in its pages President, public servants and citizens of all ages have continued to find the principles on which we have built the American way of life.

One of my distinguished predecessors once said that if our democracy is to remain the greatest hope of humanity, it must continue abundantly in the faith of the Bible. The truth of these words is made consistently clear, and chapter after chapter of our history attests to their meaning in our lives.

> —RICHARD NIXON, 37th U.S. president.
> In a letter from the White House to the ABS,
> November 1971. ABS Archives.

As a memorial of your pious labors to the end of placing a copy of the Bible in every household of the habitable world and first of all in every household of your own beloved country—and as a sacred deposit this copy will be transmitted by me to my successors to be their intimate counselor and their sure guide in the arduous duty of administering the executive affairs of the Union.

> —FRANKLIN PIERCE, 14th U.S. president.
> In a letter from Washington to the ABS,
> February 5, 1857. ABS Archives.

I feel that a comprehensive study of the Bible is a liberal education for anyone. Nearly all of the great men of our country have been well versed in teachings of the Bible, and I sincerely hope that the habit of Bible study will be developed among the people. I want to congratulate you for your effort among the people of our country.

> —FRANKLIN D. ROOSEVELT, 32nd U.S. president.
> In a letter from the executive chamber, state of New York.
> To George William Brown, Esq., general secretary, ABS,
> October 21, 1929. ABS Archives.

It is fitting that Universal Bible Sunday be observed annually on a day selected for that purpose by the American Bible Society. I congratulate the Society for sponsoring such an universal observance.

Everyone of us must gain satisfaction and strength through the practical application of the teachings of Christianity, for they affect the individual lives of men and women everywhere.

> —FRANKLIN D. ROOSEVELT, 32nd U.S. president.

In a letter from the White House to Mr. George William Brown,
general secretary, ABS, November 4, 1933. ABS Archives.

And through all the ages since Moses received on Mount Sinai the
Ten Commandments and the Law and God entered into a covenant with Israel men, in increasing numbers, have sought the solace, the consolation and the guidance which the Bible affords.
Today, after the lapse of a prodigious period of time the power
and influence of the Scriptures are undiminished and destined in
the light of past conquests, to permeate an ever widening sphere.

—FRANKLIN D. ROOSEVELT, 32nd U.S. president.
In a letter from the White House to Rev. Francis C. Stifler,
editorial secretary, ABS, November 2, 1938. ABS Archives.

It is not without significance that the American Bible Society
has chosen for its theme in the observance of Universal Bible
Sunday this year the text from St. John's Gospel which proclaims
truth as the medium through which men are made free. . . .
"Ye shall know the truth and the truth shall make you free." . . .
Let us hope that the American Bible Society will continue its
good work in disseminating the Sacred Scriptures and pray in
the fullness of time that all the world will accept the unchang-
ing truths which the Book of Books proclaims.

—FRANKLIN D. ROOSEVELT, 32nd U.S. president.
In a letter from the White House to Rev. Francis C. Stifler,
editorial secretary, ABS, November 13, 1939. ABS Archives.

Never before in nineteen hundred years did men more need the
emancipation from error promised in the simple declaration:
"Ye shall know the truth and the truth shall make you free."

Those of us who believe in the democratic way of life therefore take heart and courage from the fact that the Bible, after centuries of circulation, still holds its place as the world's best seller. I believe that all of the differences that rend the world today would find speedy solution if men and nations would but return in all humility to the plain teaching of the Sermon on the Mount. There indeed are the truths that set men free.

—FRANKLIN D. ROOSEVELT, 32nd U.S. president.
In a letter from the White House to Rev. Francis C. Stifler,
editorial secretary, ABS, November 13, 1939. ABS Archives.

The tragic events being enacted over wide areas of the earth with their attendant suffering, anguish and horror but confirm our conviction that acceptance of the plain teachings of the Bible would restore peace and happiness in a war-torn world. Despite all that we see today of the tragedy which man's selfishness has wrought in the world we know that the ancient truths of the Bible will prevail over all error because they constitute the teachings of God.

Righteousness alone exalteth a nation and the great truths of the Sermon on the Mount are as potent a guide today as when they were first uttered nineteen centuries ago.

—FRANKLIN D. ROOSEVELT, 32nd U.S. president.
In a letter from the White House to Rev. Francis C. Stifler,
editorial secretary, ABS, October 29, 1940. ABS Archives.

My hearty congratulations to all friends of the American Bible Society on the one hundred and twenty-fifth anniversary of its founding.

Best of all is the fact that after a century and a quarter of vigorous work the Society is planning to enlarge rather than to curtail its activities. I trust that success will crown its efforts and that the Society will pass from strength to strength through all the years to come.

> —FRANKLIN D. ROOSEVELT, 32nd U.S. president.
> In a letter from the White House to Rev. Francis C. Stifler,
> editorial secretary, ABS, April 28, 1941. ABS Archives.

I am glad to learn that in the face of the tragic conflict which rends the world today, our American Bible Society is prepared to increase rather than to curtail its beneficent activities. . . . Fortunate indeed is it that the American Bible Society can take over the work of distribution of the Sacred Scriptures which some of the European agencies have been obliged to curtail, because of the disorganization and dislocations which war has brought about.

> —FRANKLIN D. ROOSEVELT, 32nd U.S. president.
> In a letter from the White House to Rev. Francis C. Stifler,
> editorial secretary, ABS, September 20, 1941. ABS Archives.

More than any single work, the Bible is the repository of the moral and religious teachings of our western tradition. It is a book not for a day or a week but for eternity. In the great moral crisis of ancient Israel the prophet Isaiah cried out, "They that wait upon the Lord shall renew their strength; they shall mount up with wings as eagles; they shall run, and not be weary; and they shall walk, and not faint."

In that spirit we shall fortify our souls for the uncertainties of the future. With that spirit sustaining us, we shall not falter and we shall not fail.

> —FRANKLIN D. ROOSEVELT, 32nd U.S. president.
> In a letter from the White House to Rev. Francis C. Stifler,
> editorial secretary, ABS, October 14, 1942. ABS Archives.

I am happy again to give my warm endorsement to the setting aside of December thirteenth next as Universal Bible Sunday. These days of crisis have brought strain and anguish to American homes, but they have brought also a quickened sense of the strength which religion alone can give to our people.

The crisis of the world today is a moral crisis. The essential war is a war of values, and the stake for which mankind is contending is the right to be free. The Christian conception of man created in the image of God, that tradition of human freedom and dignity which over many centuries has gradually achieved democracy as its secular expression, is challenged today by the Nazi conception of man created in the image of the beasts of the field. We are defending humanity against systematic and calculated brutalization. We are fighting to make the future safe for decency and brotherhood.

—FRANKLIN D. ROOSEVELT, 32nd U.S. president.
In a letter from the White House to Rev. Francis C. Stifler,
editorial secretary, ABS, October 14, 1942. ABS Archives.

The Bible has special values in a time of war. For our fighting men it is testimony to the eternal truth that righteousness is won and maintained only at the cost of continual struggle against the powers of darkness. For the populations despoiled and tortured by our common enemies, it is an indestructible monument to the ideal of retributive justice: that the unjust aggressor shall not be permitted to escape the punishment due his crimes. For all of us at home, it is a source of strength in privation and bereavement, and a testimony to the reality of that better world desired by all men of good will.

—FRANKLIN D. ROOSEVELT, 32nd U.S. president.

In a letter from the White House to Rev. Francis C. Stifler,
editorial secretary, ABS, October 12, 1943. ABS Archives.

I am informed that you have just agreed to give the National
War Work Council of the Y.M.C.A. one million New Testaments which they will distribute. I know that you have already,
since the war began, printed and sent out for distribution to
our soldiers and sailors nearly half a million Testaments and
portions of the Scriptures. . . .

Every soldier and sailor of the United States should have a
Testament, and the American Bible Society is the organization
through which the work can be done in best shape.

THEODORE ROOSEVELT, 26th U.S. president.
In a letter from his New York office to Mr. David Hinshaw,
ABS, September 4, 1917. ABS Archives.

The Bible, the embodiment of the wealth and the wisdom of
the ages, happily is still the world's best seller. That fact alone
augurs well for the success of your crusade to promote world
Bible reading.

I am afraid that we of this generation do not know our Bible
as well as did our fathers and mothers. It is well for us to
remember that the Old and New Testaments remain as they
have always been, a source of strength and comfort and inspiration to all who will seek the wisdom which they hold.

—HARRY S. TRUMAN, 33rd U.S. president. In a letter from the
White House to the ABS, October 29, 1946. ABS Archives.

I think it is well for this troubled world, so torn with divisions
and dissensions, that your society is again appealing this year
for world-wide reading of the Bible from Thanksgiving to

Christmas. I hope our American people will join heartily in this crusade to read and ponder and carry in their hearts the ineffable truths of the Sacred Scriptures. . . .

As we prepare to go forward with the tasks which lie ahead we shall find strength and courage if we gird ourselves with "the Sword of the Spirit which is the Word of God."

—HARRY S. TRUMAN, 33rd U.S. president. In a letter from the
White House to the ABS, October 20, 1947. ABS Archives.

The age in which we live is a troubled one and one beset with perplexing problems, domestic and international. But above the din of discord and ill will is heard a still, small voice, saying: " . . . what doth the Lord require of thee, but to do justly, and to love mercy, and to walk humbly with thy God?"

Again when the sages and the scientists, the philosophers and the statesmen have exhausted their studies of atomic energy, one solution and one alone will be left. That solution lies in the application to twentieth century life of the plain teaching of the Sermon on the Mount—the substitution of conscience for force in the government of man.

—HARRY S. TRUMAN, 33rd U.S. president. In a letter from the
White House to the ABS, October 4, 1948. ABS Archives.

The Bible is the book that guided the souls and molded the hearts of generations of good men and valiant women. It became the rock on which rested the everlasting reality of religion. It also formed the style that gave our English tongue its most facile expression.

—HARRY S. TRUMAN, 33rd U.S. president. In a letter from the
White House to the ABS, October 5, 1949. ABS Archives.

I think the American Bible Society's annual appeal for assidious [sic] reading of the Scriptures between Thanksgiving and Christmas Days has great merit. Never was a weary world more in need of the message which the Bible alone could bring to nations rent by anger, hatred and ill will.

May God continue to bless and increase the reading of his Word.

—HARRY S. TRUMAN, 33rd U.S. president. In a letter from the White House to the ABS, October 5, 1949. ABS Archives.

... the Bible remains, after the lapse of all the centuries since it came into being, the greatest book ever written.

The Bible has an ever increasing claim upon us. A book of Divine Inspiration it not only comprises history but it unifies history, ancient and modern. This unique and incomparable work is in two parts which supplement each other: The Old Testament and the New. Obscure and mysterious in its origin as things divine often are, the Old Testament relates the majestic chronicle of the coming to the people of Israel—the chosen people—and through them to the rest of mankind, of knowledge of the one, ever living and true God, Creator of heaven and Earth under whose ruling hand all creatures live and without whose will not a sparrow falls.

—HARRY S. TRUMAN, 33rd U.S. president. In a letter from the White House to the ABS, November 10, 1951. ABS Archives.

In these troubled times, the truths which the Bible teaches are of greater and greater importance to mankind. God's message of love is the only final answer to the forces of organized hate which now threaten the civilized world.

—HARRY S. TRUMAN, 33rd U.S. president. In a letter from the White House to the ABS, September 5, 1952. ABS Archives.

This book [the Bible] speaks both the voice of God and the voice of humanity, for there is told in it the most convincing story of human experience that has ever been written, take it all in all, and those who heed that story will know that strength and happiness and success are all summed up in the exhortation, "Fear God and keep his commandments."

—WOODROW WILSON, 28th U.S. president.
In a letter from the White House to the ABS, June 6, 1917,
sent through the Maryland Bible Society. ABS Archives.

I am glad to have the opportunity to endorse the effort of the American Bible Society to procure a fund of $400,000 to cover the expenses of supplying the men in the National Army with Bibles. . . . They will need the support of the only book from which they can get it.

—WOODROW WILSON, 28th U.S. president.
In a letter on White House stationery from
the *U.S.S. Mayflower* to Rev. Dr. John Fox,
corresponding secretary, ABS, September 1, 1917.
ABS Archives.

I think vital Religion has always suffer'd, when Orthodoxy is more regarded than Virtue. And the Scripture assures me, that at the last Day, we shall not be examin'd [on] what we *thought*, but what we *did*; and our Recommendation will not be that we said *Lord, Lord*, but that we did GOOD to our Fellow Creatures. See Matth. 26.

—BENJAMIN FRANKLIN, member of the Second Continental
Congress. To Josiah and Abiah Franklin, April 13, 1738.
Labaree, *Papers of Benjamin Franklin*, vol. 2, p. 204.

The work of sending all abroad throughout this extended land and throughout all lands of the habitable globe, the holy Scriptures, in the vernacular of the peoples and tribes of every tongue, is, surely, a work the glory of which will outshine the sun. . . .

—ENOCH L. FANCHER, ABS president, and justice for the Supreme Court of New York. In letter of December 14, 1885. To A.D.F. Randolph, William H. Crosby, and Hiram M. Forrester, accepting the presidency of ABS. Corresponding Secretary Files, ABS Archives.

The older I grow, and the more I read the holy Scriptures, the more reverence I have for them, and the more convinced I am that they are not only the best guide for the conduct of this life, but the foundation of all hope respecting a future state of existence.

—DANIEL WEBSTER, American orator, lawyer, and statesman. In a letter of May 7, 1840. To Lord Ashley, the seventh Earl of Shaftsbury, expressing thanks for a copy of the Bible. Letter originally published in the biography of Lord Ashley, and quoted in the *Bible Society Record*, vol. 36, no. 1, January 15, 1891, p. 11.

Philosophical argument, especially that drawn from the vastness of the universe, in comparison with the insignificance of this globe, has sometimes shaken my reason for the faith that is in me; but my heart has always assured and reassured me that the gospel of Jesus Christ must be a Divine Reality. The Sermon on the Mount cannot be a merely human production. This belief enters into the very depth of my conscience. The whole history of man proves it.

—DANIEL WEBSTER, American orator, lawyer, and statesman. An inscription that he said was to be placed on his monument, drawn up and signed a few day before his death. George Ticknar Curtis. *Life of Daniel Webster*, Appleton, 1870, p. 684.

... cultivate an acquaintance with, and a firm belief in, the holy Scriptures; this is your certain interest.

—BENJAMIN FRANKLIN, member of the Second Continental Congress. William Makepeace Thayer, *The Printer Boy: or, How Benjamin Franklin Made His Mark*, (Oxford University, 1860), p. 264.

Religious thoughts of all ages should be impressed upon the minds of children—the story of Joseph, and the Sermon on the Mount, and the wonderful writings of St. Paul. An educated man who has not those in his memory is to be pitied.

—ANDREW D. WHITE, educator and diplomat. In a lecture at Cornell University on the need of a better education. "Character Teaching for Common Schools," James Terry White, *The School Journal*, (E.L. Kelloge & Co., 1906), p. 17.

... Above all, the pure and benign light of Revelation has had a meliorating influence on mankind, and increased the blessings of society.

—GEORGE WASHINGTON, 1st U.S. president. "Letter to the governors of States," June 8, 1783, in *The American Historical Review* by American Historical Association, 1887, p. 545.

The first and almost the only book deserving of universal attention is The Bible . . . I speak as a man of the world . . . , and I say
to you, "Search the Scriptures."

—JOHN QUINCY ADAMS, 6th U.S. president and diplomat.
Letter to the officers of the Franklin Association of Baltimore,
June 22, 1838. In *The American Quarterly Register*, Bela B.
Edwards, ed., American Education Society, 1840.

The very principles of our republic, the ethics whereby we live,
the culture that makes us civilized, all derive from the holy
Scriptures. No person can call himself educated who does not
maintain proper familiarity with the contents of the Bible. Yet
it is necessary from time to time that some special measure be
taken to remind us of these truths.

—THOMAS E. DEWEY, governor of New York.
Thomas Edmund Dewey, *Public Papers of Thomas E. Dewey:
Fifty-first governor of the State of New York, 1943 [-1954]*,
(Williams Press, 1944), p. 307.

The Bible is Word of Life. I beg that you will read it and find
this out for yourselves—read not little snatches here and
there, but long passages that will really be the road to the
heart of it. You will find it full of real men and women not
only, but also of the things you have wondered about and
troubled about all your life, as men have always been; and the
more you read, the more it will become plain to you what
things are worth while and what are not; what things make
men happy—loyalty, right dealing, speaking the truth, readiness to give everything for what they think their duty, and,
most of all, the wish that they may have the approval of the
Christ, who gave everything for them;—and the things that

are guaranteed to make men unhappy—selfishness, coward-
ice, greed, and everything that is low and mean. When you
have read the Bible you will know that it is the Word of God,
because you will have found the key to your own heart, your
own happiness, and your own duty.

—WOODROW WILSON, 28th U.S. president.
The Politics of Woodrow Wilson, August 1917.

I have read on my knees the story of Gethsemane, where the
Son of God prayed in vain that the cup of bitterness might pass
from him. I am in the garden of Gethsemane now, and my cup
is overflowing.

—ABRAHAM LINCOLN, 16th U.S. president. In comment after
his election in 1860 to Judge Joseph Gillespie, reproduced in
*The Life of Abraham Lincoln: Drawn From Original Sources
and Containing Many Speeches, Letters and Telegrams
Hitherto Unpublished and with Many Reproductions from
Original Paintings, Photographs, etc.*, Ida Minerva Tarbell,
Lincoln History Society, 1900, p. 200.

The teaching of the Bible to children is, of course, a matter of
special interest to those of us who have families—and, incidentally,
I wish to express my profound belief in large families. Older folks
often fail to realize how readily a child will grasp a little askew something they do not take the trouble to explain. We cannot be too
careful in seeing that the Biblical learning is not merely an affair of
rote, so that the child may understand what is being taught.

—THEODORE ROOSEVELT, 26th U.S. president. Inglehart,
Ferdinand Cowle, "Theodore Roosevelt: The Man As I Knew
Him," *The Christian Herald*, 1919, p. 310.

We plead for a closer and wider and deeper study of the Bible, so that our people may be in fact as well as in theory "doers of the word and not hearers only."

—THEODORE ROOSEVELT, 26th U.S. president.
Inglehart, Ferdinand Cowle, "Theodore Roosevelt: The Man As I Knew Him," *The Christian Herald*, 1919, pp. 313-314.

Brothers, sisters, friends, we have this Bible. It is our priceless heritage. Let us read it more. Let us study it more. Let us love it more. Let us live it more; and let us join hands with this Society in giving it to all the world, to every creature.

—DR. JACOB CHAMBERLAIN. From a sermon preached before the ABS in 1878, in Fourth Avenue P resbyterian Church, New York. Jacob Chamberlain, *The Bible Tested: Is It the Book for To-day and for the World? or the Bible in India*, ABS, 1918, p. 32.

I think that it will be comforting to you to remember, as you listen to your clocks ticking, that at every tick of the clock a volume of the Scriptures goes forth to accomplish God's purpose for it in the world!

—JAMES WOOD, president of the ABS. Excerpt from Address at the ABS Centennial Celebration in Washington, D.C., *Bible Society Record*, vol. 61, no. 6, June, 1916, p. 124.

Sometimes, in rightly putting the stress that we do upon intelligence, we forget the fact that there is something that counts more. It is a good thing to be clever, to be able and smart; but it is a better thing to have the qualities that find expression in the Decalogue and the Golden Rule.

—THEODORE ROOSEVELT, 26th U.S. president. Address to the Long Island Bible Society, June 11, 1901. p. 309.

The Old Testament tells us to be strong and of good courage; fear not nor be dismayed. And with God as my judge and as my guide, each day I try with all that is within me to do what is right and do what is just for my country and for all the people of America.

—LYNDON B. JOHNSON, 36th U.S. president. "Remarks Before Two Groups at the Fifth Regiment Armory in Baltimore," October 24, 1964.

The Prophet Isaiah tells us, "They that wait upon the Lord shall renew their strength; they shall mount up with wings as eagles; they shall run, and not be weary; and they shall walk, and not faint."

I believe that with all my heart, but in these troubled times I am sustained by much more than my own prayers. I am sustained by the prayers of hundreds of Americans who daily take the time to look up from their own problems in order to try to give me a little encouragement in mine.

—LYNDON B. JOHNSON, 36th U.S. president. Remarks at the 14th Annual Prayer Breakfast, February 17, 1966.

If God is on your side—and he will be if you are on his—no man, no woman, can ever defeat you. As the Bible said, "God be for us, who can be against us."

—GERALD FORD, 38th U.S. president. Remarks at the
Professional Athletes Prayer Brunch, February 15, 1976.

The supreme value of every person to whom life is given by God is a belief that comes to us from the holy Scriptures confirmed by all the great leaders of the church.

—GERALD FORD, 38th U.S. president.
Remarks at the conclusion of the International Eucharistic
Congress in Philadelphia, August 8, 1976.

We're breaking through the material conditions of existence to a world where man creates his own destiny. Even as we explore the most advanced reaches of science, we're returning to the age-old wisdom of our culture, a wisdom contained in the book of Genesis in the Bible: In the beginning was the spirit, and it was from this spirit that the material abundance of creation issued forth.

—RONALD REAGAN, 40th U.S. president.
Remarks and a Question and Answer Session with Students and
Faculty at Moscow State University, May 31, 1988.

Dear God, we humbly give you our heartfelt thanks. We thank you for bringing the war to a quick end. We thank you for sparing the lives of so many of our men and women who went to the Gulf. We ask you to bring comfort to the families of those who gave their lives for their country. We ask you to protect the innocents who this very day are suffering in Iraq and elsewhere. We give thanks for the bravery and steadfast support of our coalition partners, and yes, we pray for our enemies, that a just peace may come to their troubled land.

We are not an arrogant nation, a gloating nation. For we know: "Blessed are the meek, for they shall inherit the Earth." On this special day, this grateful nation says, "Thank you, God."

—GEORGE H.W. BUSH, 41st U.S. president.
Remarks Commemorating the National Days of Thanksgiving in
Houston, Texas, April 7, 1991.

In the Book of Kings, we find the wonderful story of the prophet Elijah, who climbs a mountain to seek the voice of God. A wind shatters rocks in pieces, but the Bible says, the Lord is not in the wind. Then, there's an earthquake and then a fire, but God is not in the earthquake or in the fire. But then, the Scripture says, "after the fire, a still, small voice."

It is that still, small voice that spoke to those six good men, that moved their souls to service and sacrifice. The still, small voice that endures through the ages, that inspires the songs and words we have all shared today, that must now carry this group of grieving families through their grief to going on.

—WILLIAM CLINTON, 42nd U.S. president.
Remarks by the president at a memorial service for
Worcester Firefighters, December 9, 1999.

How did people keep on going? Rodney reminded me when, back when I was governor, and Rodney worked for me—he didn't have such a big, fancy office, and he wasn't so far away—we used to talk all the time about Bible verses and first one thing and another, and he knew that one of my favorite verses was the ninth verse of the sixth chapter of St. Paul's Letter to the Galatians. And he mentioned it to me tonight because of the Middle

East peace talks—"Let us not grow weary in doing good for in due season we shall reap if we do not lose heart."

—WILLIAM CLINTON, 42nd U.S. president.
Remarks by the president at the 160th anniversary celebration of the Metropolitan African Methodist Episcopal Church, October 23, 1998.

The sermon today was on the unity of the church, and our unity with God in the church. I would like to add only one point—I believe our faith calls upon us to seek unity with people across the world of different races and backgrounds and creeds. In the Book of Acts, the twenty-sixth verse, it is said that God has made from one blood every nation to dwell on the surface of the Earth. I believe that is true. Therefore, I believe that Chinese and Americans are brothers and sisters as children of God. We come here in that spirit today, grateful for your welcome.

—WILLIAM CLINTON, 42nd U.S. president.
Remarks by the president at a church service, Chongwenmen Church in Beijing, June 28, 1998.

And so, as I leave South Africa, I would leave you with one verse of Scripture that has throughout my working life been one of the very most important to me. When you are discouraged, when you are frustrated, when you are angry, when you wonder whether you can make the most of your freedom for these children, remember what St. Paul said to the Galatians: "Let us not grow weary in doing good. For in due season, we shall reap if we do not lose heart."

—WILLIAM CLINTON, 42nd U.S. president.
Remarks by the president at a church service, Regine Mundi Church in Johannesburg, South Africa, March 29, 1998.

I was thinking last night about what we really want out of this prayer breakfast. And I was up late reading and I came across something King David said in the fourth Psalm. You know, David knew something about leadership and courage and human failing. He said in his psalm to God, "Thou hast enlarged me when I was in distress." So I pray that when we leave here today, by the words of Senator Nunn, the readings of the scripture, the remarks of others, we shall all be enlarged in spirit—not only for our public work, but for our private trials. I look out here and I see friends of mine in both parties whom I know today have trials in their own families, in challenges of the heart they must face. And we leave here in the prayer that we will be enlarged.

—WILLIAM CLINTON, 42nd U.S. president.
Remarks by the president at the National Prayer Breakfast,
February 1, 1991.

This is a special service that reaffirms our relationship to our God and our God-given responsibility to serve our fellow human beings. The scripture from Isaiah that is the basis of this service today is something we would all do well to read and live by on a regular basis, and to echo the words of Isaiah, "Here am I Lord, send me." Because as all of you who are here know already, service to others is something everyone can do and something everyone should do because of our relationship to our God, our responsibility to others and our responsibility to ourselves.

—WILLIAM CLINTON, 42nd U.S. president.
Remarks by the president at church services with Americorps
National Civilian Community Corps and Base Personnel,
September 11, 1994.

We need our faith as a source of challenge because, if we read the Scriptures carefully, it teaches us that all of us must try to live by what we believe; or in more conventional terms, to live out the admonition of president Kennedy, that here on Earth God's work must truly be our own.

—WILLIAM CLINTON, 42nd U.S. president. Remarks by the president at the Prayer Breakfast, February 4, 1993.

And so, my fellow Americans, at the edge of the 21st century, let us begin with energy and hope, with faith and discipline, and let us work until our work is done. The scripture says, "And let us not be weary in well-doing, for in due season, we shall reap, if we faint not."

—WILLIAM CLINTON, 42nd U.S. president. Inaugural Speech, January 20, 1993.

In the aftermath of the attacks, the words of the Psalms brought comfort to many. We trust God always to be our refuge and our strength, an ever-present help in time of trouble. Believing that One greater than ourselves watches over our lives and over this Nation, we continue to place our trust in him.

—GEORGE W. BUSH, 43rd U.S. president. National Days of Prayer and Remembrance, August 31, 2002.

CHRISTIANITY

I deem the present occasion sufficiently important and solemn to justify me in expressing to my fellow-citizens a profound reverence for the Christian religion and a thorough conviction that sound morals, religious liberty, and a just sense of religious responsibility are essentially connected with all true and lasting happiness; and to that good Being who has blessed us by the gifts of civil and religious freedom, who watched over and prospered the labors of our fathers and has hitherto preserved to us institutions far exceeding in excellence those of any other people, let us unite in fervently commending every interest of our beloved country in all future time.

—WILLIAM HENRY HARRISON, 9th U.S. president.
Inaugural Address, March 4, 1841.

A proper history of the United States would have much to recommend it: in some respects it would be singular, or unlike all others; it would develop the great plan of Providence, for causing this extensive part of our world to be discovered, and these "uttermost parts of the earth" to be gradually filled with civilized and *Christian* people and nations. The means or second causes by which this great plan has long been and still is accomplishing, are materials for history, of which the writer ought well to know the use and bearings and proper places. In my opinion, the historian, in the course of the work, is never to lose sight of that great plan.

—JOHN JAY, president of the Continental Congress, 1778-1779;
and 1st chief justice of the U.S. Supreme Court, 1789-1795.
To Jedediah Morse, August 16, 1809. Johnston,
Correspondence of Jay, vol. 4, p. 322.

It is well known, that both cathedrals and meetinghouses have heretofore exhibited individuals who have been universally and justly celebrated as *real* and useful Christians; and it is also well known, that at present not a few, under similar circumstances and of similar characters, deserve the like esteem and commendation. As real Christians are made so by him without whom we "can do nothing," it is equally certain that he receives them into his family, and that in *his* family mutual love and uninterrupted concord never cease to prevail. There is no reason to believe or suppose that this family will be divided into separate classes, and that separate apartments in the mansions of bliss will be allotted to them according to the different sects from which they had proceeded.

—JOHN JAY, president of the Continental Congress, 1778-1779;
and 1st chief justice of the U.S. Supreme Court, 1789-1795.
To the ABS, May 13, 1824. Vol. 4, p. 495.

The Christian religion . . . is the brightness of the glory and the express portrait of the character of the eternal, self-existent, independent, benevolent, all powerful and all merciful creator, preserver, and Father of the universe, the first good, first perfect, and first fair. It will last as long as the world. Neither savage nor civilized man, without a revelation, could ever have discovered or invented it. Ask me not, then, whether I am a Catholic or

Protestant, Calvinist or Arminian. As far as they are Christians, I wish to be a fellow disciple with them all.

—JOHN ADAMS, 2nd U.S. president.
Letter to Benjamin Rush, January 21, 1810.

Why should we shut our eyes to the whole history of Christianity? Is it not the preaching of the minister of the gospel that has evangelized the more civilized part of the world? Why do we at this day enjoy the rights and benefits of Christianity ourselves? And where was Christianity ever received—where were its truths ever poured into the human heart—where did its waters, springing up into everlasting life, ever burst forth—except in the track of the Christian ministry?

DANIEL WEBSTER, American orator, lawyer, and statesman.
The Christian Life and Character of the Civil Institutions of the United States, p. 234.

There is nothing we look for with more certainty that this principle, that Christianity is a part of the law of the land. Every thing declares this.

—DANIEL WEBSTER, American orator, lawyer, and statesman.
Ibid., p. 245.

When a *Christian* people feel themselves to be overtaken by a great public calamity, it becomes them to humble themselves under the dispensation of Divine Providence to recognize his righteous government over the children of men, to acknowledge his goodness in times past, as well as their own unworthiness, and to supplicate his merciful protection for the future.

—JOHN TYLER, 10th U.S. president.
Recommendation, April 13, 1841. Ibid., p. 688.

It would seem as if one of the designs of Providence in permitting the existence of so many Sects of Christians was that each Sect might be a depository of some great truth of the Gospel, and that it might by that means be better preserved. . . . Let the different Sects of Christians not only bear with each other, but love each other for this kind display of God's goodness whereby all the truths of their Religion are so protected that none of them can ever become feeble or be lost. When united they make a great whole, and that whole is the salvation of all men.

—BENJAMIN RUSH, member of the Continental Congress, 1776-1777. "Commonplace Book," August 14, 1811. Corner, *Autobiography of Rush*, pp. 339-340.

Being no bigot myself to any mode of worship, I am disposed to indulge the professors of Christianity in the church, that road to heaven, which to them shall seem the most direct, plainest, easiest, and least liable to exception.

—GEORGE WASHINGTON, 1st U.S. president. Letter to the Marquis de Lafayette, August 15, 1787. Fitzpatrick, *Writings of Washington*, vol. 29, p. 259.

Every tyro knows that heathen philosophy and Jewish ceremonies have been intermixed with Christianity. But what then? If Christianity has been corrupted? What then? What has not?

—JOHN ADAMS, 2nd U.S. president. Marginal note on Bolingbroke's essay, "Concerning Authority in Matters of Religion," n.d. Haraszti, *Prophets of Progress*, p. 70.

My religion you know is not exactly conformable to that of the greatest part of the Christian World. It excludes superstition.

But with all the superstition that attends it, I think the Christian the best that is or has been.

> —JOHN ADAMS, 2nd U.S. president. To Abigail Adams,
> January 28, 1799. Adams Papers (online edition),
> Massachusetts Historical Society.

The Christian Religion was intended to give Peace of Mind to its Disciples in all cases whatsoever: but not to send civil or political Peace upon earth but a sword, and a sword it has sent: and peace of Mind too to Millions, by conquering death and taking away his sting.

> —JOHN ADAMS, 2nd U.S. president. To Benjamin Rush,
> November 29, 1812. Old Family Letters, p. 320.

In the heavenly doctrines of Christianity, reduced to its primitive simplicity, you and I agree as well, I believe, as any two christians in the world.

> —JOHN ADAMS, 2nd U.S. president. To Francis van der Kemp,
> October 4, 1813. Adams Papers (microfilm), reel 95,
> Library of Congress.

The Christian is the religion of the heart: but the heart is deceitful above all things; and unless controuled by the dominion of the head will lead us into Salt Ponds.

> —JOHN ADAMS, 2nd U.S. president. To Benjamin Waterhouse,
> December 19, 1815. Ibid., reel 122.

It is no slight testimonial, both to the merit and worth of Christianity, that in all ages since its promulgation the great mass of those who have risen to eminence by their profound wisdom and integrity have recognized and reverenced Jesus of Nazareth as the Son of the living God.

—JOHN QUINCY ADAMS, 6th U.S. president and diplomat.

The Christian religion is, above all the Religions that ever prevailed or existed in ancient or modern times, the religion of Wisdom, Virtue, Equity, and humanity. Let the Blackguard Paine say what he will; it is Resignation to God, it is Goodness itself to Man.

—JOHN ADAMS, 2nd U.S. president. July 26, 1796.
Writing in his diary a disapproval of Thomas Paine's assertions,
Norman Cousins, *In God We Trust—The Religious Beliefs and Ideas of the American Founding Fathers* (New York: Harper & Brothers, 1958), p. 99.

Let divines and philosophers, statesmen and patriots, unite their endeavors to renovate the age by impressing the minds of men with the importance of educating their little boys and girls, inculcating in the minds of youth the fear and love of the Deity... and leading them in the study and practice of the exalted virtues of the Christian system.

—SAMUEL ADAMS, Massachusetts delegate to the Continental Congress, 1775-1781. Letter to John Adams, October 4, 1790, *The Life and Public Services of Samuel Adams*, vol. III, pp. 300-302.

I would describe myself as a man who was raised a Christian, who sought redemption and found it in Jesus Christ. And that's important by the way, for someone running for public office. It's a humbling experience to make that admission. I admit I'm a lowly sinner. It's that admission that led me to redemption and led me to Christ. Without making that admission, I don't think there's such a thing as redemption.

—GEORGE W. BUSH, 43rd U.S. president.
Interview with the Baptist Press, August 31, 2000.

We should live our lives as though Christ were coming this afternoon.

—JIMMY CARTER, 39th U.S. president. Speech
at a Bible class in Plains, Georgia, March 1976.
In *Boston Sunday Herald Advertiser*, April 11, 1976.

Christianity is an active, affectionate and social religion, chiefly consisting in a discharge of duties to our fellow creatures. It therefore requires no separation from them. Tho enjoining that we "be not conformed to the world," in following this direction, the utmost attention is necessary lest distinctions from others by plainness of manners and customs assume the place of virtues, and become snares. Such distinctions are not in the least value in themselves because they are no part of the Divine Laws.

—JOHN DICKINSON, member of the First Continental
Congress. "Religious Instruction for Youth," undated.
R. K. Logan Papers, Historical Society of Pennsylvania.

History will also afford frequent Opportunities of showing . . . the Excellency of the CHRISTIAN RELIGION above all others ancient or modern.

—BENJAMIN FRANKLIN, member of the Second Continental
Congress. "Proposals Relating to the Education of Youth in
Pennsylvania," 1749. Labaree, *Papers of Benjamin Franklin*,
vol. 3, p. 413.

He who shall introduce into public affairs the principles of primitive Christianity will change the face of the world.

> —BENJAMIN FRANKLIN, member of the Second Continental Congress. Remark to the French ministry, March 1778.

I hope you will renew your Christian faith and duties. It is a great comfort to trust God—even if his providence is unfavorable. Prayer steadies one when he is walking in slippery places—even if things asked for are not given.

> —BENJAMIN HARRISON, 23rd U.S. president and ABS vice president. Letter to Russell Harrison, August 8, 1887.

What a great mistake the man makes who goes about to oppose this religion! What a crime, if we may judge of men's acts by their results! Nay, what a great mistake is made by him who does not support the religion of the Bible!

> —RUTHERFORD B. HAYES, 19th U.S. president and ABS vice president, 1880 until his death in 1893. Diary, October 15, 1884.

I am not a subscriber to any creed. I belong to no church. But in a sense, satisfactory to myself and believed by me to be important, I try to be a Christian, or rather I want to be a Christian and to help do Christian work.

> —RUTHERFORD B. HAYES, 19th U.S. president and ABS vice president, 1880 until his death in 1893. Diary, May 17, 1890.

I am a Christian according to my conscience in belief, not of course in character and conduct, but in purpose and wish;—not of course by the orthodox standard. But I am content, and have a feeling of trust and safety.

—RUTHERFORD B. HAYES, 19th U.S. president and ABS vice president, 1880 until his death in 1893. Diary, January 8, 1893.

This is all the inheritance I can give my dear family. The religion of Christ can give them one which will make them rich indeed.

—PATRICK HENRY, American patriot and governor of Virginia. The Last Will and Testament of Patrick Henry.

It cannot be emphasized too clearly and too often that this nation was founded, not by religionists, but by Christians; not on religion, but on the gospel of Jesus Christ. For this very reason, peoples of other faiths have been afforded asylum, prosperity, and freedom of worship here.

—PATRICK HENRY, American patriot and governor of Virginia. May 1765 Speech to the House of Burgesses.

Amongst other strange things said of me, I hear it is said by the deists that I am one of the number; and, indeed, that some good people think I am no christian. This thought gives me much more pain than the appellation of tory; because I think religion of infinitely higher importance than politics; and I find much cause to reproach myself, that I have lived so long, and have given no decided and public proofs of my being a christian. But, indeed, my dear child, this is a character which I prize far above all this world has or can boast.

—PATRICK HENRY, American patriot and governor of Virginia. To Betsy Aylett, August 20, 1796. William Win, *The Life of Patrick Henry* (New York: M'Elrath & Bangs, 1831), pp. 402-403.

I have long been of opinion that the Evidence of the Truth of Christianity requires only to be carefully examined to produce conviction in candid minds.

> —JOHN JAY, president of the Continental Congress, 1778-1779;
> and 1st chief justice of the U.S. Supreme Court, 1789-1795.
> To Uzal Ogden, February 14, 1796. Jay Papers (online edition),
> Columbia University Library.

One of them asked me if I believed in Christ. I answered that I did, and that I thanked God that I did. Nothing further passed between me and them or any of them on that subject.

> —JOHN JAY, president of the Continental Congress, 1778-1779;
> and 1st chief justice of the U.S. Supreme Court, 1789-1795.
> To John Bristed, April 23, 1811. Ibid.

I am a *real Christian*, that is to say, a disciple of the doctrines of Jesus, very different from the Platonists, who call *me* infidel, and *themselves* Christians and preachers of the gospel, while they draw all their characteristic dogmas from what it's Author never said nor saw. They have compounded from the heathen mysteries a system beyond the comprehension of man, of which the great reformer of the vicious ethics and deism of the Jews, were he to return on earth, would not recognise one feature.

> —THOMAS JEFFERSON, 2nd U.S. president. To Charles
> Thomson, January 9, 1816. Adams, *Jefferson's Extracts*, p. 365.

Our saviour did not come into the world to save metaphysicians only. His doctrines are levelled to the simplest understandings and it is only by banishing hierophantic mysteries and Scholastic subtleties, which they have nick-named Christianity, and getting back to the plain and unsophisticated precepts of Christ, that we become *real* Christians.

—THOMAS JEFFERSON, 2nd U.S. president.
To Salma Hale, July 26, 1818. Ibid., p. 385.

Had the doctrines of Jesus been preached always as purely as they came from his lips, the whole civilised world would now have been Christian.

—THOMAS JEFFERSON, 2nd U.S. president.
To Benjamin Waterhouse, June 26, 1822. Ibid., p. 405.

I am looking with anxiety to see the dawn of primitive Christianity here, where, if it once appears, it will soon beam like the rising sun and restore reason to her day! "Thy kingdom come" is therefore my prayer; and my confidence is that it will come.

—THOMAS JEFFERSON, 2nd U.S. president.
To Benjamin Waterhouse, October 15, 1822.
Jefferson Papers, Library of Congress.

Christianity is the highest perfection of humanity.

—SAMUEL JOHNSON. Letter to William Drummond,
August 13, 1766. James Boswell, *The Life of Samuel Johnson*, 1791.

The best & purest religion, the Christian Religion itself.

—JAMES MADISON, 4th U.S. president. To Jasper Adams,
September 1833. Dreisbach, *Religion and Politics*, p. 117.

The true Christian is the true citizen, lofty of pose, resolute in endeavor, ready for a hero's but never looking down on his task because it is cast in the day of small things; scornful of baseness, awake to his own duties as well as to his rights, following the higher law with reverence, and in this world doing all that in him lies, so that when death comes he may feel that mankind is in some degree better because he has lived.

—THEODORE ROOSEVELT, 26th U.S. president.
In a speech at the YMCA, "Christian Citizenship,"
in New York City, December 30, 1900.

... Christianity is the only true and perfect religion, and that in proportion as mankind adopts its principles, and obeys its precepts, they will be wise, and happy.

—BENJAMIN RUSH, member of the Continental Congress,
1776-1777. "A Defense of the Use of the Bible as a School Book."
Rush, *Essays: Literary, Moral, and Philosophical*, p. 55.

In spreading the blessings of liberty and religion, our Divine Master forbids us, in many of his parables and precepts, to have either friends or country. The globe is the native country, and the whole human race the fellow citizens of a Christian.

—BENJAMIN RUSH, member of the Continental Congress,
1776-1777. To Granville Sharp, August 1791. Butterfield,
Letters of Benjamin Rush, vol 1, p. 609.

Let the children who are sent to those schools be taught to read and write and above all, let both sexes be carefully instructed in the principles and obligations of the Christian religion. This is the most essential part of education.

—BENJAMIN RUSH, member of the Continental Congress,
1776-1777. "To the citizens of Philadelphia: A Plan for Free
Schools," *Letters of Benjamin Rush*, March 28, 1787.

A veneration for the religion of a people who profess and call themselves Christians, and a fixed resolution to consider a decent respect for Christianity among the best recommendations for the public service.

—JOHN ADAMS, 2nd U.S. president.
Inaugural Address, March 4, 1797. Richardson, *Messages and Papers of the presidents*, vol. 1, p. 222.

Providence has given to our people the choice of their rulers, and it is the duty as well as the privilege and interest of our Christian nation to select and prefer Christians for their rulers.

—JOHN JAY, president of the Continental Congress,
1778-1779; and 1st chief justice of the U.S. Supreme Court,
1789-1795. To John Murray, Jr., October 12, 1816. Johnston,
Correspondence of Jay, vol 4, p. 393.

Whether our religion permits *Christians* to vote for *infidel* rulers, is a question which merits more consideration than it seems yet to have generally received, either from the clergy or the laity. It appears to me, that what the prophet said to Jehoshaphat about his attachment to Ahab affords a salutary lesson . . . "Shouldest thou help the ungodly, and love them that hate the Lord?" *2 Chron.* xix, 2.

—JOHN JAY, president of the Continental Congress, 1778-1779;
and 1st chief justice of the U.S. Supreme Court, 1789-1795.
To Jedidiah Morse January 1, 1813. Ibid., vol. 4, p. 365.

Whatever makes men good Christians, makes them good citizens.

—DANIEL WEBSTER, American orator, lawyer, and statesman.
Speech at Plymouth, Massachusetts, December 22, 1820.

In all disputes between conflicting governments it is our interest not less than our duty to remain strictly neutral, while our geographical position, the genius of our institutions and our people, the advancing spirit of civilization, and, above all, the dictates of religion direct us to the cultivation of peaceful and friendly relations with all other powers.

—ZACHARY TAYLOR, 12th U.S. president.
Inaugural Address, March 5, 1849.

CHRISTMAS MESSAGES

In love, which is the very essence of the message of the Prince of Peace, the world would find a solution for all its ills. I do not believe there is one problem in this country or in the world today which could not be settled if approached through the teaching of the Sermon on the Mount.

—HARRY S. TRUMAN, 33rd U.S. president.
Address at the lighting of the national community
Christmas tree on the White House grounds,
December 24, 1945.

Happily for all mankind, the spirit of Christmas survives travail and suffering because it fills us with hope of better things to come. Let us then put our trust in the unerring Star which guided the Wise Men to the Manger of Bethlehem. Let us hearken again to the Angel Choir singing: "Glory to God in the highest, and on earth peace, good will toward men."

—HARRY S. TRUMAN, 33rd U.S. president.
Address at the lighting of the national community
Christmas tree on the White House grounds,
December 24, 1947.

The message of Bethlehem best sums up our hopes tonight. If we as a nation, and the other nations of the world, will accept it, the star of faith will guide us into the place of peace as it did the shepherds on that day of Christ's birth long ago.

—HARRY S. TRUMAN, 33rd U.S. president.
Address at the lighting of the national community
Christmas tree on the White House grounds,
December 24, 1946.

The moving event of the first Christmas was the bringing forth of the first born in the stable in Bethlehem. There began in humble surroundings the home life of the holy Family glorified in song and story and in the hearts of men down through the centuries. The great joys and mysteries of that event have forever sanctified and enriched all home life.

—HARRY S. TRUMAN, 33rd U.S. president.
Remarks on the occasion of the lighting of the
community Christmas tree on the White House grounds,
December 24, 1948.

And as we go about our business of trying to achieve peace in the world, let us remember always to try to act and live in the spirit of the Prince of Peace. He bore in his heart no hate and no malice—nothing but love for all mankind. We should try as nearly as we can to follow his example.

—HARRY S. TRUMAN, 33rd U.S. president.
Remarks upon lighting the national community
Christmas tree, December 24, 1952.

Each succeeding Christmas will, we pray, see ever greater striving by each of us to rekindle in our hearts and minds zeal for America's progress in fulfilling her own high purposes. In doing so, our veneration of Christmas and its meaning will be better understood throughout the world and we shall be true to ourselves, to our Nation, and to the Man whose birth, 2,000 years ago, we now celebrate.

—DWIGHT D. EISENHOWER, 34th U.S. president,
Remarks at the Pageant of Peace Ceremonies, December 23, 1960.

At this special time of year, we reflect on the miraculous life that began in a humble manger 2,000 years ago. That single life changed the world, and continues to change hearts today.

—GEORGE W. BUSH, 43rd U.S. president.
Christmas Message, December 23, 2006.

More than 2,000 years ago, a virgin gave birth to a Son, and the God of heaven came to Earth. Mankind had received its Savior, and to those who had dwelled in darkness, the light of hope had come. Each Christmas, we celebrate that first coming anew, and we rejoice in the knowledge that the God who came to Earth that night in Bethlehem is with us still and will remain with us forever.

—GEORGE W. BUSH, 43rd U.S. president.
Christmas Message, December 19, 2005.

For 2,000 years, Christmas has proclaimed a message of hope: the patient hope of men and women across centuries who listened to the words of prophets and lived in joyful expectation; the hope of Mary, who welcomed God's plan with great faith; and the hope of wise men, who set out on a long journey guided only by a slender promise traced in the stars. Christmas reminds us that the grandest purposes of God can be found in the humblest places. And it gives us hope that all the love and gifts that come to us in this life are the signs and symbols of an even greater love and gift that came on a holy night.

—GEORGE W. BUSH, 43rd U.S. president.
Christmas Message, December 23, 2004.

As families and friends gather to celebrate Christmas, we remember all the blessings that fill our lives, beginning with the great blessing that came on a holy night in Bethlehem. For Christians around the world, the birth of Jesus is a central religious event; an example of God's profound love for humanity; and the pathway to hope and to new life. Today, the Christmas story still speaks to every generation.

—GEORGE W. BUSH, 43rd U.S. president.
Christmas Message, December 19, 2003.

During Christmas, we gather with family and friends to celebrate the birth of our Savior, Jesus Christ. As God's only Son, Jesus came to Earth and gave his life so that we may live. His actions and his words remind us that service to others is central to our lives and that sacrifice and unconditional love must guide us and inspire us to lead lives of compassion, mercy, and justice.

—GEORGE W. BUSH, 43rd U.S. president.
Christmas Message, December 20, 2002.

But amidst all these traditions, we remember that the true message of Christmas is in the Child whose birth we celebrate the living proof of God's mercy and unending love. Christ's message—of renewal and reconciliation is as fresh and powerful today as it was on that first Christmas two thousand years ago.

—WILLIAM CLINTON, 42nd U.S. president.
Christmas Message, December 2000.

Saint Matthew's Gospel tells us that, on the first Christmas 2000 years ago, a bright star shone vividly in the eastern sky, heralding the birth of Jesus and the beginning of his hallowed mission as teacher, healer, servant, and savior. Jesus' birth in poverty proclaimed the intrinsic dignity and brotherhood of all humanity, and his luminous teachings have brought hope and joy to generations of believers.

—WILLIAM CLINTON, 42nd U.S. president.
Christmas Message, December 21, 1999.

May the spirit of the season be with you today and throughout the new year. From our family to yours, Merry Christmas, happy New Year, and God bless you all.

—WILIAM CLINTON, 42nd U.S. president.
Christmas Message, December 1998.

The beloved Christmas story itself is a story of light for, as the Gospel of John tells us, Jesus came into the world as "the true light" that illumines all humankind.

—WILLIAM CLINTON, 42nd U.S. president.
Christmas Message, December 1997.

As we gather with family and friends again this year to celebrate Christmas, let us welcome God wholeheartedly into our daily lives. Let us learn to recognize him not only in the faces of our loved ones, but also in the faces of those who, like Jesus, are familiar with poverty, hardship, and rejection. And let us be inspired by his example to serve one another with generous hearts and open hands. In this way we will approach the dawn of a new century and a new millennium confident in God's abundant grace and strengthened by his timeless promise of salvation.

—WILLIAM CLINTON, 42nd U.S. president.
Christmas Message, December 1996.

Through his words and example, Christ made clear the redemptive value of giving of oneself for others, and his life proved that love and sacrifice can make a profound difference in the world.

—GEORGE H.W. BUSH, 41st U.S. president.
Christmas Message, December 8, 1992.

Americans have the talent and power to do anything. And so when history remembers Christmas, 1991, let it remember that we promise to bring God's light to our brothers and sisters in need. Let it record that on Christmas, 1991, this Nation united to ask God for peace on Earth, goodwill to all. And let it record that a new age of goodness and hope began here and now.

—GEORGE H.W. BUSH, 41st U.S. president.
Christmas Message, December 23, 1991.

Each Christmas Day, we close our eyes in prayer and think of what Harry Truman called the humble surroundings of the Nativity and how from a straw-littered stable shone a light which for nearly twenty centuries has given men strength, comfort, and peace.

—GEORGE H.W. BUSH, 41st U.S. president.
Christmas Message, December 24, 1990.

During the beautiful and holy season of Christmas, our hearts are filled with the same wonder, gratitude, and joy that led the psalmist of old to ask, "When I consider Thy heavens, the work of Thy fingers, the moon and the stars, which Thou hast ordained; What is man, that Thou art mindful of him? And the son of man, that Thou visitest him?" At Christmas, we, too, rejoice in the mystery of God's love for us—love revealed through the gift of Christ's birth.

—GEORGE H.W. BUSH, 41st U.S. president.
Christmas Message, December 18, 1989.

As we come home with gladness to family and friends this Christmas, let us also remember our neighbors who cannot go home themselves. Our compassion and concern this Christmas and all year long will mean much to the hospitalized, the homeless, the convalescent, the orphaned—and will surely lead us on our way to the joy and peace of Bethlehem and the Christ Child Who bids us come. For it is only in finding and living the eternal meaning of the Nativity that we can be truly happy, truly at peace, truly home.

—RONALD REAGAN, 40th U.S. president.
Christmas Message, December 19, 1988.

At Christmastime we accompany shepherds and Wise Men to the stable as of old, where we relearn the timeless and priceless lessons of love, humility and sacrifice, where we see the Christmas spirit as God's love flowing through so many people all at once.

—RONALD REAGAN, 40th U.S. president.
Christmas Message, December 23, 1987.

May our prayers this Christmas call forth that serenity of heart and confidence in the future that are the best of all possible gifts. May the song of our people be one of thanks for God's blessings on America and of petition for his continued blessings upon us, especially on those who face this Christmas in want or loneliness. Let us raise our hearts and voices in common song for the reign of peace and the rule of goodwill, that in the words of the carol, all may celebrate "everywhere, everywhere, Christmas tonight."

—RONALD REAGAN, 40th U.S. president.
Christmas Message, December 11, 1986.

Amid all the hubbub and hustle this time of year always brings, we should not forget the simple beauty of that first Christmas long ago. Joseph and Mary, far from home and huddled in a place barely fit for habitation, felt the universal love that binds all families together and a unique awe at the special purpose for which God had chosen them. Gathering around them first the shepherds and later, the Magi—poor and rich, humble and great, native and foreign—each bowed before the King whose dominion knows no boundaries. Above them was the Star, the guiding light which would shine down through the centuries for everyone seeking the Way, the Truth, and the Life.

—RONALD REAGAN, 40th U.S. president.
Christmas Message, December 18, 1985.

Today, as we gather with our family and friends to honor Christ, we can experience the same peace and joy as the shepherds and the Magi did almost two thousand years ago. If we make that peace and joy a part of our lives, our example will serve as a guide and an inspiration for everyone we meet. Nancy and I pray that the joy of this holiday season will remain with us all throughout the coming year. May God bless you.

—RONALD REAGAN, 40th U.S. president.
Christmas Message, December 21, 1984.

Sometimes, in the hustle and bustle of holiday preparations we forget that the true meaning of Christmas was given to us by the angelic host that holy night long ago. Christmas is the commemoration of the birth of the Prince of Peace, Jesus Christ, whose message would truly be one of good tidings and great joy, peace and good will. During this glorious festival let us renew our determination to follow his example.

—RONALD REAGAN, 40th U.S. president.
Christmas Message, December 20, 1983.

On this, the birthday of the Prince of Peace, you and your comrades serve to protect the peace he taught us. You may be thousands of miles away, but to us here at home, you've never been closer.

—RONALD REAGAN, 40th U.S. president. Christmas Day
Radio address to the Nation, December 25, 1982.

The Nativity story of nearly twenty centuries ago is known by all faiths as a hymn to the brotherhood of man. For Christians, it is the fulfillment of age-old prophecies and the reaffirmation of God's great love for all of us. Through a generous heavenly Father's gift of his Son, hope and compassion entered a world weary with fear and despair and changed it for all time.

—RONALD REAGAN, 40th U.S. president.
Christmas Message, December 24, 1981.

Together let us thank God for all the blessings he has given us and ask him to sustain and strengthen us as individuals and as a nation. Let us also offer our prayers for those who live where there is strife, hunger, persecution, or injustice. May the year ahead be better for them and for their families and loved ones.

—JIMMY CARTER, 39th U.S. president.
Christmas Message, December 2, 1980.

At this time of traditional joy and family festivity, as we join in thanking God for his blessings to us as a nation and as individuals, we ask that you offer a special prayer for the Americans who are being held hostage in Iran and for their families. We remember also the plight of all people, whatever their nationality, who suffer from injustice, oppression, hunger, war, or terrorism.

—JIMMY CARTER, 39th U.S. president.
Christmas Message, December 14, 1979.

We also join in this Season's traditional expression of appreciation to God for his blessings in the past year. And we ask for his continuing guidance and protection as we face the challenges of 1979.

—JIMMY CARTER, 39th U.S. president.
Christmas Message, December 18, 1978.

The celebration of the birth of Jesus is observed on every continent. The customs and traditions are not always the same, but feelings that are generated between friends and family members are equally strong and equally warm.

—GERALD FORD, 38th U.S. president. Remarks at the lighting of the National community Christmas tree, December 16, 1976.

I know this will be a particularly happy Christmas for me. I celebrate it surrounded by those I love and who love me. I celebrate it by joining with all of our citizens in observing a Christmas when Americans can honor the Prince of Peace in a nation at peace.

—GERALD FORD, 38th U.S. president.
Christmas Message, December 24, 1975.

Mrs. Ford and I send our warmest holiday greetings to all our fellow citizens. We hope that each of you will share the traditional joys of this holy season with your family and friends. And we pray that the Christmas spirit of generosity and renewal will be with you throughout the coming year.

—GERALD FORD, 38th U.S. president.
Christmas Message, December 17, 1974.

We pause to give special thought to those in need, and to the universal bonds that link all mankind in brotherhood under God. In doing so, we touch something basic and good in the human spirit: that special grace that makes this a time of giving, and of forgiving—a time of goodwill, when we know the true peace that lodges in the heart.

—RICHARD NIXON, 37th U.S. president.
Christmas Message, December 23, 1971.

May this season of giving be particularly satisfying for you who have given so much to all of us. May you derive comfort and courage from your very special gift to the American people: your sacrifices in the cause of peace and freedom. It is a gift that we can never fully return. But because of it, we are free to worship the Prince of Peace in this holy season; and we are nearer to the peace on earth we seek.

—RICHARD NIXON, 37th U.S. president.
Christmas message to hospitalized veterans, December 16, 1970.

At this moment of Christmas, we Americans join our prayers with all our human brothers, in a spirit of hope. We pray for an early and durable settlement of the war that has called many brave young men to duty far from our shores and who cannot be in their homes this Christmas. In the hour of the Prince of Peace, we pray for them, for ourselves, and for all our fellows on this earth.

—LYNDON B. JOHNSON, 36th U.S. president. Remarks at the
lighting of the nation's Christmas Tree, December 16, 1968.

The first Christmas season of our independence lives in our literature and our legend as a time that tried men's souls. Service to country was the test of a patriot. "He that stands it now," wrote Thomas Paine, "deserves the love and thanks of man and Woman." . . .

"The fate of unborn millions," General Washington said, "will now depend under God on the courage and conduct of this army."

His words carry across the years. Their message is undimmed in our time.

—LYNDON B. JOHNSON, 36th U.S. president. Christmas message
to the men and women of the armed forces, December 16, 1967.

Christmas is a time for hope. It is also a season for renewed inspiration from Christ's universal message of peace on earth, good will toward men.

—LYNDON B. JOHNSON, 36th U.S. president.
Christmas message to the men and women of the armed forces,
December 18, 1966.

This is a season of hope and rejoicing as we celebrate the birth of the Prince of Peace. It is a time for renewing ties of brotherhood with all men of good will, everywhere on earth.

—LYNDON B. JOHNSON, 36th U.S. president.
Christmas message to the men and women of the armed forces,
December 18, 1965.

To all Americans I say that loving our neighbor as we love ourselves is not enough—that we as a Nation and as individuals will please God best by showing regard for the laws of God. There is no better way of fostering goodwill toward man than by first fostering goodwill toward God. If we love him we will keep his Commandments.

—FRANKLIN D. ROOSEVELT, 32nd U.S. president.
Christmas message on Christmas Eve, December 24, 1942.

We are confident in our devotion to country, in our love of freedom, in our inheritance of courage. But our strength, as the strength of all men everywhere, is of greater avail as God upholds us.

—FRANKLIN D. ROOSEVELT, 32nd U.S. president.
Christmas Eve message to the nation, December 24, 1941.

And so I greet you with the greeting of the Angels on that first Christmas at Bethlehem which, resounding through centuries, still rings out with its eternal message: "Glory to God in the highest; and on earth peace, good-will to men."

> —FRANKLIN D. ROOSEVELT, 32nd U.S. president.
> Christmas greeting to the nation, December 24, 1935.

The glow of Christmas, however, should come from a power source which we will never run short of, our abiding faith and our love of God.

> —GERALD FORD, 38th U.S. president. Remarks at the lighting
> of the national community Christmas tree, December 17, 1974.

Our country is entering a period of healing and of hope. We are joining together as a people again, realizing the strength of a common purpose. We are blessed with warm fires and warm memories and the voices of children singing of joy in the night. I think that God in his great wisdom knew that we needed these things to help us face the cold and sometimes lonely times.

> —JIMMY CARTER, 39th U.S. president. Christmas Pageant
> of Peace remarks on lighting the national community
> Christmas tree, December 14, 1978.

CHURCH & STATE

New England has in many Respects the Advantage of every other Colony in America, and indeed of every other Part of the World, that I know any Thing of. The Institutions in New England for the Support of Religion, Morals and Decency, exceed any other, obliging every Parish to have a Minister, and every Person to go to Meeting.

—JOHN ADAMS, 2nd U.S. president. To Abigail Adams, October 29, 1775. Butterfield, *Adams Family Correspondence*, vol. 1, p. 318–319.

Americans are the most religious people on Earth. And we have always instinctively sensed that God's purpose was bound up with the cause of liberty. The Founders understood this. As Jefferson put it, "Can the liberties of a nation be thought secure when we have removed their only firm basis, a conviction in the minds of the people that these liberties are the gift of God?" That conviction is enshrined in our Declaration of Independence and in our Constitution. And it's no accident that in drafting our Bill of Rights, the Founders dedicated the first portion of our first amendment to religious liberty. We rightly emphasize the opening clause of that amendment, which forbids government from establishing religion. In fact, I believe the establishment clause has been a great boon to our country's religious life. One reason religion flourishes in America is that worship can never be controlled by the state.

But in recent times we have too often ignored the clause that follows, which forbids government from prohibiting the free exercise of religion. This myopia has in some places resulted in an aggressive campaign against religious belief itself. Some people seem to believe that freedom of religion requires government to keep our lives free from religion. Well, I believe they're just plain wrong. Our government was founded on faith. Government must never promote a religion, of course, but it is duty bound to promote religious liberty. And it must never put the believer at a disadvantage because of his belief. That is the challenge that our administration has undertaken. To be succinct, it is my conviction that children have a right to voluntary prayer in the public schools.

—GEORGE H.W. BUSH, 41st U.S. president. Remarks to the National Association of Evangelicals in Chicago, Illinois, March 3, 1992.

One of our most fervent commitments was to the complete separation of church and state. This was an issue of great importance, and we studied Christian martyrs who had sacrificed their lives rather than let any secular leader encroach on religious freedom. Although individual Christians (including my father) were free to take part in public affairs, we abhorred the concept of church congregations becoming involved in the partisan political world. We also believed in religious freedom, compassion for unbelievers, and respect for all persons as inherently equal before God.

—JIMMY CARTER, 39th U.S. president.
Our Endangered Values, 2005, p. 18.

Despite what I consider to be a constitutional and biblical requirement for the separation of church and state, I must acknowledge that my own religious beliefs have been inextricably entwined with the political principles I have adopted.

—JIMMY CARTER, 39th U.S. president.
Ibid., pp. 5-6.

Religion and Government are certainly very different Things, instituted for different Ends; the design of one being to pro mote our temporal happiness; the design of the other to procure the Favour of God, and thereby the Salvation of our Souls. While these are kept distinct and apart, the Peace and welfare of Society is preserved, and the Ends of both are answered. By mixing them together, feuds, animosities and persecutions have been raised, which have deluged the World in Blood, and disgraced human Nature.

—JOHN DICKINSON, member of the First Continental
Congress. Writing over the signature "A.B."
Pennsylvania Journal, May 12, 1768.

. . . that the impious presumption of legislators and rulers, civil as well as ecclesiastical, who, being themselves but fallible and uninspired men, have assumed dominion over the faith of others, setting up their own opinions and modes of thinking as the only true and infallible, and as such endeavoring to impose them on others, hath established and maintained false religions over the greatest part of the world and through all time: That to compel a man to furnish contributions of money for the propagation of opinions which he disbelieves and abhors, is sinful and tyranni-cal... that the opinions of men are not the object of civil govern-ment, nor under its jurisdiction; that to suffer the civil magistrate to intrude his powers into the field of opinion and to restrain the profession or propagation of principles on the supposition of their ill tendency is a dangerous fallacy, which at once destroys all religious liberty... that it is time enough for the rightful pur-poses of civil government for its officers to interfere when prin-ciples break out into overt acts against peace and good order.

—THOMAS JEFFERSON, 2nd U.S. president.
"A Bill for Establishing Religious Freedom," 1777.
Boyd, *Papers of Thomas Jefferson*, vol. 2, pp. 545-546.

The legitimate powers of government extend to such acts only as are injurious to others. But it does me no injury for my neigh-bour to say there are twenty gods, or no god. It neither picks my pocket nor breaks my leg.... It is error alone which needs the support of government. Truth can stand by itself.... Subject opinion to coercion: whom will you make your inquisitors? Fal-lible men; men governed by bad passions, by private as well as public reasons. And why subject it to coercion? To produce uni-formity. But is uniformity desireable? No more than face and stature.... Is uniformity attainable? Millions of innocent men, women, and children, since the introduction of Christianity, have been burnt, tortured, fined, imprisoned: yet we have not advanced one inch towards uniformity.

—THOMAS JEFFERSON, 2nd U.S. president. *Notes on the State of Virginia*, 1781. Peden, *Notes on Virginia*, pp. 159-160.

I contemplate with sovereign reverence that act of the whole American people which declared that *their* legislature should make no law respecting an establishment of religion, or prohibiting the free exercise thereof, thus building a wall of eternal separation between church and state.

—THOMAS JEFFERSON, 2nd U.S. president.
Draft letter to the Danbury Baptist Association,
January 1, 1802. Jefferson Papers, Library of Congress.

In matters of religion, I have considered that its free exercise is placed by the constitution independent of the powers of the general government. I have therefore undertaken, on no occasion, to prescribe the religious exercises suited to it; but have left them, as the constitution found them, under the direction and discipline of state or church authorities acknowledged by the several religious societies.

—THOMAS JEFFERSON, 2nd U.S. president.
Second Inaugural Address, March 4, 1805.
Paul Leicester Ford, ed., *The Works of Thomas Jefferson*, 12 vols.
(New York: G.P. Putnam's Sons, 1904-1905), vol. 10, p. 131.

It yet remains a problem to be solved in human affairs, whether any free government can be permanent, where the public worship of God, and the support of religion, constitute no part of the policy or duty of the state in any assignable shape. The future experience of Christendom, and chiefly of the American states, must settle this problem, as yet new in the history of the world, abundant, as it has been, in experiments in the theory of government.

—JOSEPH STORY, U.S. Supreme Court justice.
Commentaries on the Constitution, 1833. Retrieved from

www.marksquotes.com/Founding-Fathers; Retrieved from
press-pubs.uchicago.edu/founders.

One of the beautiful boasts of our *municipal jurisprudence* is
that Christianity is a part of the Common Law. . . . There never
has been a period in which the Common Law did not recognize
Christianity as lying at its foundations. . . . I verily believe
Christianity necessary to the support of *civil* society.

—JOSEPH STORY, U.S. Supreme Court justice.
William W. Story, *Life and Letters of Joseph Story*,
vol. II, pp. 8, 92. Retrieved from
http://www.generationjoshua.org/dnn/Default.aspx?tabid=103.

I believe in an America where the separation of church and
state is absolute—where no Catholic prelate would tell the
president (should he be a Catholic) how to act and no Protestant minister would tell his parishioners for whom to vote—
where no church or church school is granted any public funds
or political preference—and where no man is denied public
office merely because his religion differs from the president
who might appoint him or the people who might elect him.

—JOHN F. KENNEDY, 35th U.S. president. In a speech before
the Greater Houston Ministerial Association,
Houston, Texas, September 12, 1960.

We maintain therefore that in matters of Religion, no man's
right is abridged by the institution of Civil Society and that Religion is wholly exempt from its cognizance. . . . The Bill implies
either that the Civil Magistrate is a competent Judge of Religious Truth; or that he may employ Religion as an engine of
Civil policy. The first is an arrogant pretension falsified by the
contradictory opinions of Rulers in all ages, and throughout the

world: the second an unhallowed perversion of the means of salvation.... To say that ... is a contradiction to the Christian Religion itself, for every page of it disavows a dependence on the powers of this world: it is a contradiction to fact; for it is known that this Religion both existed and flourished, not only without the support of human laws, but in spite of every opposition from them, and not only during the period of miraculous aid, but long after it had been left to its own evidence and the ordinary care of Providence...., During almost fifteen centuries has the legal establishment of Christianity been on trial. What have been its fruits? More or less in all places pride and indolence in the Clergy, ignorance and servility in the laity, in both, superstition, bigotry and persecution. Enquire of the Teachers of Christianity for the ages in which it appeared in its greatest lustre; those of every sect, point to the ages prior to its incorporation with Civil policy.

—JAMES MADISON, 4th U.S. president. "Memorial and
Remonstrance against Religious Assessments," June 20, 1785.
Rakove, *Madison Writings*, pp. 30-33.

There remains in others a strong bias towards the old error, that without some sort of alliance or coalition between Govt. & religion neither can be duly supported. Such indeed is the tendency to such a coalition, and such is the corrupting influence on both parties, that the danger cannot be too carefully guarded ag[ain]st.... Every new & successful example therefore of a perfect separation between ecclesiastical and civil matters, is of importance. And I have no doubt that every new example, will succeed, as every past one has done, in shewing that religion & Govt. will both exist in greater purity, the less they are mixed together.... I cannot speak particularly of any of the cases excepting that of Virg[ini]a where it is impossible to deny that

Religion prevails with more zeal, and a more exemplary priesthood than it ever did when established and patronised by Public authority. We are teaching the world the great truth that Govts. do better without Kings & Nobles than with them. The merit will be doubled by the other lesson that Religion flourishes in greater purity, without than with the aid of Govt.

—JAMES MADISON, 4th U.S. president.
To Edward Livingston, July 10, 1822. Ibid.,
pp. 788-789.

I must admit, moreover, that it may not be easy, in every possible case, to trace the line of separation, between the rights of Religion & the Civil authority, with such distinctness, as to avoid collisions & doubts on unessential points. The tendency to a usurpation on one side, or the other, or to a corrupting coalition or alliance between them, will be best guarded against by an entire abstinence of the Government from interference, in any way whatever, beyond the necessity of preserving public order, & protecting each sect against trespasses on its legal rights by others.

—JAMES MADISON, 4th U.S. president.
To Jasper Adams, September 1833. Dreisbach,
Religion and Politics, p. 120.

We are a nation under God. I've always believed that this blessed land was set apart in a special way, that some divine plan placed this great continent here between the oceans to be found by people from every corner of the Earth who had a special love for freedom and the courage to uproot themselves, leave homeland and friends, to come to a strange land. And coming here they created something new in all the history of mankind—a land where man is not beholden to government, government is beholden to man.

George Washington believed that religion, morality, and brotherhood were the pillars of society. He said you couldn't have morality without religion. And yet today we're told that to protect the first amendment, we must expel God, the source of all knowledge, from our children's classrooms. Well, pardon me, but the first amendment was not written to protect the American people from religion; the first amendment was written to protect the American people from government tyranny.

> —RONALD REAGAN, 40th U.S. president. Remarks at a Spirit of America Rally in Atlanta, Georgia, January 26, 1984.

In the United States we view your religious establishment with horror, and the man who would attempt to defend it publicly or privately would be consigned to a physician, instead of a casuist or politician, to be cured of his error.

> —BENJAMIN RUSH, member of the Continental Congress, 1776-1777 To Richard Price, April 24, 1790. Butterfield, *Letters of Rush*, vol. 1, p. 564.

Were it possible for St. Paul to rise from his grave at the present juncture, he would say to the clergy who are now so active in settling the political affairs of the world: "Cease from your political labors—your kingdom is not of *this* world. Read my Epistles. In no part of them will you perceive me aiming to depose a pagan emperor or to place a Christian upon a throne. Christianity disdains to receive support from human governments. From this it derives its preeminence over all the religions that ever have or ever shall exist in the world. Human governments may receive support from Christianity, but it must be only from the love of justice and peace which it is calculated to produce in the minds of men. By promoting these and all other Christian virtues by your precepts and examples, you will much sooner overthrow errors of all kinds and establish our pure and holy religion in the world than by aiming to produce by your preaching or pamphlets any change in the political state of mankind." A certain Dr. Owens, an eminent minister of the Gospel among the dissenters in England, and a sincere friend of liberty, was once complained of by one of Cromwell's time serving priests, "that he did not preach to the *times*." "My business *and duty*" said the disciple of St. Paul, "is to preach to *Eternity*, not to the times."

—BENJAMIN RUSH, member of the Continental Congress,
1776-1777. To Thomas Jefferson, October 6, 1800.
Ibid., vol. 2, p. 824.

Although in our political institutions there is no union of Church and State, yet the religion of our Divine Saviour is not the less an all pervading principle of the laws, the sentiments, the moral and social existence of the people of the United States. Christianity animates our nationality; it is the true spirit of good government; it is the characteristic and peculiar quality of modern civilization; it is the noble bond of connexion, which, by community of religious convictions, attaches together, and elevates into relative superiority of intelligence and power, the sovereign States of Europe and America. And wherever Christianity diffuses itself among all the nations of the earth, it goes to be the herald of civilization as well as of salvation.

Of this last and best gift of the merciful Creator to his creatures, the holy Book is the inspired record. It is full of all human wisdom, but still more of that loftier, heavenly wisdom which descends to us from on high as the audible voice of the Almighty.

—FRANKLIN PIERCE, 14th U.S. president.
To Theodore Frelinghuysen, ABS president and U.S. senator,
in letter acknowledging receipt of a presentation Bible,
February 5, 1857. *Bible Society Record*,
vol. II, no. 5, May 1857, pp. 79-80.

The values that spring from our faith certainly tell us a lot about our country. And consider that for more than two centuries Americans have endorsed, and properly so, the separation of church and state. But we've also shown how both religion and government can strengthen a society. After all, our Founding Fathers' documents begin with these words: All men are endowed by their Creator with certain unalienable rights. And Americans are religious people, but a truly religious nation is a tolerant nation.

—GEORGE H.W. BUSH, 41st U.S. president.
Remarks at the Annual National Prayer Breakfast,
February 1, 1990.

The Constitution
& Declaration of
Independence

___

The second day of July, 1776, will be the most memorable epoch in the history of America. I am apt to believe that it will be celebrated by succeeding generations as the great anniversary festival. It ought to be commemorated as the day of deliverance, by solemn acts of devotion to God Almighty. It ought to be solemnized with pomp and parade, with shows, games, sports, guns, bells, bonfires, and illuminations, from one end of this continent to the other, from this time forward forevermore.

—JOHN ADAMS, 2nd U.S. president. Second Letter to
Abigail Adams, July 3, 1776. Morse, *John Adams*,
Houghton Mifflin Co., 1894, p. 128.

When, in the course of human events, it becomes necessary for one people to dissolve the political bands which have connected them with another, and to assume among the powers of the earth the separate and equal station to which the laws of nature and of nature's God entitle them, a decent respect to the opinions of mankind requires that they should declare the causes which impel them to the separation. We hold these truths to be self-evident; that all men are created equal; that they are endowed by their creator with certain unalienable rights; that among these are life, liberty and the pursuit of happiness; that to secure these rights, governments are instituted among men, deriving their just powers from the consent of the governed; that whenever any form of government becomes destructive of these ends, it is the right of the people to alter or to abolish it, and to institute new government, laying its foundation on such principles, and organizing its powers in such form, as to them shall seem most likely to effect their safety and happiness.

—THOMAS JEFFERSON, 2nd U.S. president.
Declaration of Independence, July 4, 1776.

And for the support of this declaration, with a firm reliance on the protection of divine providence, we mutually pledge to each other our lives, our fortunes, and our sacred honor.

—THOMAS JEFFERSON, 2nd U.S. president.
Declaration of Independence, July 4, 1776.

Congress shall make no law establishing religion, or to prevent the free exercise thereof, or to infringe the rights of conscience.

—FISHER AMES, member of Congress from Massachusetts,
1789-1797. August 20, 1789, Fisher Ames of Massachusetts
introduced language for the First Amendment.
Wells Bradley, "Religion and Government: The Early Days"
(Tulsa, OK: *Tulsa Christian Times,* October 1992), p. 7.;
also *Annals of Congress,* vol. 1, p. 766.

The late revolution, my respected audience, in which we this day rejoice, is big with events, that are daily unfolding themselves, and pressing in thick succession, to the astonishment of a wondering world! It has been marked with the certain characteristics of a Divine over-ruling hand, in that it was brought about and perfected against all human reasoning, and apparently against all human hope. . . Divine Providence, throughout the government of this world, appears to have impressed many great events with the undoubted evidence of his own almighty arm. He putteth down kingdoms, and he setteth up whom he pleaseth, and it has been literally verified in us, that "no king prevaileth by the power of his own strength."

—ELIAS BOUDINOT, president of the Continental Congress, 1782-1783, and ABS president. "Oration to the Society of the Cincinnati," July 4, 1793. Jane J. Boudinot, ed., *The Life, Public Services, Addresses, and Letters of Elias Boudinot* (New York: DaCapo Press, 1971), p. 361.

Almighty God himself will look down upon your righteous contest with gracious approbation. You will be a "band of brothers," cemented by the dearest ties—and strengthened with inconceivable supplies of force and constancy, by that sympathetic ardor, which animates good men, confederated in a good cause. Your *honor* and *welfare* will be, as they now are, most intimately concerned; and besides—*you are assigned by divine providence*, in the appointed order of things, *the protectors of unborn ages*, whose *fate* depends upon your *virtue*.

—JOHN DICKINSON, member of the First Continental Congress. Letter from a Farmer in Pennsylvania to the Inhabitants of the British Colonies. Paul H. Ford, ed., *The Writings of John Dickinson* (Philadelphia: Historical Society of Pennsylvania, 1895), vol. 1, p. 405.

The American Revolution was the grand operation, which seemed to be assigned by the Deity to the men of this age in our country.

—PATRICK HENRY, American patriot and governor of Virginia. To Henry Lee, June 27, 1795. Campbell, *Henry*.

I have sworn upon the altar of God, eternal hostility against every form of tyranny over the mind of man.

—THOMAS JEFFERSON, 2nd U.S. president. Letter to Benjamin Rush, September 23, 1800.

If my endeavours to avert the evil, with which this country was threatened, by a deliberate plan of Tyranny, should be crowned with the success that is wished; the praise is due to the *Grand Architect* of the Universe who did not see fit to Suffer his Superstructures, and justice, to be subjected to the ambition of the princes of this World, or to the rod of oppression, in the hands of any power upon Earth.

—GEORGE WASHINGTON, 1st U.S. president. To Watson & Cassoul, August 10, 1782. Fitzpatrick, *Writings of Washington*, vol. 24, p. 497.

The man must be bad indeed, who can look upon the events of the American Revolution without feeling the warmest gratitude towards the great Author of the Universe whose divine interposition was so frequently manifested in our behalf.

—GEORGE WASHINGTON, 1st U.S. president. To Samuel Langdon September 28, 1789. Ibid., vol. 30, p. 416.

The highest of the American Revolution was this: "It connected in one dissoluble glory bond the principles of civil government with the principles of Christianity."

—JOHN ADAMS, 2nd U.S. president. July 4, 1821.

We wish that this column, rising towards heaven among the pointed spires of so many temples dedicated to God, may contribute also to produce in all minds a pious feeling of dependence and gratitude. We wish, finally, that the last object to the sight of him who leaves his native shore, and the first to gladden his who revisits it, may be something which shall remind him of the liberty and the glory of his country.

—DANIEL WEBSTER, American orator, lawyer, and statesman, Address on Laying the Cornerstone of the Bunker Hill Monument, June 17, 1825.

I always considered the settlement of America with Reverence and Wonder, as the Opening of a grand scene and design of Providence, for the Illumination of the Ignorant and the Emancipation of the slavish part of Mankind.

—JOHN ADAMS, 2nd U.S. president. "Dissertation on the Canon and Feudal Law" (draft), February 1765. Butterfield, Diary and Autobiography of John Adams, vol. 1, p. 257.

The American Union will last as long as God pleases. It is the duty of every American Citizen to exert his utmost abilties and endeavours to preserve it as long as possible and to pray with submission to Providence "esto perpetua".

—JOHN ADAMS, 2nd U.S. president. To Charles Carroll, August 2, 1820. Adams Papers (microfilm), reel 124, Library of Congress.

Under the auspices and direction of Divine Providence, your forefathers removed to the wilds and wilderness of America. By their industry they made it a fruitful, and by their virtue a happy country. And we should still have enjoyed the blessings of peace and plenty, if we had not forgotten the source from which those blessings flowed; and permitted our country to be contaminated by the many shameful vices which have prevailed among us.

—JOHN JAY, president of the Continental Congress, 1778-1779; and 1st chief justice of the U.S. Supreme Court, 1789-1795. Address of the Convention of New York, 1776. Johnston, *Correspondence of Jay*, vol. 1, p. 101.

I shall need, too, the favor of that Being in whose hands we are, who led our fathers, as Israel of old, from their native land and planted them in a country flowing with all the necessaries and comforts of life; who has covered our infancy with his providence and our riper years with his wisdom and power, and to whose goodness I ask you to join in supplications with me that he will so enlighten the minds of your servants, guide their councils, and prosper their measures that whatsoever they do shall result in your good, and shall secure to you the peace, friendship, and approbation of all nations.

—THOMAS JEFFERSON, 2nd U.S. president. Second Inaugural Address, March 4, 1805. Richardson, *Messages and Replies*, vol. 1, p. 370.

Equal and exact justice to all men, of whatever state or persuasion, religious or political; peace, commerce, and honest friendship with all nations, entangling alliances with none. . . . Freedom of religion; freedom of the press, and freedom of person under the protection of the habeas corpus, and trial by juries impartially selected. These principles form the bright constellation which has gone before us, and guided our steps through an age of revolution and reformation. The wisdom of our sages and the blood of our heroes have been devoted to their attainment. They should be the creed of our political faith, the text of civil instruction, the touchstone by which to try the services of those we trust; and should we wander from them in moments of error or alarm, let us hasten to retrace our steps and to regain the road which alone leads to peace, liberty, and safety.

—THOMAS JEFFERSON, 2nd U.S. president.
First Inaugural Address, March 4, 1801.

The God who gave us life, gave us liberty at the same time.

THOMAS JEFFERSON, 2nd U.S. president.
Summary View of the Rights of British America, 1774.

Indeed, I tremble for my country when I reflect that God is just.

—THOMAS JEFFERSON, 2nd U.S. president.
Notes on the State of Virginia, p. 18.

The great governor of the Universe has led us too long and too far on the road to happiness and glory, to forsake us in the midst of it.

—GEORGE WASHINGTON, 1st U.S. president.
To Benjamin Lincoln, June 29, 1788. Fitzpatrick,
Writings of Washington, vol. 30, p. 11.

No People can be bound to acknowledge and adore the invisible hand, which conducts the Affairs of men more than the People of the United States. Every step, by which they have advanced to the character of an independent nation, seems to have been distinguished by some token of providential agency.

—GEORGE WASHINGTON, 1st U.S. president.
First Inaugural Address, April 30, 1789. Ibid.,
vol. 30, p. 293.

God grants liberty only to those who love it, and are always ready to guard and defend it.

—DANIEL WEBSTER, American orator,
lawyer, and statesman. Remarks in the Senate,
June 3, 1834. *The Writings and Speeches of Daniel Webster*,
1903, vol. 7, p. 47.

From the height of this place and the summit of this century, let us go forth. May God strengthen our hands for the good work ahead, and always, always bless our America.

—WILLIAM CLINTON, 42nd U.S. president.
Second Inaugural Address, January 20, 1997.

And let us not trust to human effort alone, but humbly acknowledging the power and goodness of Almighty God, who presides over the destiny of nations, and who has at all times been revealed in our country's history, let us invoke his aid and his blessings upon our labors

—GROVER CLEVELAND, 22nd & 24th U.S. president.
First Inaugural Address, March 4, 1885.

Above all, I know there is a Supreme Being who rules the affairs of men and whose goodness and mercy have always followed the American people, and I know he will not turn from us now if we Humbly and reverently seek his powerful aid.

—GROVER CLEVELAND, 22nd & 24th U.S. president.
Second Inaugural Address, March 4, 1893.

The emancipated race has already made remarkable progress. With unquestioning devotion to the Union, with a patience and gentleness not born of fear, they have "followed the light as God gave them to see the light." They are rapidly laying the material foundations of self-support, widening their circle of intelligence, and beginning to enjoy the blessings that gather around the homes of the industrious poor. They deserve the generous encouragement of all good men. So far as my authority can lawfully extend they shall enjoy the full and equal protection of the Constitution and the laws.

—JAMES A. GARFIELD, 20th U.S. president.
Inaugural Address, March 4, 1881.

Beyond that I only look to the gracious protection of the Divine Being whose strengthening support I humbly solicit, and whom I fervently pray to look down upon us all. May it be among the dispensations of his providence to bless our beloved country with honors and with length of days. May her ways be ways of pleasantness and all her paths be peace!

—MARTIN VAN BUREN, 8th U.S. president.
Inaugural Address, March 4, 1837.

Looking for the guidance of that Divine hand by which the destinies of nations and individuals are shaped, I call upon you, Senators, Representatives, judges, fellow-citizens, here and everywhere, to unite with me in an earnest effort to secure to our country the blessings, not only of material prosperity, but of justice, peace, and union—a union depending not upon the constraint of force, but upon the loving devotion of a free people; "and that all things may be so ordered and settled upon the best and surest foundations that peace and happiness, truth and justice, religion and piety, may be established among us for all generations."

> —RUTHERFORD B. HAYES, 19th U.S. president and
> ABS vice president. 1880 until his death in 1893.
> Inaugural Address, March 5, 1877.

But first and above all, our thanks are due to Almighty God for the numerous benefits which he has bestowed upon this people, and our united prayers ought to ascend to him that he would continue to bless our great Republic in time to come as he has blessed it in time past.

> —JAMES BUCHANAN, 15th U.S. president.
> Annual message, December 8, 1857.

But let not the foundation of our hope rest upon man's wisdom. It will not be sufficient that sectional prejudices find no place in the public deliberations. It will not be sufficient that the rash counsels of human passion are rejected. It must be felt that there is no national security but in the nation's humble, acknowledged dependence upon God and his overruling providence.

> —FRANKLIN PIERCE, 14th U.S. president.
> Inaugural Address, March 4, 1853.

Although disease, assuming at one time the characteristics of a widespread and devastating pestilence, has left its sad traces upon some portions of our country, we have still the most abundant cause for reverent thankfulness to God for an accumulation of signal mercies showered upon us as a nation. It is well that a consciousness of rapid advancement and increasing strength be habitually associated with an abiding sense of dependence upon him who holds in his hands the destiny of men and nations.

—FRANKLIN PIERCE, 14th U.S. president.
First Annual message, December 5, 1853.

We have no government armed with power capable of contending with human passions unbridled by morality and religion. Avarice, ambition, revenge, or gallantry, would break the strongest cords of our Constitution as a whale goes through a net. Our Constitution was made only for a moral and religious people. It is wholly inadequate to the government of any other.

—JOHN ADAMS, 2nd U.S. president. To the Officers of the First Brigade of the 3rd Division of the Massachusetts Militia, October 11, 1798. Adams Papers (microfilm), reel 119, Library of Congress.

I beg I may not be understood to infer, that our General Convention was divinely inspired, when it form'd the new federal Constitution . . . yet I must own I have so much faith in the general Government of the world by Providence, that I can hardly conceive a Transaction of such momentous Importance to the Welfare of Millions now existing, and to exist in the Posterity of a great Nation, should be suffered to pass without being in some degree influenc'd, guided, and governed by that omnipotent, omnipresent, and beneficent Ruler, in whom all inferior Spirits live, and move, and have their Being.

—BENJAMIN FRANKLIN, member of the Second Continental Congress. "A Comparison of the Conduct of Ancient Jews and Anti-federalists in the United States of America," 1788. Smyth, *Writings of Franklin*, vol. 9, p. 702.

For my own part, I sincerely esteem it [the Constitution] a system which without the finger of God, never could have been suggested and agreed upon by such a diversity of interests.

—ALEXANDER HAMILTON, member of the Continental Congress and 1st secretary of the treasury, 1787, after the Constitutional Convention.

Would it be wonderful if, under the pressure of all these difficulties, the convention should have been forced into some deviations from that artificial structure and regular symmetry which an abstract view of the subject might lead an ingenious theorist to bestow on a Constitution planned in his closet or in his imagination? The real wonder is that so many difficulties should have been surmounted, and surmounted with a unanimity almost as unprecedented as it must have been unexpected. It is impossible for any man of candor to reflect on this circumstance without partaking of the astonishment. It is impossible for the man of pious reflection not to perceive in it a finger of that Almighty hand which has been so frequently and signally extended to our relief in the critical stages of the revolution.

—JAMES MADISON, 4th U.S. president. Federalist 37, January 11, 1788. Edward M. Earle, ed., *The Federalist* (New York: Modern Library, 1937), p. 231.

Many pious people wish the name of the Supreme Being had been introduced somewhere in the new Constitution. Perhaps an acknowledgement may be made of his goodness or of his providence in the proposed amendments.

—BENJAMIN RUSH, member of the Continental Congress, 1776-1777. To John Adams, June 15, 1789. Butterfield, *Letters of Rush*, vol. 1, p. 517.

. . . we may, with a kind of grateful and pious exaltation, trace the finger of Providence through those dark and mysterious events, which first induced the States to appoint a general Convention and then led them one after another (by such steps as were best calculated to effect the object) into an adoption of the system recommended by that general Convention; thereby, in all human probability laying a lasting foundation for tranquility and happiness; when we had but too much reason to fear that confusion and misery were rapidly coming upon us. That the same good Providence may still continue to protect us and prevent us from dashing the cup of national felicity just as it has been lifted to our lips, is the earnest prayer of My Dear Sir, your faithful friend, &c.

—GEORGE WASHINGTON, 1st U.S. president. To Jonathan Trumbull, July 20, 1788. Fitzpatrick, *Writings of Washington*, vol. 30, p. 22.

We have reason to rejoice in the prospect that the present national Government, which by the favor of Divine Providence, was formed by the common counsels and peaceably established with the common consent of the People, will prove a blessing to every denomination of them.

—GEORGE WASHINGTON, 1st U.S. president. To the

Religious Society Called Quakers, September 1789.
Washington Papers, Library of Congress.

... This nation, under God, shall have a new birth of freedom ...

—ABRAHAM LINCOLN, 16th U.S. president.
Lincoln at Gettysburg: An Address, November 19, 1863.

I know that there is a God and that he hates injustice and slavery.... I know that I am right, because I know that liberty is right; for Christ teaches it, and Christ is God.

—ABRAHAM LINCOLN, 16th U.S. president. Ernst Foster,
Abraham Lincoln, Cassell, 1893, p. 81.

With malice toward none, with charity for all, with firmness in the right as God gives us to see the right, let us strive on... to do all which may achieve and cherish a just peace among ourselves and with all nations.

—ABRAHAM LINCOLN, 16th U.S. president.
Second Inaugural Address, March 4, 1865.

The annual observance of Universal Bible Sunday is a valuable aid in spreading knowledge of the Book of Books, from the pages of which have come those ideals that root our government and our national life firmly in the consciences of men and women.

—HERBERT HOOVER, 31st U.S. president.
Letter from The White House to
Mr. George William Brown, general secretary of the ABS.
Presidential Autograph Collection, ABS Archives.

Almost every man who has based his life-work added to the sum of human achievement of which the race is proud, of which our people are proud, almost every such man has based his life-work largely upon the teachings of the Bible.

> —THEODORE ROOSEVELT, 26th U.S. president. Address to the Long Island Bible Society, 1901. Ferdinand Cowle Inglehart, "Theodore Roosevelt: The Man As I Knew Him," *The Christian Herald*, 1919, p. 308.

There is no other book so various as the Bible, nor one so full of concentrated wisdom. Whether it be of law, business, morals or that vision which leads the imagination in the creation of constructive enterprises for the happiness of mankind, he who seeks for guidance . . . may look inside its covers and find illumination.

> —HERBERT HOOVER, 31st U.S. president. Message to the National Federation of Men's Bible Classes Convention, Baltimore, May 5, 1929.

I am interested to know that December 6th is to be observed as Universal Bible Sunday. Our institutions and common life are grounded in spiritual ideals. I hope that the observation of Bible Sunday will quicken the spiritual impulses of our people and contribute to the spiritual advancement which underlies our stability, service and progress as a nation and as individuals.

> —HERBERT HOOVER, 31st U.S. president. Message to the ABS on Universal Bible Sunday, December 4, 1931.

Democracy is first and foremost a spiritual force. It is built
upon a spiritual basis—and on a belief in God and an observance of moral principles. And in the long run only the church
can provide that basis. Our founders knew this truth—and we
will neglect it at our peril.

—HARRY S. TRUMAN, 33rd U.S. president.
Remarks in Alexandria, Virginia, at the cornerstone laying of the
Westminster Presbyterian Church, November 23, 1952.

You will see, as you make your rounds, that this Nation was
established by men who believed in God. You will see that our
Founding Fathers believed that God created this Nation. And I
believe it, too. They believed that God was our strength in time
of peril and the source of all our blessings.

—HARRY S. TRUMAN, 33rd U.S. president. Address
to the Washington Pilgrimage of American Churchmen,
September 28, 1951.

On this day, in this year, as we concede these shortcomings, let
each of us pray that through our failures we may derive the
wisdom, the courage, and the strength to secure for every one
of our citizens the full measure of dignity, freedom, and brotherhood for which all men are qualified by their common fatherhood under God.

—JOHN F. KENNEDY, 35th U.S. president.
Proclamation 3559—National Day of Prayer, October 8, 1963.

We of this land have so much to be grateful for. The God above
us has been good to us from the very beginning of this Republic.
 With the duties which rest upon us, we have much to pray

for—that we may, as a nation, be just in our strength, wise in our actions, and faithful in our trust.

—LYNDON B. JOHNSON, 36th U.S. president. Remarks at the 12th Annual presidential Prayer Breakfast, February 5, 1964.

The Constitution is the supreme law of our land and it governs our actions as citizens. Only the laws of God, which govern our consciences, are superior to it.

—GERALD FORD, 38th U.S. president. Remarks on signing a proclamation granting pardon to Richard Nixon, September 8, 1974.

The power of clemency can look to reasons for these actions which the law cannot. Unlike God's law, man's law cannot probe into the heart of human beings.

—GERALD FORD, 38th U.S. president. Remarks on signing 18 executive warrants for clemency, November 29, 1974.

Fellow Americans, one final word: I want to be a good President. I need your help. We all need God's sure guidance. With it, nothing can stop the United States of America.

—GERALD FORD, 38th U.S. president. Address to the Joint Session of the Congress, August 12, 1974.

Let us pray, each in our own way, for the strength and the will to meet the challenges that face us today with the same profound faith in God that inspired the Founders of this Nation.

—GERALD FORD, 38th U.S. president. Proclamation 4338—National Day of Prayer, December 5, 1974.

Let us now pray—as we have done throughout our history, and as the Congress has requested (66 Stat. 64)—for the wisdom to continue the American pilgrimage, striving toward a nobler existence for all humanity. Let us ask for the strength to meet the challenges that face our Nation. Let us give thanks to God for the many blessings granted to America throughout these two centuries.

—GERALD FORD, 38th U.S. president.
Proclamation 4379—National Day of Prayer,
June 12, 1975.

We are Americans because we deliberately chose to be one nation, indivisible, and for 199 years with God's help we have gone forward together.

—GERALD FORD, 38th U.S. president.
Statement on the observance of Independence Day,
July 3, 1975.

Throughout our history, the United States has stood for the protection and promotion of human rights for all peoples. Central to these concerns are the political, social, and economic rights of all human beings. Our dedication to these rights stems from the belief that all people should be allowed to live their lives to the fullest of their capabilities, that the talent and character given each person by God should not be wasted.

—JIMMY CARTER, 39th U.S. president.
Proclamation 4589—International Literary Day,
August 21, 1978.

We want a nation, as our Constitution promises, where the only limits on our children are the talents God gave them and their own determination and hard work.

> —JIMMY CARTER, 39th U.S. president. Remarks at the
> opening session of the 1978 National Democratic Party
> Conference, December 8, 1978.

The Founding Fathers derived their principles of limited government from a belief in natural law, that is, the concept that our Creator had ordained a framework for society giving great importance to individual freedom, expression, and responsibility. They held that each person had certain natural rights bestowed on him by God.

> —RONALD REAGAN, 40th U.S. president. Proclamation
> 5003—Bill of Rights Day, Human Rights Day and Week,
> December 10, 1982.

So, the record is clear. The first Americans proclaimed their freedom because they believed God himself had granted freedom to all men. And they exercised their liberty prayerfully, avidly seeking and humbly accepting God's blessing on their new land.

> —RONALD REAGAN, 40th U.S. president. Remarks at the
> annual convention of the National Association of Evangelicals in
> Columbus, Ohio, March 6, 1984.

Our Founding Fathers knew that their hope was in prayer. And that's why our Declaration of Independence begins with an affirmation of faith and why our Congress opens every day with prayer. It is why the First Congress of the fledgling United States in the Northwest Ordinance provided for schools that would teach "religion, morality, and knowledge"—because they knew that no man, no nation, could grow in freedom without divine guidance.

—RONALD REAGAN, 40th U.S. president. Remarks at the Annual National Prayer Breakfast, February 5, 1987.

Is there any force on Earth more powerful than that love? Is there any truth that gives more strength than knowing that God has a special plan for each one of us? Yes, man is sinful, separated from God. But there is God's promise of salvation, even for the least likely of us.

—RONALD REAGAN, 40th U.S. president. Remarks at the annual convention of the National Religious Broadcasters, February 1, 1988.

So, we ask God to bless us, to guide us, and to help us through whatever dark nights we still may face. We hope that, in the sublime resolve of those who strive so that all may live in peace and freedom, we will show how this nation has forged its very soul; and that the liberty bell of the four freedoms will ring for all people in every nation of this world.

—GEORGE H.W. BUSH, 41st U.S. president. Remarks at the 50th anniversary observance of Franklin D. Roosevelt's Four Freedoms speech, January 30, 1991.

Throughout our Nation's history, Americans have come before God with humble hearts to ask forgiveness, to seek wisdom, and to offer thanksgiving and praise. The framers of our democracy, on a quest for freedom and equality, were fueled by an abiding faith in a just and loving God, to whom they turned often for guidance and strength.

—WILLIAM CLINTON, 42nd U.S. president. Proclamation, National Day of Prayer, May 4, 2000.

We have always been a people of hope—hope that we can make tomorrow brighter than today, hope that we can fulfill our Nation's enduring promise of freedom and opportunity. And we have always known that, by the grace of God and our mutual labor, we can make our hopes reality.

—WILLIAM CLINTON, 42nd U.S. president. Remarks by the president, National Day of Hope and Renewal, January 20, 1997.

For the brave men and women of our founding generation, victory was far from certain. They were certain only of the cause they served—the belief that freedom is the gift of God and the right of all mankind. The strength of their convictions made possible the birth of the free Nation in which we are blessed to live.

—GEORGE W. BUSH, 43rd U.S. president. President's Radio address, July 1, 2006

We're a nation founded by men and women who came to these shores seeking to worship the Almighty freely. From these prayerful beginnings, God has greatly blessed the American people, and through our prayers, we give thanks to the true source of our blessings.

—GEORGE W. BUSH, 43rd U.S. president. "President Attends 54th Annual Prayer Breakfast," February 2, 2006.

This church brings the generations, grandparents, great-grandparents, and grandkids, here to work within this church—that strengthens the American family—and to give the kids not only indoctrination into faith and into the teachings of the Lord, but the church helps kids understand the larger family. We are one Nation under God. We must remember that. We must advocate that. We must continue to state that we are one Nation under God.

—GEORGE H.W. BUSH, 41st U.S. president.
Remarks at Mount Zion Missionary Baptist Church in
Los Angeles, May 7, 1992.

The fundamental basis of this nation's law was given to Moses on the Mount. The fundamental basis of our Bill of Rights comes from the teaching we get from Exodus and St. Matthew, from Isaiah and St. Paul. I don't think we emphasize that enough these days. If we don't have the proper fundamental moral background, we will finally wind up with a totalitarian government which does not believe in the right for anybody except the state.

—HARRY TRUMAN, 33rd U.S. president.
Address before the attorney general's conference on
law enforcement problems, February 15, 1950.

Providence has given to our people the choice of their rulers, and it is the duty, as well as the privilege and the interest, of a Christian nation to select and prefer Christians for their rulers.

—JOHN JAY, president of the Continental Congress, 1778-1779;
and 1st chief justice of the U.S. Supreme Court, 1789-1795. Letter
to Jedidiah Morse, February 28, 1797.

And for the support of this Declaration, with a firm reliance on the protection of divine Providence, we mutually pledge to each other our Lives, our Fortunes, and our sacred honor.

—THOMAS JEFFERSON, 2nd U.S. president.
Declaration of Independence, July 4, 1776.

... enlightened by a benign religion, professed, indeed, and practiced in various forms, yet all of them inculcating honesty, truth, temperance, gratitude and love of man; acknowledging and adoring an overruling Providence, which by all of its dispensations proves that it delights in the happiness of man here and his greater happiness hereafter.

—THOMAS JEFFERSON, 2nd U.S. president.
First Inaugural Address, March 4, 1801.
Richardson, *Messages and Papers of the presidents*,
vol. 1, p. 311.

We are not in a world ungoverned by the laws and power of a superior agent. Our efforts are in his hand and directed by it; and he will give them their effect in his own time.

—THOMAS JEFFERSON, 2nd U.S. president.
To David Barrow, May 1, 1815. Jefferson Papers,
Library of Congress.

It is a momentous thing to be the instrument, under Providence, of the liberation of a race.

—ABRAHAM LINCOLN, 16th U.S. president. Remark to
Cd. McKaye, 1863. In F. B. Carpenter, *Six Months at the
White House with Abraham Lincoln*, 1866, p. 59.

The purposes of the Almighty are perfect and must prevail, though we erring mortals may fail to accurately perceive them in advance. We hoped for a happy termination of this terrible war long before this; but God knows best, and has ruled otherwise. We shall yet acknowledge his wisdom and our own error therein. Meanwhile, we must work earnestly in the best light he gives us, trusting that so working still conduces to the great ends he ordains. Surely he intends some great good to follow this mighty convulsion, which no mortal could make, and no mortal could stay.

—ABRAHAM LINCOLN, 16th U.S. president.
Letter to Liza P. Gurney, September 4, 1864.

I assume the arduous and responsible duties of president of the United States, relying upon the support of my countrymen and invoking the guidance of Almighty God. Our faith teaches that there is no safer reliance than upon the God of our fathers, who has so singularly favored the American people in every national trial, and who will not forsake us so long as we obey his commandments and walk humbly in his footsteps.

—WILLIAM MCKINLEY, 25th U.S. president.
First Inaugural Address, March 4, 1897.

No greater thing could come to our land today than a revival of the spirit of faith—a revival that would sweep through the homes of the nation and stir the hearts of men and women of all faiths to a reassertion of their belief in God and their dedication to his will for themselves and for their world. I doubt if there is any problem—social, political, or economic—that would not melt away before the fires of such spiritual awakening

—FRANKLIN DELANO ROOSEVELT, 32nd U.S. president.

Address to the Federal Council of Churches, Constitution Hall,
Washington, D.C., 1934.

As I have heard since my arriv'l at this place, a circumstantial account of my death and dying speech, I take this early opportunity of contradicting both, and of assuring you that I now exist and appear in the land of the living by the miraculous care of Providence, that protected me beyond all human expectation, I had 4 Bullets through my Coat, and two horses shot under me, and yet escaped unhurt.

—GEORGE WASHINGTON, 1st U.S. president.
To John Augustine Washington, July 18, 1755.
Fitzpatrick, *Writings of Washington*, vol. 1, p. 152.

I go fully trusting in that providence, which has been more bountiful to me than I deserve. . . .

—GEORGE WASHINGTON, 1st U.S. president.
To Martha Washington, June 23, 1775. Ibid., vol. 3, p. 301.

. . . however, it is to be hoped, that if our cause is just, as I do most religiously believe it to be, the same Providence, which has in many Instances appear'd for us, will still go on to afford its aid.

—GEORGE WASHINGTON, 1st U.S. president.
To John Washington, May 31, 1776. Ibid., vol. 5, p 93

The hand of Providence has been so conspicuous in all this, that he must be worse than an infidel that lacks faith, and more than wicked, that has not gratitude enough to acknowledge his obligations, but, it will be time enough for me to turn preacher, when my present appointment ceases; and therefore, I shall add no more on the Doctrine of Providence.

—GEORGE WASHINGTON, 1st U.S. president.
To Thomas Nelson, August 20, 1778. Ibid., vol. 12, p. 343.

Divine Service is to be performed tomorrow in the several Brigades or Divisions. The Commander in Chief earnestly recommends that the troops not on duty should universally attend with that seriousness of Deportment and Gratitude of heart which the recognition of such reiterated and astonishing interpositions of Providence demands of us.

—GEORGE WASHINGTON, 1st U.S. president.
General Orders, October 20, 1781. Ibid., vol. 23, p. 247.

When I contemplate the interposition of Providence, as it was visibly manifested, in guiding us through the Revolution, in preparing us for the reception of a general government, and in conciliating the good will of the People of America towards one another after its adoption, I feel myself oppressed and almost overwhelmed with a sense of divine munificience. I feel that nothing is due to my personal agency in all these complicated and wonderful events, except what can simply be attributed to an honest zeal for the good of my country.

—GEORGE WASHINGTON, 1st U.S. president. To the mayor,
recorder, aldermen and common council of Philadelphia,
April 20, 1789. Washington Papers, Library of Congress.

. . . it would be peculiarly improper to omit in this first official Act, my fervent supplications to that Almighty Being who rules over the Universe, who presides in the councils of nations, and whose providential aids can supply every human defect. . . . No People can be bound to acknowledge and adore the invisible hand, which conducts the Affairs of men more than the People of the United States. Every step, by which they have advanced to the character of an independent nation, seems to have been distinguished by some token of providential agency.

—GEORGE WASHINGTON, 1st U.S. president.
Inaugural Address, April 30, 1789. Fitzpatrick,
Writings of Washington, vol. 30, pp. 292-293.

The time is now near at hand which must probably determine whether Americans are to be Freemen or Slaves; whether they are to have any property they can call their own; whether their houses and farms are to be pillaged and destroyed, and themselves consigned to a State of Wretchedness from which no human efforts will deliver them. The fate of unborn Millions will now depend, under God, on the Courage and Conduct of this army. Our cruel and unrelenting Enemy leaves us no choice but a brave resistance, or the most abject submission. . . . We have, therefore, to resolve to conquer or die.

—GEORGE WASHINGTON, 1st U.S. president. Address to
the Continental Army before the Battle of Long Island,
August 27, 1776.

To trust altogether in the justice of our cause without our own utmost exertions would be tempting Providence.

—GEORGE WASHINGTON, 1st U.S. president.
In a letter to Jonathan Trumbull, August 7, 1776.

It is the duty of all nations to acknowledge the providence of Almighty God, to obey his will, to be grateful for his benefits, and humbly to implore his protection and favour.

—GEORGE WASHINGTON, 1st U.S. president.
In a Thanksgiving Proclamation, October 3, 1789.

If such talents as I possess have been called into action by great events, and those events have terminated happily for our country, the glory should be ascribed to the manifest interposition of an overruling Providence.

—GEORGE WASHINGTON, 1st U.S. president.
In a letter to the Synod of the Reformed Dutch Church
in North America, October 9, 1789.

The ways of Providence are unscrutable, mortals must submit.

—GEORGE WASHINGTON, 1st U.S. president.
In a letter to Thaddeus Kosciuszko, August 31, 1797.

I think one would go crazy if he did not believe in Providence. It would be a maze without a clue. Unless there were some supreme guidance we would despair of the results of human counsel.

—WOODROW WILSON, 28th U.S. president.
Reply to a committee of the National Council of Evangelical
Free Churches, London, England, December 28, 1918.

CREATION

The adorable Creator of the World is infinitely benevolent, tho it is impossible for our finite Capacities to comprehend all of his dispensations. However, we know enough to excite our warmest gratitude and firmest confidence. My belief is unhesitating, that by his superintending Providence a Period greatly favorable is commencing in the Destinies of the human Race. That he may be pleased to honour Thee, as an Instrument for advancing his gracious Purposes, and that he may be thy Guide and Protector, is the ardent Wish, the fervent Prayer, of thy truly affectionate Friend.

—JOHN DICKINSON, member of the First Continental
Congress. To Thomas Jefferson, February 21, 1801.
Jefferson Papers, Library of Congress.

That there is one God, who made all things. That he governs the world by his providence. That he might be worshipped by adoration, prayer, and thanksgiving. But that the most acceptable service of God is doing good to Man. That the Soul is immortal. And that God will certainly reward virtue and punish vice, either here or hereafter.

—BENJAMIN FRANKLIN, member of the Second Continental
Congress. "Observations on my reading history, in Library,
May 19th, 1731." *Autobiography*. 1798.

FAITH

In contemplating what may be the life and adventures of one whole generation of the race of man, the only members of the animal creation susceptible of the perception of good and evil, of virtue and vice, of right and wrong, there are in this, as there have been in all former ages, observing and reflecting men, especially in the decline of life, prone to depreciate the moral and physical character of the present age, and to glorify the past. Far more pleasing, and, I believe, more correct is the conclusion, that the race of man in his fallen state is placed by successive generations on the earth to improve his own condition and that of his kind, and that this book has been furnished him by the special providence of his Maker to enable him, by faith in his Redeemer, and by works conformable to that faith, to secure salvation in a future world, and to promote his well-being in the present.

—JOHN QUINCY ADAMS, 6th U.S. president and diplomat. Address at a meeting of the ABS on February 27, 1844, held at the Capitol in Washington. Bible Society Record, vol. 1, no. 3, March 1844, p. 41.

This is the hour to rededicate ourselves to the faith in God that gives us confidence as we face the challenge of the years ahead.

—HARRY S. TRUMAN, 33rd U.S. president. Annual message to the Congress on the State of the Union, January 7, 1948.

If we do not hold to our faith in God, we cannot prevail against the dangers from abroad and the fears and distrust that those dangers create among us here at home.

—HARRY S. TRUMAN, 33rd U.S. president. Remarks on laying the cornerstone of the new temple of the Washington Hebrew Congregation, November 16, 1952.

You can help build a society where the demands of morality, and the needs of the spirit, can be realized in the life of the Nation. So, will you join in the battle to give every citizen the full equality which God enjoins and the law requires, whatever his belief, or race, or the color of his skin?

—LYNDON B. JOHNSON, 36th U.S. president. Remarks at the University of Michigan, May 22, 1964.

I realize that people whom we will never meet have this deep religious faith which has run through the destiny of this land from the beginning. I realize that we carry on our shoulders their hopes, but more important, we are sustained by their prayers.

—RICHARD NIXON, 37th U.S. president. Remarks at the 17th Annual Prayer Breakfast, January 30, 1969.

But also remember that the greatest service that you can render is to help to reinstill in America's young people a love of country, a faith in God, a faith in themselves that is essential if a nation is to be truly a great nation.

—RICHARD NIXON, 37th U.S. president.
Remarks at the convention of the National Federation of
Republican Women, October 22, 1971.

The chance America now has to lead the way to a lasting peace in the world may never come again.

With faith in God and faith in ourselves and faith in our country, let us have the vision and the courage to seize the moment and meet the challenge before it slips away.

—RICHARD NIXON, 37th U.S. president.
Remarks on accepting the presidential nomination of the
Republican National Convention, August 23, 1972.

All of us have the responsibility to stand and support the standards we believe in. As religious people, stand up for your faith. I stand with you. We believe in the same God.

—GERALD FORD, 38th U.S. president.
Remarks at the annual meeting of the National Baptist
Convention in St. Louis, September 12, 1975.

Your holiness, I'm reminded of the passage from the Bible of Saint Peter walking out on the water after Christ. We know that as long as he kept his eyes on our Savior, as long as his faith was strong, he was held up, but as soon as his faith faltered, he began to sink. Your holiness, with gentle chidings and powerful exhortations you have continually directed our thoughts to the spiritual source of all true goodness and happiness.

—RONALD REAGAN, 40th U.S. president. Remarks following discussions with Pope John Paul II in Vatican City, June 6, 1987.

I have learned what I suppose every president has learned, and that is that one cannot be president of our country without faith in God and without knowing with certainty that we are one nation under God. So, I think I should have made that clear—more clear that God is our rock and salvation, and we must trust him and keep faith in him.

—GEORGE H.W. BUSH, 41st U.S. president. Remarks at the National Prayer Breakfast, January 31, 1991.

What an extraordinary moment this is. Eighty-three years ago this day, this hour, our predecessors here laid a cornerstone. Now, eight decades later, we look at Mount St. Alban and say: here we have built our church—not just a church, a house of prayer for a nation built on the rock of religious faith, a nation we celebrate as "one nation under God," a nation whose founding President, George Washington, said: "No people can be bound to acknowledge and adore the invisible hand which conducts the affairs of men more than the people of the United States."

—GEORGE H.W. BUSH, 41st U.S. president. Remarks at the Washington National Cathedral Dedication Ceremony, September 29, 1990.

And I am convinced that faith and family can help us honor God in a most profound and personal way—daily, as human beings—by the conduct of our lives.

—GEORGE H.W. BUSH, 41st U.S. president.
Remarks at the Annual National Prayer Breakfast, May 4, 1989.

Our faith in God lifts our spirits, and many Americans step back from the concerns of daily life to reflect on the power of our religious traditions and on the values they teach us. During this time of renewal, let us all thank God for the countless wonders of creation and rededicate ourselves to the common ideals that have made ours a land of infinite blessings.

—WILLIAM CLINTON, 42nd U.S. president.
Easter Sunday, April 11, 1995.

Our Founding Fathers knew the importance of freedom of religion to a stable and lasting Union. Our Constitution protects individuals' rights to worship as they choose. Today, we continue to welcome the important contributions of people of faith in our society. We reject religious bigotry in every form, striving for a society that honors the life and faith of every person. As we maintain the vitality of a pluralistic society, we work to ensure equal treatment of faith-based organizations and people of faith.

—GEORGE W. BUSH, 43rd U.S. president. Proclamation by the
president, Religious Freedom Day, January 15, 2005.

In times of tragedy, faith assures us that death and suffering are not the final word; that love and hope are eternal. Religious faith not only comforts, it challenges. Faith teaches that every person is equal in God's sight, and must be treated with equal dignity here on earth.

—GEORGE W. BUSH, 43rd U.S. president. Remarks at the Religious Broadcaster's Convention, February 10, 2003.

Faith teaches us that God has a special concern for the poor, and that faith proves itself through actions and sacrifice, through acts of kindness and caring for those in need. For some people, Jesus's admonition to care "for the least of these" is an admirable moral teaching. For many Baptists, it is a way of life.

—GEORGE W. BUSH, 43rd U.S. president. Remarks by the president via satellite to the Southern Baptist Convention 2002 Annual Meeting, June 11, 2002.

Throughout our history, Americans of faith have always turned to prayer—for wisdom, prayer for resolve, prayers for compassion and strength, prayers for commitment to justice and for a spirit of forgiveness.

—GEORGE W. BUSH, 43rd U.S. president. National Hispanic Prayer Breakfast, May 16, 2002.

America is a country of faith. And throughout our history, in times of crisis and in times of calm, Americans have always turned to prayer.

—GEORGE W. BUSH, 43rd U.S. president. "President Commemorates National Day of Prayer," May 2, 2002.

Faith teaches humility, and with it, tolerance. Once we have recognized God's image in ourselves, we must recognize it in every human being.

—GEORGE W. BUSH, 43rd U.S. president.
Remarks at the National Prayer Breakfast, February 7, 2002.

I'm a Methodist. I'm an active church member . . . I attend church, I like church. . . I've heard great preachers, I've heard not-so-great preachers. I love the hymns, I read the Bible daily . . . I pray on a daily basis. I've got a structure to my life where religion plays a role. I understand religion is a walk, it's a journey. And I fully recognize that I'm a sinner, just like you. That's why Christ died. He died for my sins and your sins.

—GEORGE W. BUSH, 43rd U.S. president.
"*George W. Bush: Running on His Faith,*" US News Online.

I believe in tolerance, not in spite of my faith, but because of it. I believe in a God who calls us, not to judge our neighbors, but to love them.

—GEORGE W. BUSH, 43rd U.S. president. Acceptance speech,
Republican Convention, Philadelphia, August 3, 2000.

The Scriptures tell us we need faith as a source of strength. "The assurance of things hoped for, and the conviction of things unseen," the Scripture says. We need our faith as a source of hope. Faith teaches us that each of us is capable of redemption and, therefore, that progress is possible. Not perfection, but progress. I have always been touched by the living example of Jesus Christ. All the religious leaders of his day were suspicious of him and always tried to trap him because he was so at ease with the hurting, the hungry, the lonely and, yes, the sinners. In one of the attempts to trick Christ, he was asked what is the greatest commandment. And he answered, quoting Moses, "You shall love the Lord your God with all your heart and with all your soul and with all your mind." And then he added, as we should add, "This is the great and foremost commandment, and the second is like it. You shall love your neighbor as yourself."

—WILLIAM CLINTON, 42nd U.S. president.
Remarks at the National Prayer Breakfast, February 4, 1993.

It is only when men begin to worship that they begin to grow.

—CALVIN COOLIDGE, 30th U.S. president.
In a speech at Fredericksburg, Virginia, July 6, 1922.

Q. What is Faith?
A. An humble and hearty Assent to the Truths of Revelation—"the substance (confidence) of things hoped for, the Evidence of Things not seen"—so that we firmly believe in the Power and will of God to save Us from the Guilt and dominion of Sin, and accept Jesus Christ as he is proposed to us for our Saviour.

—JOHN DICKINSON, member of the First Continental
Congress. "Religious Instruction for Youth," undated.
R. R. Logan Papers, Historical Society of Pennsylvania.

Morality or Virtue is the End, Faith only a Means to obtain that End: And if the End be obtained, it is no matter by what Means.... Faith in Christ, however, may be and is of great Use to produce a good Life, but that it can conduce nothing towards Salvation where it does not conduce to Virtue is, I suppose, plain.... St. James, in his second Chapter, is very zealous against these Cryers-up of Faith, and maintains that Faith without Virtue is useless, *Will thou know, O vain Man*, says he, *that Faith without Works is dead and, shew me your Faith without your Works, and I will shew you mine by my Works*. Our Saviour, when describing the last Judgment, and declaring what shall give Admission into Bliss, or exclude from it, says nothing of Faith but what he says against it, that is, that those who cry *Lord, Lord*, and profess to have *believed* in his Name, have no Favour to expect on that Account; but declares that 'tis the Practice, or the omitting the Practice of the Duties of Morality, *Feeding the hungry, cloathing the Naked, visiting the sick &c.* In short, 'tis the Doing or not Doing all the Good that lies in our Power, that will render us the heirs of happiness or Misery.

—BENJAMIN FRANKLIN, member of the Second Continental Congress. "Dialogue between Two Presbyterians," April 10, 1735. Labaree, *Papers of Benjamin Franklin*, vol. 2, p. 30.

A philosopher may regard the present course of things in Europe as some great providential dispensation. A Christian can hardly view it in any other light. Both these descriptions of persons must approve a national appeal to heaven for protection. The politician will consider this as an important means of influencing Opinion, and will think it a valuable resource in a contest with France to set the Religious Ideas of his Countrymen in active Competition with the Atheistical tenets of their enemies. This is an advantage which we shall be very unskilful, if we do not improve to the utmost. And the impulse cannot be too early given. I am persuaded a day of humiliation and prayer besides being very proper would be extremely useful.

—ALEXANDER HAMILTON, member of the Continental Congress and 1st secretary of the treasury.

To William Loughton Smith, April 10, 1797. Syrett,
Papers of Alexander Hamilton, vol. 21, p. 41.

That the government of a State should have authority to appoint "particular days for rendering thanks to God" for any signal blessing, or imploring his assistance "in any public calamity," is certainly proper.

—JOHN JAY, president of the Continental Congress, 1778-1779;
and 1st chief justice of the U.S. Supreme Court, 1789-1795.
To Edward Livingston, July 28, 1822. Johnston,
Correspondence of Jay, vol. 4, p. 465.

My fundamental principle would be the reverse of Calvin's, that we are to be saved by our good works which are within our power, and not by our faith which is not within our power.

—THOMAS JEFFERSON, 2nd U.S. president. To
Thomas B. Parker, May 15, 1819. Adams, *Jefferson's Extracts*, p. 386.

No man has the right to abandon the care of his salvation to another.

—THOMAS JEFFERSON, 2nd U.S. president.
1776, Ford, ed, *Notes on Religion*, p. 141.

Religious proclamations by the Executive recommending thanksgivings & fasts . . . altho' recommendations only, they imply a religious agency, making no part of the trust delegated to political rulers. . . . The last & not the least objection is the liability of the practice to a subserviency to political views; to the scandal of religion, as well as the increase of party animosities. Candid or incautious politicians will not always disown such views. In truth it is difficult to frame such a religious Proclamation generally suggested by a political State of things, without referring to them in terms having some bearing on party questions.

—JAMES MADISON, 4th U.S. president. Detached Memoranda, 1819. Rakove, *Madison Writings,* pp. 764 765.

My reticence about public displays of religious faith flows both from the style of my family's religious observances and from a belief that God's will is expressed by men through their actions toward and on behalf of others. In living a Christian life, faith is the first step. Acknowledging your faith is the second. But the most important step is using the energy and creativity faith gives you to make the world a better place.

—RICHARD NIXON, 37th U.S. president. Richard Nixon, *In the Arena: A Memoir of Victory, Defeat and Renewal,* (Simon & Schuster, 1990), p. 89.

Again, do we rightly understand the way in which we are to obtain deliverance out of this our ruined and miserable condition. viz., by faith in Jesus Christ, which implies a firm belief of the Gospel report concerning him, a hearty approbation of the whole method of salvation thro' him, a cheerful consent and desire to be saved in this way, and a reliance of soul on his merits, and the mercy of God thro' him, for the whole of salvation, both from sin and hell, to be made holy as well as happy; acknowledging the whole to be of mere grace, and testifying our acceptance thereof, by a life of holy obedience to his commands.

—ROGER SHERMAN, member of the Continental Congress. Short Sermon, p. 5.

My life would not be worth living if it were not for the driving power of religion, for faith, pure and simple. I have seen all my life the arguments against it without ever having been moved by them . . . never for a moment have I had one doubt about my religious beliefs. There are people who believe only so far as they understand—that seems to me presumptuous and sets their understanding as the standard of the universe. . . . I am sorry for such people.

—WOODROW WILSON, 28th U.S. president.
Letter to Nancy Toy, 1915.

GOD

Under the blessings of Divine Providence. . . . It becomes us in humility to make our devout acknowledgments to the Supreme Ruler of the Universe for the inestimable civil and religious blessings with which we are favored,

—JAMES K. POLK, 11th U.S. president.
First Annual message, December 2, 1845.

And I look at some of the things that those ancestors of ours had to contend with, and I wonder how in the world they ever did it.

I will tell you how they did it. They did it because there was an incentive. They brought with them ideals. They brought with them an idea of God. They brought with them an idea of liberty. And as a result we have, I think, the greatest republic on which the sun has ever shone.

—HARRY S. TRUMAN, 33rd U.S. president.
Remarks at the National Conference on Family Life,
May 6, 1948.

I believe in God in his wisdom and benevolence: and I cannot conceive that such a Being could make such a species as the human merely to live and die on this earth. If I did not believe [in] a future state, I should believe in no God.

—JOHN ADAMS, 2nd U.S. president.
In a letter to Thomas Jefferson, December 8, 1818.

Grateful to Almighty God for the blessings which, through Jesus Christ our Lord, he has conferred on my beloved country in her emancipation, and in permitting me, under circumstances of mercy, to live to the age of eight-nine years, and to survive the fiftieth year of American Independence, adopted by Congress on the 4th of July, 1776, which I originally subscribed on the 2nd day of August of the same year, and of which I am now the last surviving signer, I do hereby recommend to the present and future generations the principles of that important document as the best inheritance their ancestors could bequeath to them, and pray that the civil and religious liberties that have secured to my country may be perpetuated to remotest posterity and extended to the whole family of man.

—CHARLES CARROLL, member of the Continental Congress.
August 2, 1826. *The Christian Life and Character of the Civil Institutions of the United States*, p. 180.

We should always remember that the many remarkable and unexpected means and events by which our wants have been supplied and our enemies repelled or restrained are such strong and striking proofs of the interposition of heaven, that our having been hitherto delivered from the threatened bondage of Britain ought to be forever ascribed to its true cause (the favor of God), and, instead of swelling our breasts with arrogant ideas of our prowess and importance, kindle in them a flame of gratitude and piety which may consume all remains of vice and irreligion.

—JOHN JAY, president of the Continental Congress, 1778-1779; and 1st chief justice of the U.S. Supreme Court, 1789-1795. *The Christian Life and Character of the Civil Institutions of the United States*, p. 183.

The resurrection of the Saviour of mankind is commemorated by keeping the first day of the week, not only as a certain memorial of his first coming in a state of humiliation, but the positive evidence of his future coming in glory.

—ELIAS BOUDINOT, president of the Continental Congress, 1782-1783, and ABS president. *The Christian Life and Character of the Civil Institutions of the United States*, p. 187.

Without religion, I believe that learning does real mischief to the morals and principles of mankind.

—BENJAMIN RUSH, member of the Continental Congress, 1776-1777. L.H. Butterfield, *Letters of Benjamin Rush*, vol. 1, p. 294. To John Armstrong on March 19, 1783 Retrieved from *www.generationjoshua.org*.

You might as well put out the sun and think to enlighten the world with tapers, destroy the attraction of gravity and think to wield the universe by human powers, as to extinguish the moral illumination of the Sabbath, and break this glorious mainspring of the moral government of God.

—DANIEL WEBSTER, American orator, lawyer, and statesman. *The Christian Life and Character of the Civil Institutions of the United States*, p. 235.

God has infinite Wisdom, goodness and power. He created the Universe. His duration is eternal, a parte Ante, and a parte post. His presence is as extensive as Space. What is Space? An infinite, spherical Vaccuum. He created this Speck of Dirt and the human Species for his glory: and with the deliberate design of making, nine tenths of our Species miserable forever, for his glory. This is the doctrine of Christian Theologians in general: ten to one. Now, my friend, can Prophecies, or miracles convince You, or Me, that infinite Benevolence, Wisdom and Power, created and preserves, for a time, innumerable millions to make them miserable, forever; for his own Glory? Wretch! What is his Glory? Is he ambitious? Does he want promotion? Is he vain? tickled with Adulation? Exulting and tryumphing in his Power and the Sweetness of his Vengeance? Pardon me, my Maker, for these Aweful Questions. My Answer to them is always ready: I believe no such Things. My Adoration of the Author of the Universe is too profound and too sincere. The Love of God and his Creation; delight, Joy, Tryumph, Exultation in my own existence, 'tho but an Atom, a Molecule Organique, in the Universe; are my religion. Howl, Snarl, bite, ye Calvinistick! Ye Athanasian Divines, if You will. Ye will say, I am no Christian: I say Ye are no Christians: and there the Account is ballanced. Yet I believe all the honest men among you are Christians in my sense of the Word... It has been long, very long a settled opinion in my Mind that there is now, never will be, and never was but one being who can Understand the Universe. And that it is not only vain but wicked for insects to pretend to comprehend it.

—JOHN ADAMS, 2nd U.S. president.
To Thomas Jefferson, September 14, 1813. Cappon,
Adams-Jefferson Letters, vol. 2, pp. 373-374.

There are instances of, I would say, an almost astonishing providence in our favor; so that we may truly say that it is not our own arm which has saved us. The hand of heaven appears to have led us on to be, perhaps, humble instruments and means in the great providential dispensation which is completing.

—SAMUEL ADAMS, Massachusetts delegate to the Continental Congress, 1775-1781. Speech on American independence, August 1, 1776, Philadelphia. Retrieved from www.bartleby.com.

There is a just God who presides over the destinies of nations; and who will raise up friends to fight our battles for us.

—PATRICK HENRY, American patriot and governor of Virginia. "Give Me Liberty or Give Me Death" speech, March 23, 1775. Retrieved from the James Madison Center, www.jmu.edu.

I have the most animating confidence that the present noble struggle for liberty will terminate gloriously for America. And let us play the man for our God, and for the cities of our God; while we are using the means in our power, let us humbly commit our righteous cause to the great Lord of the Universe, who loveth righteousness and hateth iniquity. And having secured the approbation of our hearts, by a faithful and unwearied discharge of our duty to our country, let us joyfully leave our concerns in the hands of him who raiseth up and pulleth down the empires and kingdoms of the world as he pleases; and with cheerful submission to his sovereign will, devoutly say: "Although the fig tree shall not blossom, neither shall fruit be in the vines; the labor of the olive shall fail, and the field shall yield no meat; the flock shall be cut off from the fold, and there shall be no herd in the stalls; yet we will rejoice in the Lord, we will joy in the God of our salvation."

—JOHN HANCOCK, president of the Second Continental Congress, 1775-1777. Boston Massacre Oration, March 5, 1774. Delivered at Boston, Massachusetts, on the anniversary of the Boston Massacre of 1770. Retrieved from America's homepage, http://ahp.gatech.edu/boston_mass_orat_1774.html.

History can hardly produce such a series of events as has taken place in favor of American opposition. The hand of heaven seems to have directed every occurrence. Had such an event as lately occurred at Essex happened to Cromwell, he would have published it as a miracle in his favor, and excited his soldiers to enthusiasm and bravery.

—ELBRIDGE GERRY, U.S. vice president, member of the Continental Congress and U.S. Congress. Letter to Samuel Adams, December 13, 1775.

May that Omnipotent Being who with infinite wisdom and justice presides over the destinies of nations, confirm the heroic patriotism which has glowed in the breasts of the national rulers, and convince the enemy that, whilst a disposition to peace on honorable and equitable terms will ever prevail in their public councils, one spirit, animated by the love of country, will inspire every department of the national government.

—ELBRIDGE GERRY, U.S. vice president, member of the Continental Congress and U.S. Congress. Addressing the Senate, 1814.

Those of us who are vested with civil authority ought also with much care to promote religion and good morals among all under their government. If we give credit to the holy Scriptures, he that ruleth must be just, ruling in the fear of God.

—JOHN WITHERSPOON, member of the Continental Congress. *The Christian Life and Character of the Civil Institutions of the United States.*

He had no doubt that God who, in former ages, had hardened Pharaoh's heart, and that he might show his power and glory in the redemption of his chosen people, for similar purposes had permitted the flagrant outrages which had occurred throughout the continent. It was for them now to determine whether they were worthy of divine interference—whether they would accept the high boon now held out to them by heaven;—that, if they would, though it might lead them through a sea of blood, they were to remember that the same God whose power divided the Red Sea for the deliverance of Israel still reigned in all his glory, unchanged and unchangeable—was still the enemy of the oppressor and the friend of the oppressed—that he would cover them from their enemies by a pillar of cloud by day, and guide them through the night by a pillar of fire.

—PATRICK HENRY, American patriot and governor of Virginia. April 1775. *The Christian Life and Character of the Civil Institutions of the United States*, p. 148.

At a season when the providence of God has manifested itself in the visitation of a fearful pestilence which is spreading itself throughout the land, it is fitting that a people whose reliance has ever been in his protection should humble themselves before his throne, and, while acknowledging past transgressions, ask a continuancy of the Divine mercy.

—ZACHARY TAYLOR, 12th U.S. president.
Recommendation, July 3, 1849. *The Christian Life and Character of the Civil Institutions of the United States*, p. 689.

In this hour of our calamity and peril, to whom shall we resort for relief but to God of our fathers? His omnipotent arm only can save us from the awful effects of our own crimes and follies—our own ingratitude and guilt towards our heavenly Father.

—JAMES BUCHANAN, 15th U.S. president.
A Recommendation, December 14, 1860. Ibid., p. 694.

My only hope of salvation is in the infinite transcendent love of God manifested to the world by the death of his Son upon the Cross. Nothing but his blood will wash away my sins. I rely exclusively upon it. Come, Lord Jesus! Come quickly!

—BENJAMIN RUSH, member of the Continental Congress, 1776-1777. George W. Corner, *The Autobiography of Benjamin Rush*, p. 166. Retrieved from www.generationjoshua.org.

I believe that there is only one living and true God, existing in three persons, the Father, the Son, and the holy Ghost, the same in substance equal in power and glory. That the scriptures of the old and new testaments are a revelation from God and a complete rule to direct us how we may glorify and enjoy him. . . . I believe the souls of believers are at their death made perfectly holy and immediately taken to glory: that at the end of this world there will be a resurrection of the dead and a final judgment of all mankind when the righteous shall be publicly acquitted by Christ the Judge and admitted to everlasting life and glory, and the wicked be sentenced to everlasting punishment.

—ROGER SHERMAN, member of the Continental Congress.
Lewis Henry Boutell, *The Life of Roger Sherman*, pp. 272-273.
Retrieved from www.generationjoshua.org.

Our country has been provided with the resources with which it can enlarge its intellectual, moral, and spiritual life. The issue is in the hands of the people. Our faith in man and God is the justification for the belief in our continuing success.

—CALVIN COOLIDGE, 30th U.S. president.
Sixth Annual message, December 4, 1928.

No occasion could be conceived more worthy, more truly and comprehensively American, than that which is chosen to commemorate this divinely appointed captain. The contemplation of his life and work will forever strengthen our faith in our country and in our country's God.

—CALVIN COOLIDGE, 30th U.S. president.
Address at the celebration of the 150th anniversary of George Washington taking command of the Continental Army, Cambridge, Massachusetts, July 3, 1925.

When an election is so held, when a choice is so made, it results in the real rule of the people, it warrants and sustains the belief that the voice of the people is the voice of God.

—CALVIN COOLIDGE, 30th U.S. president. Radio address from the White House on the duties of citizenship, November 3, 1924.

The principle of equality is recognized. It follows inevitably from belief in the brotherhood of man through the fatherhood of God.

—CALVIN COOLIDGE, 30th U.S. president.
Address to the Holy Name Society, Washington, D.C.,
September 21, 1924.

Now, therefore, I, Woodrow Wilson, president of the United States of America, do hereby proclaim Thursday, the thirtieth day of May, a day already freighted with sacred and stimulating memories, a day of public humiliation, prayer and fasting, and do exhort my fellow-citizens of all faiths and creeds to assemble on that day in their several places of worship and there, as well as in their homes, to pray to Almighty God that he may forgive our sins and shortcomings as a people and purify our hearts to see and love the truth, to accept and defend all things that are just and right, and to purpose only those righteous acts and judgments which are in conformity with his will; beseeching him that he will give victory to our armies as they fight for freedom, wisdom to those who take counsel on our behalf in these days of dark struggle and perplexity, and steadfastness to our people to make sacrifice to the utmost in support of what is just and true, bringing us at last the peace in which men's hearts can be at rest because it is founded upon mercy, justice and good will.

—WOODROW WILSON, 28th U.S. president.
Proclamation, Day of Prayer, May 11, 1918.

A supreme moment of history has come. The eyes of the people have been opened and they see. The hand of God is laid upon the nations. He will show them favor, I devoutly believe, only if they rise to the clear heights of his own justice and mercy.

—WOODROW WILSON, 28th U.S. president.
Address to a Joint Session of Congress Calling for War with
Austria-Hungary, December 4, 1917.

The way to success in this great country, with its fair judgments, is to show that you are not afraid of anybody except God and his final verdict. If I did not believe that, I would not believe in democracy. If I did not believe that, I would not believe that people can govern themselves. If I did not believe that the moral judgment would be the last judgment, the final judgment, in the minds of men as well as the tribunal of God, I could not believe in popular government. But I do believe these things, and, therefore, I earnestly believe in the democracy not only of America but of every awakened people that wishes and intends to govern and control its own affairs.

—WOODROW WILSON, 28th U.S. president.
Address at Independence Hall, "The Meaning of Liberty,"
July 4, 1914.

When we say God is a Spirit, we know what we mean as well as we do when we say that the Pyramids of Egypt are Matter. Let us be content therefore to believe him to be a Spirit, that is, an Essence that we know nothing of, in which originally and necessarily reside all energy; all Power, all Capacity, all Activity, all Wisdom, all Goodness.

—JOHN ADAMS, 2nd U.S. president.
To Thomas Jefferson, January 20, 1820. vol. 2, p. 560.

Question 1. Is this stupendous and immeasurable universe governed by eternal fate? 2. Is it governed by chance? 3. Is it governed by caprice anger resentment and vengeance? 4. Is it governed by intelligence wisdom and benevolence? The three first of these questions I have examined with as close attention as I am capable of & have decided them all forever in the negative. The 4th I have meditated with much more satisfaction & comfort to myself & decided unequivocally in the affirmative & from this last decision I have derived all my system of divinity.

—JOHN ADAMS, 2nd U.S. president.
To Louisa Catherine Adams, November 11, 1821.
Adams Papers (microfilm), reel 124, Library of Congress.

But what do we mean by the ideas, the thoughts, the reason, the intelligence, or the speech of God? His intelligence is a subject too vast, too incomprehensible for Plato, Philo, Paul or Peter, Jews, Gentiles, or Christians. Let us adore, not presume nor dogmatize. Even the great Teacher may not reveal this subject. There never was, is not, and never will be more than one Being in the universe capable of comprehending it. At least this is the humble adoring opinion of the writer of this note.

Moses says, God spoke the world into being. He said "Let there be Light" and there was Light. Plato and Philo seem to teach that God thought the world into existence. Which is the most sublime? Which the most incomprehensible? But if God's idea was of itself almighty and produced a world, the world must be eternal because God must have had an idea of it from eternity. These are all the effects of great minds grasping at ideas too vast for their comprehension. The will of God must come into consideration. Moses seems to have understood it best.

God had the idea from eternity. At length he willed the existence of the world, expressed his will by a word, and it was done. The world existed and stood fast. Thinking, or willing a world into existence is as sublime as speaking it. A thought is more simple than a word! But these are incorrect figures to express inadequate ideas. Admire and adore the Author of the telescopic universe, love and esteem the work, do all in your power to lessen ill, and increase good: but never assume to comprehend.

—JOHN ADAMS, 2nd U.S. president.
Marginalia in Joseph Priestley's *Early Opinions Concerning Jesus Christ*, Haraszti, *Prophets of Progress*, p. 288.

"Blessed, forever blessed, be the name of God!"

—JOHN QUINCY ADAMS, 6th U.S. president and diplomat. In a diary entry, after hearing that his efforts to rescind the infamous *Gag Rule* had finally succeeded, December 3, 1844. Champ Bennet Clark, *John Quincy Adams: "Old Man Eloquent"* (Boston: Little, Brown, & Co., 1932), p. 407.

God governs the world and all things *must* be right and just.

—ELIAS BOUDINOT, president of the Continental Congress, 1782-1783, and ABS president. To Susan Boudinot, October 22, 1781. Boudinot Papers, Princeton University Library.

Our God has provided for us hitherto, is the same yesterday, today & forever. His hand is not shortened: but is yet mighty to save.

—ELIAS BOUDINOT, president of the Continental Congress, 1782-1783, and ABS president. To James Milnor, March 22, 1820. Boudinot Papers, ABS.

He sits at the head of these threatening floods; and on a throne whose dominion neither earth, nor the powers of darkness, can disturb. Happy for us, that in the word of God, the true exponent of his counsels, we may learn, and cause others to know, how nations and men can best secure a defence against the assaults of violence, and best prepare for the inroads of change and decay.

—THEODORE FRELINGHUYSEN, U.S. senator and
ABS president, address of the president at the annual meeting,
May 11, 1848. *ABS Annual Report*, 1848, ABS Archives, p. 95.

The enemies of foreign missions have spoken tauntingly of the slowness of the work and of its great and disproportionate cost, and we have too exclusively consoled ourselves and answered the criticism by the suggestion that with God a thousand years is as one day. We should not lose sight of the other side of that truth—one day with him is as a thousand years. God has not set a uniform pace for himself in the work of bringing in the kingdom of his Son. He will hasten it in his day . . . .

—BENJAMIN HARRISON, 23rd U.S. president
and ABS vice president. Arthur Judson Brown, *The How and Why
of Foreign Missions*, Young People's Missionary Movement of
The United States and Canada, 1908, p. 176.

We still remain true to the faith of our fathers who established religious liberty when the nation began. We must remember, too, that our forebears in every generation, and wherever they established their homes, made prompt and generous provision for the institutions of religion. We must continue their stead-fast reliance upon the Providence of God.

—FRANKLIN D. ROOSEVELT, 32nd U.S. president.
Greeting to the National Eucharistic Congress, October 1, 1938.

When every succeeding day brings sad news of suffering and disaster abroad we are especially conscious of the Divine Power and of our dependence upon God's merciful guidance. With this consciousness in our hearts it is seemly that we should, at a time like this, pray to Almighty God for his blessing on our country and for the establishment of a just and permanent peace among all the nations of the world.

> —FRANKLIN D. ROOSEVELT, 32nd U.S. president.
> Proclamation 2418 for a Day of Prayer, August 7, 1940.

But in this critical moment of our history, we must be more than ever conscious of the true meaning of the "community spirit" which it expresses. It is a spirit which comes from our community of interests, our community of faith in the democratic ideal, our community of devotion to God.

> —FRANKLIN D. ROOSEVELT, 32nd U.S. president.
> Radio address for the mobilization for human needs,
> October 13, 1940.

I look forward, as does Your holiness, to that bright day when the peace of God returns to the world. We are convinced that this will occur only when the forces of evil which now hold vast areas of Europe and Asia enslaved have been utterly destroyed. On that day we will joyfully turn our energies from the grim duties of war to the fruitful tasks of reconstruction. In common with all other Nations and forces imbued with the spirit of good will toward men, and with the help of Almighty God, we will turn our hearts and our minds to the exacting task of building a just and enduring peace on earth.

> —FRANKLIN D. ROOSEVELT, 32nd U.S. president.
> Message to Pope Pius XII on the invasion of Italy, July 10, 1943.

God, the Father of all living, watches over these hallowed graves and blesses the souls of those who rest here. May he keep us strong in the courage that will win the war, and may he impart to us the wisdom and the vision that we shall need for true victory in the peace which is to come.

> —FRANKLIN D. ROOSEVELT, 32nd U.S. president.
> Armistice Day Address, November 11, 1942.

The belief in the four freedoms of common humanity—the belief in man, created free, in the image of God—is the crucial difference between ourselves and the enemies we face today. In it lies the absolute unity of our alliance, opposed to the oneness of the evil we hate. Here is our strength, the source and promise of victory.

> —FRANKLIN D. ROOSEVELT, 32nd U.S. president.
> Radio address on United Flag Day, June 14, 1942.

The Almighty God has blessed our land in many ways. He has given our people stout hearts and strong arms with which to strike mighty blows for freedom and truth. He has given to our country a faith which has become the hope of all peoples in an anguished world.

> —FRANKLIN D. ROOSEVELT, 32nd U.S. president.
> Inaugural Address, January 20, 1945.

The creed of our democracy is that liberty is acquired, liberty is kept by men and women who are strong, self-reliant, and possessed of such wisdom as God gives to mankind—men and women who are just, men and women who are understanding.

> —FRANKLIN D. ROOSEVELT, 32nd U.S. president.
> Address at Soldier's Field, Chicago, Illinois, October 28, 1944.

We owe it to our posterity, we owe it to our heritage of freedom, we owe it to our God, to devote the rest of our lives and all of our capabilities to the building of a solid, durable structure of world peace.

—FRANKLIN D. ROOSEVELT, 32nd U.S. president.
Radio address from the White House, October 5, 1944.

This nation has placed its destiny in the hands and heads and hearts of its millions of free men and women; and its faith in freedom under the guidance of God.

—FRANKLIN D. ROOSEVELT, 32nd U.S. president.
Annual message to Congress—the Four Freedoms speech,
January 6, 1941.

I am certain that out of the hearts of every man, woman and child in this land, in every waking minute, a supplication goes up to Almighty God; that all of us beg that suffering and starving, that death and destruction may end—and that peace may return to the world. In common affection for all mankind, your prayers join with mine—that God will heal the wounds and the hearts of humanity.

—FRANKLIN D. ROOSEVELT, 32nd U.S. president.
Fireside chat—on national defense—radio address,
May 26, 1940.

And in the difficult hours of this day—through dark days that may be yet to come—we will know that the vast majority of the members of the human race are on our side. Many of them are fighting with us. All of them are praying for us. But, in representing our cause, we represent theirs as well—our hope and their hope for liberty under God.

—FRANKLIN D. ROOSEVELT, 32nd U.S. president.
Fireside chat on the Declaration of War with Japan,
December 9, 1941.

We have humility for the guidance that has been given us of God in serving his will as a leader of freedom for the world.

—HARRY S. TRUMAN, 33rd U.S. president.
Statement by the president, July 4, 1945.

That we now have this Charter at all is a great wonder. It is also a cause for profound thanksgiving to Almighty God, who has brought us so far in our search for peace through world organization.

—HARRY S. TRUMAN, 33rd U.S. president.
Address in San Francisco at the Closing Session of the
United Nations conference, June 26, 1945.

For the triumph of spirit and of arms which we have won, and for its promise to peoples everywhere who join us in the love of freedom, it is fitting that we, as a nation, give thanks to Almighty God, who has strengthened us and given us the victory.

—HARRY S. TRUMAN, 33rd U.S. president.
President's news conference on V-E Day, May 8, 1945.

As we are about to undertake our heavy duties, we beseech our Almighty God to guide us in the building of a permanent monument to those who gave their lives that this moment might come.

—HARRY S. TRUMAN, 33rd U.S. president. Address to the United Nations conference in San Francisco, April 25, 1945.

Now, I am confident that the Divine Power which has guided us to this time of fateful responsibility and glorious opportunity will not desert us now. With that help from Almighty God which we have humbly acknowledged at every turning point in our national life, we shall be able to perform the great tasks which he now sets before us.

—HARRY S. TRUMAN, 33rd U.S. president. Annual message to the Congress on the State of the Union, January 5, 1949.

Our American heritage of human freedom is born of the belief that man is created in the image of God and therefore is capable of governing himself. We have created here a government dedicated to the dignity and the freedom of man. It is a government whose creed is derived from the word of God, and its roots are deep in our spiritual foundations. Our democracy is an expression of faith in the spirit of man, and it is a declaration of faith in man as created by God.

—HARRY S. TRUMAN, 33rd U.S. president. Address at the unveiling of a memorial carillion in Arlington National Cemetery.

The only sure bedrock of human brotherhood is the knowledge that God is the Father of mankind.

—HARRY S. TRUMAN, 33rd U.S. president. Address at a luncheon of the National Conference of Christian and Jews.

The basic source of our strength as a nation is spiritual. We believe in the dignity of man. We believe that he is created in the image of God, who is the Father of us all.

—HARRY S. TRUMAN, 33rd U.S. president. Radio address as part of the program "Religion in American Life," October 30, 1949.

You know, the president has to be very careful, when he goes to church, that he goes to church for the purpose of worshiping God and not for the purpose of being a circus. A great many people, if they find that the President, not Harry Truman, but the President, is going to be in church, they will go to church. Well, that is not the right frame of mind in which to go to church, and I don't cater to that sort of program. I go because I want to go and because I think I ought to go, and not for the purpose of making a show. The First Baptist Church treats me just the way I want to be treated.

—HARRY S. TRUMAN, 33rd U.S. president.
Remarks to the members of the *Associated Church Press*,
April 21, 1949.

The summons to peace on earth, good will toward men has come ringing down the ages, giving direction to the thought and the action of every human being whose life is lived according to God's purpose.

—HARRY S. TRUMAN, 33rd U.S. president.
Exchange of message with Pope Pius XII,
December 23, 1949.

Eventually, my friends, the moral forces of the world will prevail over the unmoral forces. I am just as sure as I stand here that

Almighty God, from whom we derive all our powers, will not let his law be upset by people who do not believe in any law.

—HARRY S. TRUMAN, 33rd U.S. president.
Informal remarks in St. Louis in connection with the
30th reunion of the 35th Division Association, June 10, 1950.

We have become the leaders of the moral forces of the world, the leaders who believe that the Sermon on the Mount means what it says, the leaders of that part of the world which believes that the law is the *God* given law under which we live, that all our traditions have come from Moses at Sinai, and Jesus on the Mount.

—HARRY S. TRUMAN, 33rd U.S. president. Remarks at the
91st annual convention of the Augustana Lutheran Church,
June 7, 1950.

For a society is made up of men, who are often weak, and selfish, and quarrelsome. And yet, men are the children of God. Men have within them the Divine spark that can lead them to truth, and unselfishness, and courage to do the right.

—HARRY S. TRUMAN, 33rd U.S. president.
Address in Spokane at Gonzaga University, May 11, 1950.

The unity of our country is a unity under God. It is a unity in freedom, for the service of God is perfect freedom. If we remember our faith in God, if we live by it as our forefathers did, we need have no fear for the future.

—HARRY S. TRUMAN, 33rd U.S. president.
Address in Philadelphia at the dedication of the Chapel
of the Four Chaplains, February 3, 1951.

With the rising tide of Godless materialism it is imperative that youth and older folks as well have a vital interest in spiritual values and have faith in God. Only in this way can we hope for real brotherhood and peace.

—HARRY S. TRUMAN, 33rd U.S. president.
Statement by the president commending the "Crusade for Christian Citizenship," February 20, 1952.

And the destruction of the conditions that shrivel the soul and starve the body would add new millions to the soldiers of the faith, the faith that the children of God can live—if they so will—in the climate and the relationships that mean justice and decency and peace for all.

—DWIGHT D. EISENHOWER, 34th U.S. president.
Address at the second assembly of the World Council of Churches, Evanston, Illinois, August 19, 1954.

This is the hope that beckons us onward in this century of trial. This is the work that awaits us all, to be done with bravery, with charity, and with prayer to Almighty God.

—DWIGHT D. EISENHOWER, 34th U.S. president.
Inaugural Address, January 20, 1953.

For close to two centuries our nation has thrived under the bracing influence of belief in *God* and the dignity of the individual. Should this spiritual base of our society ever become dimmed, our faith in the destiny of America would disappear before a vain reliance on materialism, and crass political maneuver.

—DWIGHT D. EISENHOWER, 34th U.S. president.
Address at the golden jubilee dinner of the National Conference of Catholic Charities, New York City, September 26, 1960.

This University is dedicated to true education; it strives to develop wisdom. This implies, over and beyond mere knowledge, an understanding of men's relationship to their fellow men in a world created for their stewardship by a God in whose image they are all made.

—DWIGHT D. EISENHOWER, 34th U.S. president.
Address and remarks at the Baylor University
commencement Ceremonies, Waco, Texas,
May 25, 1956.

When we take all these circumstances into consideration, it is but natural that the first paragraph of the Declaration of Independence should open with a reference to Nature's God and should close in the final paragraphs with an appeal to the Supreme Judge of the world and an assertion of a firm reliance on Divine Providence.

—CALVIN COOLIDGE, 30th U.S. president. Address at
the celebration of the 150th anniversary of the Declaration
of Independence, Philadelphia, Pennsylvania, July 5, 1926.

But by gathering occasionally—and I understand this whole ceremony is something of a week long—by announcing to the world that we come up as laymen and meet, making the same acknowledgments that are made in that prayer, we are doing exactly the same thing: we are telling people that this nation is still a nation under God.

—DWIGHT D. EISENHOWER, 34th U.S. president.
Remarks at an annual breakfast of the
International Council for Christian Leadership,
February 2, 1956.

Neither dare we forget our blessings. To count them is to gain new courage and new strength, a firmer patience under test and a stouter faith in the decency of man and in the providence of God.

—DWIGHT D. EISENHOWER, 34th U.S. president.
Remarks at the Pageant of Peace ceremonies, December 17, 1954.

The real fire within the builders of America was faith—faith in a Provident God whose hand supported and guided them: faith in themselves as the children of God . . . faith in their country and its principles that proclaimed man's right to freedom and justice.

—DWIGHT D. EISENHOWER, 34th U.S. president.
Abilene homecoming, June 4, 1952.

We are delighted to welcome you to this, your house, the first house in the first land of the world, because from the time of the ancient hebrew prophets and the dispersal of the money, men of God have taught us that social problems are moral problems on a huge scale. They have demonstrated that a religion which did not struggle to remove oppression from the world of men would not be able to create the world of spirit. They have preached that the church should be the first to awake to individual suffering and the church should be the bravest in opposing all social wrongs.

—LYNDON B. JOHNSON, 36th U.S. president.
Remarks to a group of civil rights leaders, April 29, 1964.

I urge that each of us turn to God on that day—acknowledging that our country continues, as it was founded, "with a firm reliance upon the protection of divine Providence";

—thanking him for the blessings of mind and spirit which he has heaped upon us in a land of vast bounty;

—begging his forgiveness for our shortcomings;

—asking for the patience, the wisdom, the understanding, and the courage we need to carry on his work.

—LYNDON B. JOHNSON, 36th U.S. president.
Proclamation 3617—National Day of Prayer, September 22, 1964.

In each generation, with toil and tears, we have had to earn our heritage again. If we fail now then we will have forgotten in abundance what we learned in hardship: that democracy rests on faith, that freedom asks more than it gives, and the judgment of God is harshest on those who are most favored.

—LYNDON B. JOHNSON, 36th U.S. president.
Inaugural Address, January 20, 1965.

We were never meant to be an oasis of liberty and abundance in a worldwide desert of disappointed dreams. Our Nation was created to help strike away the chains of ignorance and misery and tyranny wherever they keep man less than God means him to be.

—LYNDON B. JOHNSON, 36th U.S. president. Annual message to the Congress on the State of the Union, January 4, 1965.

We work with and for those men and women not because we have to. We work because morality commands it, justice requires it, and our own dignity as men depends upon it. We work not because we fear the unjust wrath of our enemy, but because we fear the just wrath of God.

—LYNDON B. JOHNSON, 36th U.S. president.
Commencement address at Baylor University, May 28, 1965.

We are a people with an abiding faith in a merciful God and in his goodness.

—LYNDON B. JOHNSON, 36th U.S. president.
Proclamation 3657—Prayer for Peace,
Memorial Day, 1965, May 15, 1965.

There are those who say the rule of law is a fruitless and uto-pian dream. It is true that if it comes, it will come slowly. It will come through the practical and the wise resolution of number-less problems. But to deny the possibility is to deny peace itself and to deny that flowering of the spirit which we must believe God meant for man.

—LYNDON B. JOHNSON, 36th U.S. president.
Remarks to the delegates to the conference on
World Peace through Law, September 16, 1965.

This also means that each man must have a chance to share in present benefits and to share in future progress. God did not create any man to live in unseen chains, laboring through a life of pain in order to heap the table of a favored few. No farmer should be enslaved to land that he can never own. No worker should be stripped of reward for toil. No family should be com-pelled to sacrifice while others escape the obligations of their society. "Indeed," said Thomas Jefferson, "I tremble for my country when I reflect that God is just." We must surely tremble for our continent as long as any live and flourish protected by the walls of injustice.

—LYNDON B. JOHNSON, 36th U.S. president. Remarks at a ceremony commemorating the fourth anniversary of the Alliance for Progress, August 17, 1965.

On this occasion, then, I come to speak, at this time and at this place, about the morality of nations. For while I believe devotedly in the separation of church and state, I do not believe it is pleasing in the sight of God for men to separate morality from their might.

LYNDON B. JOHNSON, 36th U.S. president
Commencement address at Catholic University, June 6, 1965.

We—the heirs and trustees of a great civilization, richer and more powerful by far than any that has gone before us, cherishing freedom and the majesty of the human spirit—ask God's mercy and blessing on us now, and in all that we shall do in the years ahead.

—LYNDON B. JOHNSON, 36th U.S. president. Remarks at the presidential Prayer Breakfast, February 2, 1967.

We in America, as we meet here with all of our blessings tonight, are keenly aware that God has showered our land with abundance. The sharing of our blessings with others is a value we hold in common with Israel.

—LYNDON B. JOHNSON, 36th U.S. president. Toasts of the president and President Zalman Shazar of Israel, August 2, 1966.

We can never be so arrogant as to claim God's special blessing for America, but we can express the hope that in his eyes we have at least tried to help make possible a new vitality of the human conscience—not only here in America, our beloved land, but we have tried it and are still trying it throughout all the world.

—LYNDON B. JOHNSON, 36th U.S. president. Remarks
at the presidential Prayer Breakfast, February 1, 1968.

In our churches, in our homes, and in our private hearts, let us resolve before God to stand against divisiveness in our country and all its consequences.

—LYNDON B. JOHNSON, 36th U.S. president.
Address to the nation upon proclaiming a day of
mourning following the death of Dr. King, April 5, 1968.

But we know something better and truer in our hearts: We have in ourselves, in our institutions, the real power to show the world that we are still Americans, the place on earth which promised in the 18th century that reason and justice would triumph, that all men were born to stand equal before God and the law, the place on earth where every single child would grow with an equal chance to fulfill the talents that his Creator had given him.

—LYNDON B. JOHNSON, 36th U.S. president.
Remarks at the annual dinner of the White House
Correspondents Association, May 11, 1968.

This college symbolizes two ancient American traits: —first, a steadfast faith in God,—second, a fervent commitment to education.

—LYNDON B. JOHNSON, 36th U.S. president.
Remarks at the dedication of Thomas More College, Fort
Mitchell, Kentucky, September 28, 1968.

Let us close the springs of racial poison. Let us pray for wise and understanding hearts. Let us lay aside irrelevant differences and make our Nation whole. Let us hasten that day when our unmeasured strength and our unbounded spirit will be free to do the great works ordained for this Nation by the just and wise God who is the Father of us all.

—LYNDON B. JOHNSON, 36th U.S. president.
Radio and television remarks upon signing the
Civil Rights Bill, July 2, 1964.

Praying to be worthy of God's guidance, let us rededicate ourselves to the continuing tasks before us remembering always that the price of our liberty is eternal vigilance.

—LYNDON B. JOHNSON, 36th U.S. president. Message to the
members of the Armed Forces, November 25, 1963.

The work must be our work now. Scarred by the weaknesses of man, with whatever guidance God may offer us, we must nevertheless and alone with our mortality, strive to ennoble the life of man on earth.

—LYNDON B. JOHNSON, 36th U.S. president. Annual message
to the Congress on the State of the Union, January 12, 1966.

Above the pyramid on the great seal of the United States it says—in Latin—"God has favored our undertaking."

God will not favor everything that we do. It is rather our duty to divine his will. But I cannot help believing that he truly understands and that he really favors the undertaking that we begin here tonight.

—LYNDON B. JOHNSON, 36th U.S. president.
Special message to the Congress, March 15, 1965.

Our destiny offers not the cup of despair, but the chalice of opportunity. So let us seize it not in fear, but in gladness—and "riders on the earth together," let us go forward, firm in our faith, steadfast in our purpose, cautious of the dangers, but sustained by our confidence in the will of *God* and the promise of man.

—RICHARD NIXON, 37th U.S. president.
Inaugural Address, January 20, 1969.

This is a great Office, and I am proud and humble to hold it. This is enormous responsibility, and I accept the responsibility without fear but with also great respect.

But I can also tell you America would not be what it is today, the greatest nation in the world, if this were not a nation which has made progress under God.

—RICHARD NIXON, 37th U.S. president. Remarks at
Dr. Billy Graham's East Tennessee Crusade, May 28, 1970.

I think more people prayed last week than perhaps have prayed in many years in this country, and the very fact that they did indicates that the religious strength of this country, something we often take for granted, and something that sometimes, particularly now, seems to be weakening in some areas, that it is there in times of trouble. Let us remember that if we turn to spiritual help, if we pray for the assistance of God when we were faced with this very great potential tragedy and this great trouble, let us remember we have come a long way in this country because we have had faith in God.

—RICHARD NIXON, 37th U.S. president.
Remarks at a special church service in Honolulu, April 19, 1970.

But yet every one, whether he was a churchgoer or, as in Lincoln's case, not a churchgoer, every one recognized in the awesome position of power of the Presidency the necessity for divine guidance and also the fact that this Nation is a nation under God, and that this Nation some way from the beginning has had a spiritual strength far more important than the enormous economic potential that we have now developed or the military strength that we now possess.

—RICHARD NIXON, 37th U.S. president.
Remarks at the presidential Prayer Breakfast,
February 5, 1970.

We hope, by this journey, to know better the origins of earth, the moon, and the other planets. We hope to understand something more of the mysteries of God's great work. And, in this seeking, we hope to understand more of man himself.

—RICHARD NIXON, 37th U.S. president.
Statement following the successful launch of Apollo 15,
July 26, 1971.

We shall answer to God, to history, and to our conscience for the way in which we use these years.

—RICHARD NIXON, 37th U.S. president.
Oath of Office and Inaugural Address, January 20, 1973.

It is rather hard sometimes for us to have that respect, sometimes for each other in our political process and sometimes for other nations who have totally different political views, but I would only suggest that we go back to Lincoln—and, of course, I go back to my grandmother—and I would pray for this Nation at this time, and I hope all of you would, too, whether orally or in silence, that we try to listen more to what God wants rather than to tell God what we want, that we would try to find out what God wants America to be rather than to ask him always to see that what we believe America should be prevails.

—RICHARD NIXON, 37th U.S. president.
Remarks at the National Prayer Breakfast, January 31, 1974.

The electronic era of communications, which is only beginning—as the age of the book was only beginning when Gutenberg printed his Bible—holds unlimited opportunities for those who today tell and retell the good news of God's love for man.

—GERALD FORD, 38th U.S. president.
Remarks at the annual congressional breakfast of the National
Religious Broadcasters, January 28, 1975.

We are joined in the profound realization that none of us can go it alone, and that we do not need to go it alone if we seek the help of God and of our fellowship.

—GERALD FORD, 38th U.S. president.
Remarks at the National Prayer Breakfast, January 30, 1975.

Masonic principles—internal, not external—and our order's vision of duty to country and acceptance of God as a Supreme Being and guiding light have sustained me during my years of Government service.

—GERALD FORD, 38th U.S. president. Remarks an Unveiling Ceremony at the George Washington Masonic National Memorial, Alexandria, Virginia, February 17, 1975.

Further, it is important that all of us recall that the watchful eye of our Creator is upon us and upon those we love. We take comfort in the fact that each of us, in our own way, may call upon our God for guidance, for solace, and for strength to endure.

—GERALD FORD, 38th U.S. president. Proclamation 4413—National Day of Prayer for Americans missing in action in Southeast Asia, January 21, 1976.

Let us join the great principles of our past—spiritual and temporal—with the great promise of our future. With the help of God, America's third century will be our proud legacy to so many generations yet to come.

—GERALD FORD, 38th U.S. president. Remarks at the lighting of the national community Christmas tree, December 18, 1975.

I hope and work for the day when the human mind and the human spirit are no longer shackled by ignorance and prejudice, when all the children of God are brothers and sisters.

—GERALD FORD, 38th U.S. president. Remarks at North Carolina Central University, November 14, 1975.

In some circles it is considered very smart and very "in" to be cynical and somewhat disdainful of the basic motivations that have inspired and sustained mankind throughout the centuries. A love of family, a love of country, a love of labor, a love of learning, a love of God—these values are not outdated. And from the spirit that I feel is here today, I am sure that all of you agree most wholeheartedly.

—GERALD FORD, 38th U.S. president.
Remarks at the Dedication Ceremonies at Pepperdine University,
Malibu, California, September 20, 1975.

I have no fear for the future of America. The future is our friend, and as we go forward together, I promise you once more—as I have promised you before—to uphold the Constitution, to do what is right as God gives me to see the right, and to do the very best that I can for America. God helping me, I will not let you down.

—GERALD FORD, 38th U.S. president.
Remarks at the North Carolina State Fair in Raleigh,
October 23, 1976.

Sometimes we take for granted that an acknowledgment of sin, an acknowledgment of the need for humility permeates the consciousness of our people. But it doesn't. But if we know that we can have God's forgiveness as a person, I think as a nation it makes it much easier for us to say, "God, have mercy on me, a sinner," knowing that the only compensation for sin is condemnation.

—JIMMY CARTER, 39th U.S. president.
National Prayer Breakfast Remarks at the Annual Breakfast,
January 27, 1977.

In a civilization marred by disputes and conflicts, the ministers of God, representing all faiths, help lead the human family to an understanding of his love and his peace. Clergymen of all denominations point the way to a richer, more fulfilling life through higher moral standards.

—JIMMY CARTER, 39th U.S. president.
Proclamation 4484—International Clergy Week,
January 28, 1977.

As you solemnly review and judge your own conduct during the past year, we are all reminded that we serve God most faithfully by showing concern for our friends and neighbors.

—JIMMY CARTER, 39th U.S. president.
Jewish High Holy Days message of the president,
August 15, 1977.

To me, God is real. To me, the relationship with God is a very personal thing. God is ever-present in my life—sustains me when I am weak, gives me guidance when I turn to him, and provides for me as a Christian through the life of Christ, a perfect example to emulate in my experiences with other human beings.

—JIMMY CARTER, 39th U.S. president.
National Prayer Breakfast Remarks at the 26th Annual Breakfast,
February 2, 1978.

So, our faith in God, no matter what form it may have taken in our own individual lives, can be a basis for repairing the damage that has been done to the human spirit and should be a constant reminder that we have an equivalent responsibility to care for the environment, the ecology, the place where we live. We have a responsibility for stewardship.

The Bible says that the body is a temple of God and that we should care for our own bodies and for those around us.

—JIMMY CARTER, 39th U.S. president. Denver, Colorado. Remarks at the governor's annual prayer breakfast, May 4, 1978.

Our Nation, perhaps more than any other, has always held a special cognizance of the gifts of the Creator. We were founded upon a belief in, and reverence for, the liberty of the human spirit under God and the equality of all people before the Almighty.

—JIMMY CARTER, 39th U.S. president. Proclamation 4591—National Day of Prayer, September 1, 1978.

Many people these days feel alone. There is a Yiddish proverb, a religious proverb, that says, "God gave burdens, also shoulders." A simple proverb—it doesn't say God gave us burdens, but he gave us shoulders strong enough to bear them, it just says, "God gave burdens, also shoulders." We not only have our own shoulders to carry burdens, but we have others to help, not just to carry burdens but, sometimes, shoulders to cry on. Those shoulders let us bear the burdens of life.

—JIMMY CARTER, 39th U.S. president. Salt Lake City, Utah. Remarks at Mormon church ceremonies honoring family unity, November 27, 1978.

The bond of our common humanity is stronger than the divisiveness of our fears and prejudices. God gives us the capacity for choice. We can choose to alleviate suffering. We

can choose to work together for peace. We can make changes—
and we must.

—JIMMY CARTER, 39th U.S. president.
"Text from the Nobel lecture given by the
Nobel Peace Prize Laureate for 2002, Jimmy Carter,"
in Oslo, December 10, 2002.

Let us as a nation join together before God, aware of the trials
that lie ahead and of the need for divine guidance. With unshakable faith in God and the liberty which is our heritage, we as a
free nation will continue to grow and prosper.

—RONALD REAGAN, 40th U.S. president.
Proclamation 4897 National Day of Prayer,
February 12, 1982.

Our forefathers drew on the wisdom and strength of God when
they turned a vast wilderness into a blessed land of plenty called
the United States of America. God has truly blessed this country, but we never should fall into the trap that would detract
from the universality of God's gift. It is for all mankind. God's
love is the hope and the light of the world.

—RONALD REAGAN, 40th U.S. president.
Remarks at the Annual Prayer Breakfast, February 4, 1988.

Compelled by a deep need for God's wisdom, we began to pray.
And we prayed for God's protection in what we undertook, for
God's love to fill hearts, and for God's peace to be the moral
North Star that guided us.

—GEORGE H.W. BUSH, 41st U.S. president.
Remarks at the National Prayer Breakfast, January 30, 1992.

More than a hundred years ago, the great American poet, Henry Wadsworth Longfellow, reminded us that "nature is a revelation of God." This Earth Day, let us remember that we are only stewards in our time of the Earth God gave us for all time. And let us strengthen our resolve to preserve the beauty and the natural bounty that sustains us, and must sustain generations yet to come.

—WILLIAM CLINTON, 42nd U.S. president.
Radio address of the president to the nation, April 22, 2000.

When we pray we acknowledge our total dependence on Almighty God. We put our future in his hands, and we find that prayer lifts our spirits and changes our lives.

—GEORGE W. BUSH, 43rd U.S. president.
National Hispanic Prayer Breakfast, June 15, 2007.

At the start of this New Year, we move forward with trust in the power of the American spirit, confidence in our purpose, and faith in a loving God who created us to be free.

—GEORGE W. BUSH, 43rd U.S. president.
Message for New Year's Day 2007, December 31, 2006.

On the fiftieth anniversary of our national motto, "In God We Trust," we reflect on these words that guide millions of Americans, recognize the blessings of the Creator, and offer our thanks for his great gift of liberty.

—GEORGE W. BUSH, 43rd U.S. president.
50th anniversary of our national motto,
"In God We Trust," 2006.

In this young century, our nation has been called to great duties. I'm confident we'll meet our responsibilities so long as we continue to trust in God's purposes.

—GEORGE W. BUSH, 43rd U.S. president. President Attends
National Catholic Prayer Breakfast, April 7, 2006.

Life is a creation of God, not a commodity to be exploited by man.

—GEORGE W. BUSH, 43rd U.S. president. President's remarks
via satellite to the Southern Baptist Convention, June 15, 2004.

On this bicentennial of that event, we pause to remember and give thanks to Almighty God for our unbroken heritage of democracy, the peaceful transition of power, and the perseverance of our Government through the challenges of war and peace, want and prosperity, discord and harmony.

—GEORGE W. BUSH, 43rd U.S. president.
National Day of Prayer and Thanksgiving,
January 22, 2001.

Fifty years ago, General Eisenhower concluded his order of the day with these words: "Let us all beseech the blessing of Almighty God upon this great and noble undertaking." As we begin this new day of remembrance, let us also ask God's blessing: for all those who died for freedom fiftieth years ago, and for the Americans who carry on their noble work today. May God bless them, and may God bless America.

—WILLIAM CLINTON, 42nd U.S. president. Remarks
by the president in sunrise ceremony commemorating
those lost at sea in the Normandy Invasion, June 6, 1994.

We are here because we are all the children of God, because we know we have all fallen short of God's glory, because we know that no matter how much power we have, we have it but for a moment. And in the end, we can only exercise it well if we see ourselves as servants, not sovereigns.

—WILLIAM CLINTON, 42nd U.S. president.
Remarks by the president at the National Prayer Breakfast,
February 2, 1995.

I am guided by certain traditions. One is that there is a God and he is good, and his love, while free, has a self imposed cost: We must be good to one another.

—GEORGE H.W. BUSH, 41st U.S. president.
Republican National Convention acceptance address, 1988.

Freedom and fear, justice and cruelty have always been at war, and we know that God is not neutral between them.

—GEORGE W. BUSH, 43rd U.S. president. Address to a joint
session of Congress and the nation, September 20, 2001.

The existence of millions of distant galaxies, the evolution of species, and the big bang theory cannot be rejected because they are not described in the Bible, and neither does confidence in them cast doubt on the Creator of it all. God gave us this exciting opportunity for study and exploration, never expecting the Bible to encompass a description of the entire physical world or for scientific discoveries to be necessary as the foundation for our Christian faith.

—JIMMY CARTER, 39th U.S. president. Jimmy Carter,
Our Endangered Values, (New York: Simon & Schuster, 2005) p. 49.

I know as no one else can know my limitations, and how fixed and inexorable they are . . . but I shall trust God, as I have in the past, for strength and opportunity for further usefulness.

—GROVER CLEVELAND, 22nd & 24th U.S. president.
Letter to Rev. Wilton Merle Smith, D.D., March 21, 1906.

God is a spirit, from everlasting to everlasting, alone-self exis-tent, invisible, unchangeable, infinitely powerful, wise, just, true, merciful, good, holy, who by his word created all things, and preserves, governs and disposes of them, according to his will.

—JOHN DICKINSON, member of the First Continental
Congress. "Religious Instruction for Youth," undated.
R. R. Logan Papers, Historical Society of Pennsylvania.

Limited as our Capacities are, We are favored so far as to per-ceive, that the Sovereign of the Universe can deduce Good out of Evil; and that he is inclined to do so. But our sentiments on this head must be mingled with pure humility, for "who hath known the Mind of the Lord? Or, who hath been his Councellor?"

—JOHN DICKINSON, member of the First Continental
Congress. To Mercy Otis Warren, December 22, 1806.
Warren-Adams Letters, vol. 2, p. 349.

It might be judg'd an Affront to your Understandings should I go to prove this first Principle, the Existence of a Deity and that he is the Creator of the Universe, for that would suppose you ignorant of what all Mankind in all Ages have agreed in. I shall therefore proceed to observe: 1. That he must be a Being of great Wisdom: 2. That he must be a Being of great Goodness and

3. That he must be a Being of great Power. That he must be a Being of infinite Wisdom, appears in his admirable Order and Disposition of Things, whether we consider the heavenly Bodies, the Star and Planets, and their wonderful regular Motions, or this Earth compounded of such an Excellent mixture of all the Elements; or the admirable Structure of Animal Bodies of such an infinite Variety, and yet every one adopted to its Nature, and the Way of Life it is to be placed in, whether on Earth, in the Air or in the Waters, and so exactly that the highest and most exquisite human Reason, cannot find a fault. . . . 2. That the Deity is a Being of great Goodness, appears in his giving Life to so many Creatures, each of which acknowledge it a benefit by their unwillingness to leave it; in his providing plentiful Sustenance for them all, and making those Things that are most useful, most common and easy to be had; such as Water necessary for almost every Creature's Drink; Air without which few could subsist, the inexpressible Benefits of Light and Sunshine to almost all Animals in general. . . . 3. That he is a Being of infinite Power appears, in his being able to form and compound such Vast Masses of Matter as this Earth and the Sun and innumerable Planets and Stars, and give them such prodigious Motion, and yet so to govern them in their greatest Velocity as that they shall not flie off out of their appointed Bounds nor dash one against another, to their mutual Destruction.

—BENJAMIN FRANKLIN, member of the Second Continental Congress. "On the Providence of God in the Government of the World," 1732. Labaree, *Papers of Benjamin Franklin*, vol. 1, pp. 265-266.

I believe there is one supreme most perfect Being, Author and Father of the Gods themselves. For I believe that Man is not the most perfect Being but one, rather that as there are many Degrees of Beings his inferiors, so there are many Degrees of Beings superior to him.

> BENJAMIN FRANKLIN, member of the Second Continental Congress. "Articles of Belief and Acts of Religion," November 20, 1728

I believe in one God, creator of the Universe. That he governs it by his Providence. That he ought to be worshiped. That the most acceptable Service we render to him is doing good to his other Children. That the soul of man is immortal and will be treated with justice in another life respecting its conduct in this. These I take to be the fundamental Principles of all sound religion, and I regard them as you do in whatever Sect I meet with them.

> —BENJAMIN FRANKLIN, member of the Second Continental Congress. In a letter to Ezra Stiles, president of Yale, March 9, 1790.

In the beginning of the contest with Britain, when we were sensible of danger, we had daily prayer in this room for Divine protection. Our prayers, Sir, were heard, and they were graciously answered. . . do we imagine we no longer need his assistance?

> —BENJAMIN FRANKLIN, member of the Second Continental Congress. Constitutional Convention, Thursday, June 28, 1787.

... the benevolent and sublime reformer of that religion [Jesus] has told us only that god is good and perfect, but has not defined him. I am therefore of his theology, believing that we have neither words nor ideas adequate to that definition. And if we could all, after his example, leave the subject as undefinable, we should all be of one sect, doers of good and eschewers of evil. No doctrines of his lead to schism.

> —THOMAS JEFFERSON, 2nd U.S. president. To Ezra Shies Ely, June 25, 1819. Adams, *Jefferson's Extracts*, p. 387.

1. That there is one only God, and he all perfect. 2. That there is a future state of rewards and punishments. 3. That to love God with all thy heart and thy neighbor as thyself the sum of religion.

> —THOMAS JEFFERSON, 2nd U.S. president. Letter to Benjamin Waterhouse specifying the "doctrines of Jesus," June 26, 1822.

I hold (without appeal to revelation) that when we take a view of the Universe, in it's parts general or particular, it is impossible for the human mind not to perceive and feel a conviction of design, consummate skill, and indefinite power in every atom of it's composition. The movements of the heavenly bodies, so exactly held in their course by the balance of the centrifugal and centripetal forces, the structure of our earth itself, with its' distribution of lands, waters and atmosphere, animal and vegetable bodies, examined in all their minutest particles, insects mere atoms of life, yet as perfectly organised as man or mammoth, the mineral substances, their generation and uses, it is impossible, I say, for the human mind not to believe that there is, in all this, design, cause and effect, up to an ultimate cause, a fabricator of all things from matter and motion, their preserver and regulator while permitted to exist in their present forms, and their regenerator into new and other forms. We see, too, evident proofs of the necessity of a superintending power to maintain the Universe in it's course and order. Stars, well known, have disappeared, new ones have come into view, comets, in their incalculable courses, may run foul of suns and planets and require renovation under other laws; certain races of animals are become extinct; and, were there no restoring power, all existences might extinguish successively, one by one, until all should be reduced to a shapeless chaos. So irresistible are these evidences of an intelligent and powerful Agent that, of the infinite numbers of men who have existed thro' all time, they have believed, in proportion of a million at least to Unit, in the hypothesis of an eternal pre-existence of a creator, rather than in that of a self-existent Universe. Surely this unanimous sentiment renders this more probable than that of the few in the other hypothesis.

—THOMAS JEFFERSON, 2nd U.S. President, to John Adams, April 11, 1823. Cappon, *Adams-Jefferson Letters*, vol. 2, p. 592.

I know there is a God—and I see a storm coming; If he has a place for me, I believe that I am ready.

—JOHN F. KENNEDY, 35th U.S. president
Words written on a slip of paper found by his secretary
Evelyn Lincoln following a disappointing meeting with
Soviet Premier Nikita Khrushchev in Vienna, June 1961.
Evelyn Lincoln, *My Twelve Years with John F. Kennedy*,
(Black Pebbles, 2003.)

With a good conscience our only sure reward, with history the final judge of our deeds, let us go forth to lead the land we love, asking his blessing and his help, but knowing that here on earth God's work must truly be our own.

—JOHN F. KENNEDY, 35th U.S. president.
Inaugural Address, January 20, 1961.

I have felt his hand upon me in great trials and submitted to his guidance, and I trust that as he shall further open the way, I will be ready to walk therein, relying on his help and trusting in his goodness and wisdom.

—ABRAHAM LINCOLN, 16th U.S. president.
Remark to a White House visitor, June 1862.
In James F. Wilson, *North American Review*,
December 1896, pp. 668-669.

. . . it will probably always be found that the course of reasoning from the effect to the cause, "from Nature to Nature's God," Will be the more universal & persuasive application. The finiteness of the human understanding betrays itself on all subjects, but more especially when it contemplates such as involve infinity. What may safely be said seems to be, that the infinity of time & space forces itself on our conception, a limitation of either being inconceivable; that the mind prefers at once the idea of a self-existing cause to that of an infinite series of cause & effect, which augments, instead of avoiding the difficulty; and that it finds more facility in assenting to the self-existence of an invisible cause possessing infinite power, wisdom & goodness, than to the self-existence of the universe, visibly destitute of those attributes, and which may be the effect of them. In this comparative facility of conception & belief, all philosophical Reasoning on the subject must perhaps terminate.

—JAMES MADISON, 4th U.S. president.
To Frederick Beasley, November 20, 1825.
Gaillard Hunt, ed., *The Writings of James Madison*
(New York: G. P. Putnam's Sons, 1910), vol. 9, pp. 230–231.

Good-bye—good bye, all. It's God's way. His will, not ours, be done. Nearer my God to Thee, nearer to Thee.

—WILLIAM MCKINLEY, 25th U.S. president.
Last words before death, September 14, 1901,
in Samuel Fellows, *Life of William McKinley, Our Martyred president: With Short Biographies of Lincoln and Garfield,*
(Regan Printing House, 1901), p. 3.

To me, the greatness of the universe is too much for man to explain. I still believe that God is the creator, the first cause of all that exists. I still believe that he lives today, in some form, directing the destiny of the cosmos.

—RICHARD NIXON, 37th U.S. president.
"What Can I Believe?" (college essay), October 9, 1933,
quoted in *RN: The Memoirs of Richard Nixon*, 1978, p. 16.

I believe with all my heart that standing up for America means standing up for the God who has so blessed our land. We need God's help to guide our nation through stormy seas. But we can't expect him to protect America in a crisis if we just leave him over on the shelf in our day-to-day living.

—RONALD REAGAN, 40th U.S. president. Remarks at the annual convention of the United States League of Savings Associations in New Orleans, Louisiana. November 16, 1982.

The Founding Fathers believed that faith in God was the key to our being a good people and America's becoming a great nation.

—RONALD REAGAN, 40th U.S. president.
Remarks at a White House meeting with Women Leaders
of Christian Religious Organizations, October 13, 1983.

More and more Americans believe that loving God in their hearts is the ultimate value. Last year, not only were Year of the Bible activities held in every State of the Union, but more than twenty-five States and five hundred cities issued their own Year of the Bible proclamations. One schoolteacher, Mary Gibson, in New York raised $4,000 to buy Bibles for working people in downtown Manhattan.

Nineteen eighty-three was the year more of us read the Good Book. Can we make a resolution here today?—that 1984 will be the year we put its great truths into action?

My experience in this office I hold has only deepened a belief I've held for many years: Within the covers of that single Book are all the answers to all the problems that face us today if we'd only read and believe.

Let's begin at the beginning. God is the center of our lives; the human family stands at the center of society; and our greatest hope for the future is in the faces of our children. Seven thousand Poles recently came to the christening of Maria Victoria Walesa, daughter of Danuta and Lech Walesa, to express their belief that solidarity of the family remains the foundation of freedom.

God's most blessed gift to his family is the gift of life. He sent us the Prince of Peace as a babe in a manger. I've said that we must be cautious in claiming God is on our side. I think the real question we must answer is, are we on his side?

—RONALD REAGAN, 40th U.S. president.

Remarks at the annual convention of the
National Religious Broadcasters, January 30, 1984.

I know one thing I'm sure most of us agree on: God, source of
all knowledge, should never have been expelled from our children's classrooms. The great majority of our people support
voluntary prayer in schools.

—RONALD REAGAN, 40th U.S. president. Ibid.

I believe that faith and religion play a critical role in the political
life of our nation—and always has—and that the church—and
by that I mean all churches, all denominations—has had a
strong influence on the state. And this has worked to our benefit
as a nation.

Those who created our country—the Founding Fathers and
Mothers—understood that there is a divine order which tran-
scends the human order. They saw the state, in fact, as a form of
moral order and felt that the bedrock of moral order is religion.

... Religion played not only a strong role in our national
life; it played a positive role. The abolitionist movement was at
heart a moral and religious movement; so was the modern civil
rights struggle. And throughout this time, the state was tolerant of religious belief, expression, and practice. Society, too,
was tolerant.

... We establish no religion in this country, nor will we ever.
We command no worship. We mandate no belief. But we poison
our society when we remove its theological underpinnings.

... Without God, there is no virtue, because there's no
prompting of the conscience. Without God, we're mired in the
material, that flat world that tells us only what the senses perceive. Without God, there is a coarsening of the society. And

without God, democracy will not and cannot long endure. If we ever forget that we're one nation under God, then we will be a nation gone under.

> —RONALD REAGAN, 40th U.S. president.
> Excerpts from Reagan's remarks at the Ecumenical
> Prayer Breakfast in Dallas, Texas, August 23, 1984.

The Supreme Being, for the same reasons, often assumes to himself the violent passions, and even the features and senses of men; and yet who can suppose it proper to ascribe either of them to a Being, one of whose perfections consists in his existing as a pure unchangeable spirit.

> —BENJAMIN RUSH, member of the Continental Congress,
> 1776-1777. "An Enquiry into the Consistency of Oaths
> with Reason and Christianity," January 20, 1789.
> Rush, *Essays: Literary, Moral, and Philosophical*, p. 78.

Whereas It is the duty of all Nations to acknowledge the providence of Almighty God, to obey his will, to be grateful for his benefits, and humbly to implore his protection and favors.

> —GEORGE WASHINGTON, 1st U.S. president.
> Thanksgiving Proclamation, 1789.

No Man has a more perfect Reliance on the alwise, and powerful dispensations of the Supreme Being than I have nor thinks his aid more necessary.

> —GEORGE WASHINGTON, 1st U.S. president.
> To William Gordon, May 13, 1776. Fitzpatrick,
> *Writings of Washington*, vol. 37, p. 526.

... the supreme Dispenser of every Good.

—GEORGE WASHINGTON, 1st U.S. president.
To Philip Schuyler, January 27, 1776. Ibid., vol. 4, p. 281.

When you speak of God, or his attributes, let it be seriously, in reverence.

—GEORGE WASHINGTON, 1st U.S. president.
"Rules of Civility," maxims copied by Washington when a
schoolboy, c. 1748, quoted in *Maxims of Washington,* compiled by
John Frederick Schroeder, (Appleton & Company, 1855), p. 359.

Almighty and eternal Lord God, the great Creator of heaven
and earth, and the God and Father of our Lord Jesus Christ;
look down from heaven in pity and compassion upon me thy
servant, who humbly prostrate myself before thee.

—GEORGE WASHINGTON, 1st U.S. president.
A Prayer for Wednesday Morning, George Washington's Prayer
Journal, from William J. Johnson, *George Washington, the
Christian* (New York: Abingdon Press, 1919), pp. 24-35.

IMMORALITY

I too firmly believe that virtue will be rewarded and vice punished in a future state.

—JOHN ADAMS, 2nd U.S. president.
To Adrian van der Kemp. January 30, 1814. Adams Papers
(microfilm), reel 95, Library of Congress.

I know not how to prove physically that We shall meet and know each other in a Future State; Nor does Revelation, as I can find give Us any positive Assurance of such a felicity. My reasons for believing it, as I do, most undoubtedly, are all moral and divine. I believe in God and in his Wisdom and Benevolence; and I cannot conceive that such a Being could make such a Species as the human merely to live and die on this earth. If I did not believe a future State I should believe in no God. This Universe; this all; this ... totality; would appear with all its swelling Pomp, a boyish Fire Work. And if there be a future State why should the Almighty dissolve forever all the tender Ties which Unite Us so delightfully in this World and forbid us to see each other in the next?

—JOHN ADAMS, 2nd U.S. president.
To Thomas Jefferson, December 8, 1818. Ibid., reel 95.

I believe enough of the Apocalypse to be perfectly convinced "that be thou faithful unto the death and thou shalt receive a crown of life."

—JOHN ADAMS, 2nd U.S. president.
To Louisa Catherine Adams, May 25, 1819. Ibid., reel 447.

I am fast approaching to that last scene which will put an end to all earthly cares and concerns. I am looking to that state from which all care all solicitude and all the passions which agitate mankind are excluded. Revelation instructs us that eternal happiness, or eternal misery will be the destiny of man in the life to come, the most pious the most exemplary have trembled at the thought of the dreadful alternative: oh! what will be the fate of those, who little think of it, or thinking square not their actions accordingly.

—CHARLES CARROLL, member of the Continental Congress.
To Charles H. Wharton, July 19, 1826.
Carroll Papers (microfilm), reel 3, Library of Congress.

Your frequently repeated Wishes and Prayers for my Eternal as well as temporal happiness are very obliging. . . . I have my self no Doubts that I shall enjoy as much of both as is proper for me. That Being who gave me Existence, and thro' almost three score Years has been continually showering his Favours upon me, whose very Chastisements have been Blessings to me, can I doubt that he loves me? And if he loves me, can I doubt that he will go on to take care of me not only here but hereafter? This to some may seem Presumption; to me it appears the best grounded hope; hope of the Future; built on Experience of the Past.

—BENJAMIN FRANKLIN, member of the Second
Continental Congress. To George Whitefield, June 19, 1764.
Labaree, *Papers of Benjamin Franklin*, vol. 11, pp. 231-232.

. . . the soul of Man is immortal, and will be treated with Justice in another Life respecting its Conduct in this.

—BENJAMIN FRANKLIN, member of the Second Continental Congress. To Ezra Stiles, March 9, 1790. Franklin Papers, Library of Congress.

The laws of nature have witheld from us the means of physical knowledge of the country of the spirits and revelation has, for reasons unknown to us, chosen to leave us in the dark as we were. When I was young I was fond of the speculations which seemed to promise some insight into that hidden country, but observing at length that they left me in the same ignorance in which they had found me, I have for very many years ceased to read or think concerning them, and have reposed my head on that pillow of ignorance which a benevolent creator has made so soft for us knowing how much we should be forced to use it. I have thought it better by nourishing the good passions, and controuling the bad, to merit an inheritance in a state of being of which I can know so little, and to trust for the future to him who has been so good for the past.

—THOMAS JEFFERSON, 2nd U.S. president. To the Reverend Isaac Story December 5, 1801. Adams, *Jefferson's Extracts*, pp. 325-326.

When you and I look back on the country over which we have passed, what a field of slaughter does it exhibit! Where are all the friends who entered it with us under all the inspiring energies of health and hope? As if pursued by the havoc of war, they are strowed by the way, some earlier, some later, and scarce a few stragglers remain to count the numbers fallen, and to mark yet by their own fall the last footsteps of their party. Is it a desireable thing to bear up thro' the heat of the action, to witness the death of all of our companions, and merely be the last victim? I doubt it. We have however the traveller's consolation. Every step shortens the distance we have to go; the end of our journey is in sight, the bed wherein we are to rest, and rise in the midst of the friends we have lost. We sorrow not then as others who have no hope; but look forward to the day which "joins us to the great majority." But whatever is to be our destiny, wisdom, as well as duty, dictates that we should acquiesce in the will of him whose it is to give and to take away, and be contented in the enjoyment of those who are still permitted to be with us.

—THOMAS JEFFERSON, 2nd U.S. president. To John Page, June 25, 1804. Jefferson Papers, Library of Congress.

I believe that the souls of believers are at their death made perfectly holy, and immediately taken to glory; that at the end of this world there will be a resurrection of the dead, and a final judgment of all mankind, when the righteous shall be publickly acquitted by Christ the Judge and admitted to everlasting life and glory, and the wicked be sentenced to everlasting punishment.

—ROGER SHERMAN, member of the Continental Congress. "White Haven Church Confession of Faith" (draft), 1788. Sherman Papers, Library of Congress.

The reason why any of the human race are subjected to endless punishment, is, because they have sinned and voluntarily continue finally impenitent, which is wholly their own fault.

—ROGER SHERMAN, member of the Continental Congress. To Samuel Hopkins, June 28, 1790. American Antiquarian Society, Proceedings 5, October 1887-October 1888, p. 443.

JESUS

[Jesus] was, as you say, "the most benevolent Being that ever appeard on Earth."

—JOHN ADAMS, 2nd U.S. president. To Thomas Jefferson, February 2, 1816. Cappon, *Adams-Jefferson Letters*, vol. 2, p. 462.

The suffering Messiah known to the whole angelic host, as lying in the father's bosom from eternity, and as the great object of their love and adoration from their first existence; and who alone was capable of knowing and contemplating the Divinity in his pure essence, and who had seen the Father, being the express image of his person, and who thought it no robbery to claim an equality with God: this glorious being, becoming an expiatory sacrifice and propitiatory victim for the sins of the world, magnified the law of God; demonstrated his infinite justice and love to being in general, and made it known to the universe, when he declared, "That God so loved the world, as to give his only begotten Son, that whosoever should believe in him should not perish, but have everlasting life!" All this fully proved the infinite wisdom of the amazing plan, designed to subdue all things to, and keep them in the love of order and obedience, discovering to men and angels "the exceeding sinfulness of sin," and the awful consequences of it, even when the sacred humanity of the eternal Son of God was to be the victim, as a substitute for the aggressor.

—ELIAS BOUDINOT, president of the Continental Congress,
1782-1783, and ABS president. *The Age of Revelation*
(Philadelphia:Asbury Dickins, 1801), pp. 217-218.

It is the example of him, who being in the form of God, came down from heaven for our sakes, took upon him the form of a servant and sealed his love to us by greater suffering than any man ever endured for his friend. This example is easy and familiar, conveying instruction in instances frequently occurring in human life. Upon all occasions the conduct of our blessed saviour was open, meek, patient, sincere, kind, tender, friendly and courteous, marking out a plain path for us to "walk even as he walked." He was the modestest, humblest, best natured, most self denying and disinterested man that ever appeared in the world.

—JOHN DICKINSON, member of the First Continental
Congress. Undated note. R. R. Logan Papers,
Historical Society of Pennsylvania.

As to Jesus of Nazareth, my Opinion of whom you particularly desire, I think the System of Morals and his Religion, as he left them to us, the best the World ever saw or is likely to see; but I apprehend it has received various corrupting Changes, and I have, with most of the present Dissenters in England, some Doubts as to his Divinity; tho' it is a question I do not dogmatize upon, having never studied it, and think it needless to busy myself with it now when I expect soon an Opportunity of knowing the Truth with less Trouble.

I see no harm, however, in its being believed, if that Belief has the good Consequence, as probably it has, of making his Doctrines more respected and better observed.

—BENJAMIN FRANKLIN, member of the Second
Continental Congress. To Ezra Stiles, March 9, 1790. Smyth,
Writings of Franklin, vol. 10, p. 84

His character and doctrines have received still greater injury from those who pretend to be his special disciples, and who have disfigured and sophisticated his actions and precepts, from views of personal interest, so as to induce the unthinking part of mankind to throw off the whole system in disgust, and to pass sentence as an imposter on the most innocent, the most benevolent the most eloquent and sublime character that ever has been exhibited to man.

—THOMAS JEFFERSON, 2nd U.S. president.
To Joseph Priestley, April 19, 1803.
Adams, *Jefferson's Extracts*, p. 328.

Of all the systems of morality, ancient or modern, which have come under my observation, none appear to me so pure as that of Jesus.

—THOMAS JEFFERSON, 2nd U.S. president.
Letter to William Camby, September 18, 1813.

The doctrines of Jesus are simple, and tend to all the happiness of man.

—THOMAS JEFFERSON, 2nd U.S. president.
Letter to Benjamin Waterhouse, June 26, 1822.

I have a tender reliance on the mercy of the Almighty, through the merits of the Lord Jesus Christ. I am a sinner. I look to him for mercy; pray for me.

> —ALEXANDER HAMILTON, member of the Continental
> Congress and 1st secretary of the treasury.
> July 12, 1804, on his death.

The atonement of Jesus Christ is the only remedy and rest for my soul.

> —MARTIN VAN BUREN, 8th U.S. president. 1862, during
> his final illness. William J. Federer, *Treasury of
> Presidential Quotations*, (Amerisearch, 2004), p. 69.

Whatever diversity may exist among Christian denominations as to forms of worship, or even upon unessential points of faith, they are all prepared with one heart and one voice to declare that "other foundation can no man lay, than that is laid, which is Jesus Christ."

> —THEODORE FRELINGHUYSEN, U.S. senator and ABS
> president. At an ABS meeting, May 10, 1849. *Bible Society Record*,
> vol. 1, no. 35, May 1849, p. 450.

We miss the purport of Christ's birth if we do not accept it as a living link which joins us together in spirit as children of the ever-living and true God. In love alone—the love of God and the love of man—will be found the solution of all the ills which afflict the world today.

> —HARRY S. TRUMAN, 33rd U.S. president. Address
> in connection with lighting of the national community
> Christmas tree on White House grounds, December 24, 1949.

Let men and women of faith remember that this Nation, endowed by God with so many blessings, is also surrounded by incredible needs. At the beginning of this century in American history, let us remember Jesus, who, surrounded by needs still early in the morning, went away to a solitary place to pray.

—GERALD FORD, 38th U.S. president.
Remarks at the National Prayer Breakfast, January 29, 1976.

But it doesn't matter how you come to church; the important thing is that the feeling is the same, the feeling of being in the spirit of Jesus Christ.

—GEORGE H.W. BUSH, 41st U.S. president.
Remarks at Chongmenwen Christian Church in Beijing,
February 26, 1989.

As Christians, we have been called to share that forgiveness with others. Across the globe, in places large and small, we have witnessed the tragic consequences of humanity's refusal to forgive. Ancient feuds, ethnic tensions, old hatreds and prejudices—these have torn apart families, communities, and nations for decades and continue to bring suffering to our world. On this, the first Easter of the new millennium and in the Jubilee Year of Christ's birth, the challenge to each of us is to reflect God's love and forgiveness in all our actions.

—WILLIAM CLINTON, 42nd U.S. president.
President's Easter Message, April 21, 2000.

Christ's extraordinary sacrifice and compassion continue to inspire people around the world. His promise of new life gives hope and confidence to his followers. His service and love for his neighbors offer a profound lesson for all people.

—GEORGE W. BUSH, 43rd U.S. president.
President's Easter Message, April 13, 2006.

I send greetings to all those celebrating Easter, the Resurrection of Jesus Christ. Through his sacrifice and triumph over death, Christ lifted the sights of humanity forever. In his teachings, the poor have heard hope, the proud have been challenged, and the weak and dying have found assurance. Today, the words of Jesus continue to comfort and strengthen Christians around the world.

—GEORGE W. BUSH, 43rd U.S. president.
President's Easter Message, March 24, 2005.

Through his ministry and sacrifice, Jesus demonstrated God's unconditional love for us. He taught us the importance of helping others and loving our neighbors. His selfless devotion and mercy provide a remarkable example for all of us.

—GEORGE W. BUSH, 43rd U.S. president.
President's Easter Message, April 9, 2004.

The life and teachings of Jesus have inspired people throughout the ages to strive for a better world and a more meaningful life. Jesus' death stands out in history as the perfect example of unconditional love.

—GEORGE W. BUSH, 43rd U.S. president.
President's Easter Message, March 27, 2002.

Many traditions associated with Easter have become a part of our American way of life. Although these customs may differ, the universal message of Easter draws all Christian communities together. As families and friends gather to celebrate, we renew our commitment to follow the example of Jesus Christ in loving our neighbors and giving of ourselves for others.

—GEORGE W. BUSH, 43rd U.S. president.
President's Easter Message, April 13, 2001.

By his words and by his example, Christ has called us to share our many blessings with others. As individuals and as a Nation, in our homes and in our communities, there are countless ways that we can extend to others the same love and mercy that God showed humankind when he gave us his only Son. During this holy season and throughout the year, let us look to the selfless spirit of giving that Jesus embodied as inspiration in our own lives—giving thanks for what God has done for us and abiding by Christ's teaching to do for others as we would do for ourselves.

—GEORGE H.W. BUSH, 41st U.S. president.
Message on the Observance of Christmas,
December 11, 1991.

THE JUDICIAL SYSTEM

The Law given from Sinai [The Ten Commandments] was a
civil and municipal as well as a moral and religious code.

—JOHN QUINCY ADAMS, 6th U.S. president and diplomat.
Letters to His Son, J. M. Alden, 1850, p. 61.

PRAYER

Certainly the sincere Prayers of good Men, avail much.

—JOHN ADAMS, 2nd U.S. president. To Abigail Adams,
May 8, 1775. Butterfield, *Adams Family Correspondence*,
vol. 1, p. 196.

If I were a Calvinest, I might pray that God by a Miracle of
Divine Grace would instantaneously convert a whole Contami-
nated Nation from turpitude to purity, but even in this I should
be inconsistent, for the fatalism of Mahometnism, Materialists,
Atheists, Pantheists and Calvinests, and Church of England
Articles, appear to me to render all prayer futile and absurd.

—JOHN ADAMS, 2nd U.S. president. To Thomas Jefferson,
December 21, 1819. Cappon, *Adams-Jefferson Letters*,
vol. 2, p. 551.

Set aside some time in every day (I do mean any particular
hour, as this might be inconvenient & a snare) if it is but five
Minutes, to lift up your heart to God in Secret. This may season
your whole Time & put you on your Guard against Sin of every
kind, even in the wandering of your Thoughts. Be not content
to live one day, without some sensible Communion between

God and your Soul. Learn the sacred Art & Mystery of making Religion, or daily converse with God, an agreeable Business. It ought to be the most cheerful & delightful part of our Time. To have a God, who is Almighty all wise, all good & merciful to go to as your constant friend, as your continual Benefactor, as your Safeguard & Guide it should, it must sweeten every bitter Draught of Life.

—ELIAS BOUDINOT, president of the Continental Congress, 1782-1783, and ABS president. To Susan Bradford, December 29, 1784. Boudinot Papers, Princeton University Library.

The prayers of God's People, rich and poor of every denomination, all ranks and orders of his Children in every part of the great Sheepfold never cease night and day surrounding the Throne of the Eternal, for Blessings on their Labors. When Zion prays, God will hear and listen.

—ELIAS BOUDINOT, president of the Continental Congress, 1782-1783, and ABS president. To John Pintard, July 6, 1818. Boudinot Papers, ABS.

The liberty, prosperity, and happiness of our country will always be the object of my most fervent prayers to the Supreme Author of All Good.

—JAMES MONROE, 5th U.S. president. Second Inaugural Address, March 5, 1821.

As I said many times before, prayer always has been important in our lives. And without it, I really am convinced, more and more convinced, that no man or no woman who has the privilege of serving in the Presidency could carry out their duties without prayer.

—GEORGE H.W. BUSH, 41st U.S. president.
Remarks to the National Association of Evangelicals in
Chicago, Illinois, March 3, 1992.

The prayers of the innocent are all powerful.

—CHARLES CARROLL, member of the Continental Congress.
To Elizabeth Harper, December 22, 1820. Carroll Papers
(microfilm), reel 3, Library of Congress.

Our Saviour "spoke two Parables to this End, that Men ought allways to pray and not faint," besides repeated Commands to the same purport. . . . Tis true God needs not to be informed by Us of our Wants: But he knows that Prayer is useful for purifying our hearts, and inclining Us to Obedience. Therefore his Wisdom and Goodness are both displayed in requiring Us to seek for his Mercies, and he is kind when he demands to be asked for them, as when he grants them to Us. . . With what Disposition or Temper of Mind should our Prayers be offered that they may be acceptable? . . . With the deepest humility under a Sense of the adorable Perfection of the Glorious Being, whom by his Conde scension we are permitted to address, and a Conviction of our Guilt and Nothingness—a filial Submission to his Will as his Right and our Duty—the strictest Engagement to keep his Commandments throughout our whole Lives—the sincerest Goodwill to all Mankind & the warmest wishes for their spiritual & temporal Welfare, without the Exception of a single Individual—the firmest

Resolution to do no Injuries to any of them in future, and to make Reparation for those we have allready done.

> —JOHN DICKINSON, member of the First Continental
> Congress. "Religious Instruction for Youth," undated.
> R. R. Logan Papers, Historical Society of Pennsylvania.

And conceiving God to be the Fountain of Wisdom, I thought it right and necessary to solicit his Assistance for obtaining it; to this End I form'd the following little Prayer . . . for daily Use. O Powerful Goodness! bountiful Father! merciful Guide! Increase in me that Wisdom which discovers my truest Interests; Strengthen my Resolutions to perform what that Wisdom dictates. Accept my kind Offices to thy other Children, as the only Return in my Power for thy continual Favours to me.

> —BENJAMIN FRANKLIN, member of the Second
> Continental Congress. *Autobiography,* post-1784.
> Labaree, *Autobiography of Franklin,* p. 153.

Prayers to heaven, the only contribution of old age.

> —THOMAS JEFFERSON, 2nd U.S. president. To George Logan,
> October 15, 1815. Jefferson Papers, Library of Congress.

Prayer has sustained our people in crisis, strengthened us in times of challenge, and guided us through our daily lives since the first settlers came to this continent. Our forbearers came not for gold, but mainly in search of God and the freedom to worship in their own way.

We've been a free people living under the law, with faith in our Maker and in our future. I've said before that the most sublime picture in American history is of George Washington on his knees in the snow at Valley Forge. That image personifies a people who know that it's not enough to depend on our own courage and goodness; we must also seek help from God, our Father and Preserver.

—RONALD REAGAN, 40th U.S. president. Remarks at a White House ceremony in observance of National Day of Prayer, May 6, 1982.

Man is as necessarily a praying as he is a sociable, domestic, or religious animal. As "no man liveth and sinneth not," so no man liveth and prayeth not. Distress and terror drive even atheists to call upon God. Worldly men pray for the success of their worldly schemes. Men in deep distress even call for the prayers of their friends. . . . Prayer is an instinct of nature in man, as much so as his love of society. He cannot, he does not live without it, except in a morbid or unnatural state of his mind.

—BENJAMIN RUSH, member of the Continental Congress, 1776-1777. "Commonplace Book," August 14, 1811. Corner, *Autobiography of Rush*, p. 339.

I now make it my earnest prayer, that God would have you, and the State over which you preside, in his holy protection, that he would incline the hearts of the Citizens to cultivate a spirit of subordination and obedience to Government, to entertain a brotherly affection and love for one another, for their fellow Citizens of the United States at large, and particularly for their brethren who have served in the Field, and finally, that he would most graciously be pleased to dispose us all, to do Justice, to love mercy, and to demean ourselves with that Charity, humility and pacific temper of mind, which were the Characteristicks of the Divine Author of our blessed Religion, and without an

humble imitation of whose example in these things, we can
never hope to be a happy Nation.

—GEORGE WASHINGTON, 1st U.S. president.
Circular to the chief executives of the states, June 8, 1783.
Fitzpatrick, *Writings of Washington*, vol. 26, p. 496.

And, O Lord, give us Faith. Give us Faith in Thee; Faith in our
sons; Faith in each other; Faith in our united crusade. Let not
the keenness of our spirit ever be dulled. Let not the impacts of
temporary events, of temporal matters of but fleeting moment
let not these deter us in our unconquerable purpose.

With Thy blessing, we shall prevail over the unholy forces of
our enemy. Help us to conquer the apostles of greed and racial
arrogancies. Lead us to the saving of our country, and with our
sister Nations into a world unity that will spell a sure peace, a
peace invulnerable to the schemings of unworthy men. And a
peace that will let all of men live in freedom, reaping the just
rewards of their honest toil.

I believe in God, the Almighty Ruler of Nations, our great and
good and merciful Maker, our Father in heaven, who notes the
fall of a sparrow, and numbers the hairs of our heads. I believe in
his eternal truth and justice. I recognize the sublime truth
announced in the holy Scriptures and proven by all history that
those nations only are blest whose God is the Lord. I believe that
it is the duty of nations as well as of men to own their dependence
upon the overruling power of God, and to invoke the influence of
his holy Spirit; to confess their sins and transgressions in humble
sorrow, yet with assured hope that genuine repentance will lead
to mercy and pardon. I believe that it is meet and right to recognize and confess the presence of the Almighty Father equally in
our triumphs and in those sorrows which we may justly fear are a

punishment inflicted upon us for our presumptuous sins to the needful end of our reformation. I believe that the Bible is the best gift which God has ever given to men. All the good from the Saviour of the world is communicated to us through this book. I believe the will of God prevails. Without him all human reliance is vain. Without the assistance of his divine Being, I cannot succeed. With that assistance I cannot fail. Being a humble instrument in the hands of our heavenly Father, I desire that all my works and acts may be according to his will; and that it may be so, I give thanks to the Almighty, and seek his aid. I have a solemn oath registered in heaven to finish the work I am in, in full view of my responsibility to my God, with malice toward none; with charity for all; with firmness in the right as God gives me to see the right. Commending those who love me to his care, as I hope in their prayers they will comend me, I look through the help of God to a joyous meeting with many loved ones gone before.

—ABRAHAM LINCOLN, 16th U.S. president.
"Creed of Abraham Lincoln in His Own Words,"Barton,
The Soul of Abraham Lincoln, (George Daran Co., 1920), p. 300.

Thy will be done, Almighty God.
Amen.

—FRANKLIN D. ROOSEVELT, 32nd U.S. president.
Prayer on D-Day, June 6, 1944.

I call upon the people of the United States, of all faiths, to unite in offering their thanks to God for the victory we have won, and in praying that he will support and guide us into the paths of peace.

—HARRY S. TRUMAN, 33rd U.S. president. Proclamation
2660—Victory in the East —Day of Prayer, August 16, 1945.

May Almighty God, in his infinite wisdom and mercy, guide and sustain us as we seek to bring peace everlasting to the world.

—HARRY S. TRUMAN, 33rd U.S. president.
Address in New York City at the opening session of the
United Nations General Assembly, October 23, 1946.

But all of us—at home, at war, wherever we may be—are within reach of God's love and power. We all can pray. We all should pray.

—HARRY S. TRUMAN, 33rd U.S. president. Address recorded
for the broadcast on the occasion of the national community
Christmas tree on the White House grounds, December 24, 1950.

Before all else, we seek, upon our common labor as a nation, the blessings of Almighty God. And the hopes in our hearts fashion the deepest prayers of our whole people.

—DWIGHT D. EISENHOWER, 34th U.S. president.
Second Inaugural Address, January 21, 1957.

I am honored to be with you here again this morning. These breakfasts are dedicated to prayer and all of us believe in and need prayer.

—JOHN F. KENNEDY, 35th U.S. president. Remarks at the
11th Annual presidential Prayer Breakfast, February 7, 1963.

Recognizing our own shortcomings may we be granted forgiveness and cleansing, that God shall bless us and be gracious unto us, and cause his face to shine upon us as we stand everyone of us on this day in his Presence.

—JOHN F. KENNEDY, 35th U.S. president.
Proclamation 3436—National Day of Prayer, September 28, 1961.

The guiding principle and prayer of this Nation has been, is now, and shall ever be "In God We Trust."

—JOHN F. KENNEDY, 35th U.S. president.
Remarks at the dedication breakfast of International Christian
Leadership, Inc., February 9, 1961.

In putting my name to this paper, I cannot proclaim that all Americans will pray on October 20th. Nor would I do so even if I could. But I do hope by this action that we will remind our citizens of the blessings that God has bestowed upon them. I do ask them to remember that our reliance upon Divine Providence is a far greater force for freedom in the world than all of our wealth combined.

—LYNDON B. JOHNSON, 36th U.S. president.
Remarks upon signing proclamation "National Day
of Prayer, 1965," October 7, 1965.

On this Memorial Day, as we honor the memory of brave men who have borne our colors in war, we pray to God for his mercy. We pray for the wisdom to find a way to end this struggle of nation against nation, of brother against brother. We pray that soon we may begin to build the only true memorial to man's valor in war—a sane and hopeful environment for the generations to Come.

—LYNDON B JOHNSON, 36th U.S. president.
Proclamation 3727—Prayer for Peace, Memorial Day,
May 26, 1966.

Our prayers are to the God who has strengthened the will of a grateful people. Our remembrance is of those who created and sustained this great university, and brought here thousands of young men and women from all over the world, and gave them the power to serve their fellow man.

—LYNDON B. JOHNSON, 36th U.S. president.
Remarks at a ceremony marking the 100th anniversary of
Howard University, March 2, 1967.

I was trying to think, after the eloquent words of the Chief Justice, what prayer I could leave with this very distinguished audience and with those who are listening on television and on radio all over the world. And I was reminded of one of the favorite stories from the Old Testament. You will recall that when King David died and when Solomon ascended to the throne, God came before him in a dream and asked him what he wanted. And Solomon did not ask for power and he did not ask for wealth. He said, "Give Thy servant an understanding heart."

And so, let that be our prayer.

—RICHARD NIXON, 37th U.S. president.
Remarks at the National Prayer Breakfast, February 2, 1971.

Virtually everyone this morning who has prayed, has prayed for the president of the United States, and for that, as a person, I am deeply grateful. But as you pray in the future, as these journeys take place, will you pray primarily that this Nation, under God, in the person of its President, will, to the best of our ability, be on God's side.

—RICHARD NIXON, 37th U.S. president.
Remarks at the National Prayer Breakfast, February 1, 1972.

REPORTER. Could you tell us how your prayer for peace in the Middle East went? What was your prayer, Mr. President?

THE PRESIDENT: My prayer was one that recognized this whole world wants peace; that Christ, our Savior, is the Prince of Peace; that the Middle East has been particularly afflicted by war, which no one there wanted, constantly—almost day by day—conflict, and four major wars in the last 30 years; that yesterday Prime Minister Begin, who is a very deeply religious man, worshipped God in a Jewish temple; this morning president Sadat worshipped the same God in a Moslem mosque and later worshipped the same God in a Christian holy place where Christ was buried; and that all over the world today people are praying for peace.

—JIMMY CARTER, 39th U.S. president. Visit of president Anwar al Sadat to Israel. Exchange with reporters, November 20, 1977.

Prayer is today as powerful a force in our Nation as it has ever been. We as a Nation should never forget this source of strength. And while recognizing that the freedom to choose a Godly path is the essence of liberty, as a Nation we cannot but hope that more of our citizens would, through prayer, come into a closer relationship with their Maker.

—RONALD REAGAN, 40th U.S. president. Proclamation 4826—National Day of Prayer, March 19, 1981.

The public expression through prayer of our faith in God is a fundamental part of our American heritage and a privilege which should not be excluded by law from any American school, public or private.

—RONALD REAGAN, 40th U.S. president. Message to the Congress transmitting proposed legislation on a constitutional amendment of prayer in school, May 17, 1982.

It's said that prayer can move mountains. Well, it's certainly moved the hearts and minds of Americans in their times of trial and helped them to achieve a society that, for all its imperfections, is still the envy of the world and the last, best hope of mankind. And just as prayer has helped us as a nation, it helps us as individuals. In nearly all our lives, there are moments when our prayer and the prayers of our friends and loved ones help to see us through and keep on the right path. In fact, prayer is one of the few things in this world that hurts no one and sustains the spirit of millions.

—RONALD REAGAN, 40th U.S. president.
Radio address to the nation on prayer,
September 18, 1982.

The public expression through prayer of our faith in God is a fundamental part of our American heritage and a privilege which should not be excluded by law from any American school, public or private.

—RONALD REAGAN, 40th U.S. president.
Message to the Congress transmitting the proposed
constitutional amendment on prayer in schools,
March 8, 1983.

Prayer unites people. This common expression of reverence heals and brings us together as a Nation and we pray it may one day bring renewed respect for God to all the peoples of the world.

—RONALD REAGAN, 40th U.S. president.
Proclamation 5017—National Day of Prayer,
June 27, 1983.

And yet in a world today that is so torn with strife where the divisions seem to be increasing, not people coming together, within countries, divisions within the people, themselves and all, I wonder if we have ever thought about the greatest tool that we have—that power of prayer and God's help.

—RONALD REAGAN, 40th U.S. president.
Remarks at the Annual National Prayer Breakfast,
February 2, 1984.

We are all God's handiwork, and it is appropriate for us as individuals and as a Nation to call to him in prayer.

—RONALD REAGAN, 40th U.S. president.
Proclamation 5296—National Day of Prayer, January 29, 1985.

Prayer is deeply woven into the fabric of our history from its very beginnings. The same Continental Congress that declared our independence also proclaimed a National Day of Prayer. And from that time forward, it would be hard to exaggerate the role that prayer has played in the lives of individual Americans and in the life of the Nation as a whole.

—RONALD REAGAN, 40th U.S. president.
Proclamation 5429—National Day of Prayer, January 13, 1986.

If I had a prayer for you today, among those that have all been uttered, it is that one we're so familiar with: The Lord bless you and keep you; the Lord make his face to shine upon you and be gracious unto you; the Lord lift up his countenance upon you and give you peace.

—RONALD REAGAN, 40th U.S. president. Remarks at
the Annual National Prayer Breakfast, February 6, 1986.

Prayer, of course, is deeply personal. Many of us have been taught to pray by people we love. In my case, it was my mother. I learned quite literally at her knee. My mother gave me a great deal, but nothing she gave me was more important than that special gift, the knowledge of the happiness and solace to be gained by talking to the Lord.

—RONALD REAGAN, 40th U.S. president.
Remarks on Signing the 1987 National Day of Prayer
Proclamation, December 22, 1986.

Americans in every generation have turned to their Maker in prayer. In adoration and in thanksgiving, in contrition and in supplication, we have acknowledged both our dependence on Almighty God and the help he offers us as individuals and as a Nation.

—RONALD REAGAN, 40th U.S. president.
Proclamation 5767—National Day of Prayer,
February 3, 1988.

So many of us, compelled by a deep need for God's wisdom in all we do, turn to prayer. We pray for God's protection in all we undertake, for God's love to fill all hearts, and for God's peace to be the moral North Star that guides us. So, I have proclaimed Sunday, February 3rd, National Day of Prayer. In this moment of crisis, may Americans of every creed turn to our greatest power and unite together in prayer.

—GEORGE H.W. BUSH, 41st U.S. president.
Radio address to the nation on the National Day of Prayer,
February 2, 1991.

There is no greater peace than that which comes from prayer and no greater fellowship than to join in prayer with others.

—GEORGE H.W. BUSH, 41st U.S. president.
Remarks at the Annual National Prayer Breakfast,
February 2, 1989.

And my first act as president is a prayer. I ask you to bow your heads.

Heavenly Father, we bow our heads and thank You for Your love. Accept our thanks for the peace that yields this day and the shared faith that makes its continuance likely. Make us strong to do Your work, willing to heed and hear Your will, and write on our hearts these words: "Use power to help people." For we are given power not to advance our own purposes, nor to make a great show in the world, nor a name. There is but one just use of power, and it is to serve people. Help us remember, Lord. Amen.

—GEORGE H.W. BUSH, 41st U.S. president.
Inaugural Address, January 20, 1989.

But I can tell you from my heart that I freely acknowledge my need to hear and to heed the voice of Almighty God.

—GEORGE H.W. BUSH, 41st U.S. president.
Remarks at the National Prayer Breakfast, February 2, 1989.

Gathered in the spirit of truth and hope, in unity and peace, at the beginning of the new year, the dawn of a new century, and at the turn of the third millennium, let us offer before God our prayers and thanksgivings.

We give you thanks, oh, God, for the goodness and love you

have made known to us in creation. You fill the world with beauty. Open our eyes to see your handiwork in all creation, and in one another.

—WILLIAM CLINTON, 42nd U.S. president.
Remarks by the president and the first lady at Christmas:
Holy Eucharist Services, January 2, 2000.

And finally, I ask you to pray for all of us, including yourselves; to pray that our purpose truly will reflect God's will. To pray that we can all be purged of the temptation to pretend that our willfulness is somehow equal to God's will. To remember that all the great peacemakers in the world in the end have to let go and walk away, like Christ, not from apparent, but from genuine grievances.

—WILLIAM CLINTON, 42nd U.S. president.
Remarks by the president at the National Prayer Breakfast,
February 4, 1999.

For five years now, Hillary and I have looked forward to this day. For me it's a day in which I can be with other people of faith and pray and ask for your prayers, both as president and as just another child of God. I have done it for five years, and I do so again today.

—WILLIAM CLINTON, 42nd U.S. president.
Remarks by the president at the National Prayer Breakfast,
February 5, 1998.

From our earliest history, Americans have always looked to God for strength and encouragement in those moments when darkness seemed to encroach from every side. Our people have always believed in the power of prayer and have called upon the name of the Lord through times of peace and war, hope and despair, prosperity and decline.

—WILLIAM CLINTON, 42nd U.S. president.
Remarks by the president, National Day of Prayer Proclamation,
April 18, 1997.

A National Day of Prayer, first proclaimed by the Continental Congress in 1775, stems from the understanding that faith is a fundamental part of our Nation's social fabric.

—WILLIAM CLINTON, 42nd U.S. president.
Proclamation, National Day of Prayer, April 3, 1996.

Our Nation was built on the steadfast foundation of the prayers of our ancestors. In times of blessing and crisis, stability and change, thanksgiving and repentance, appeals for Divine direction have helped the citizens of the United States to remain faithful to our long-standing commitment to life, liberty, and justice for all.

—WILLIAM CLINTON, 42nd U.S. president.
Proclamation, National Day of Prayer, March 14, 1995.

Through prayer our people take a moment away from the concerns of everyday life to understand the greater power that gives us guidance. We come together in an act common to all religions. Prayer gives us a quiet space to remember and contemplate the greater purpose of the activity that fills our lives. As a Nation, we understand the common bonds we all share, and we recommit ourselves to serving a greater good. Prayer enables us to rejoice in our freedoms and understand the implicit responsibility that accompanies them. We return to the guiding vision that gives our Nation so much vitality.

—WILLIAM CLINTON, 42nd U.S. president.
Proclamation, National Day of Prayer, April 30, 1993.

A prayerful spirit has always been an important part of our national character, and it is a force that has guided the American people, given us strength, and sustained us in moments of joy and in times of challenge.

—GEORGE W. BUSH, 43rd U.S. president. Proclamation,
National Day of Prayer, April 20, 2007.

People who have never met you are praying for you; they're praying for your friends who have fallen and who are injured. There's a power in these prayers, real power. In times like this, we can find comfort in the grace and guidance of a loving God. As the Scriptures tell us, "Don't be overcome by evil, but overcome evil with good."

—GEORGE W. BUSH, 43rd U.S. president.
Offering condolences at Virginia Tech Memorial Convocation,
April 17, 2007.

The greatest gift a citizen of this country can give those of us entrusted with political office is to pray for us. And I thank those in our nation who lift all of us up in prayer.

—GEORGE W. BUSH, 43rd U.S. president.
Attending the National Prayer Breakfast, February 1, 2007.

On these Days of Prayer and Remembrance, we mourn with those who still mourn, and find comfort through faith. We give thanks to the Almighty for our liberty, and we pray for his blessing on all those who were lost and for strength in the work ahead. May God continue to watch over the United States of America, and may his will guide us in the days to come.

—GEORGE W. BUSH, 43rd U.S. president.
Proclamation by the president, National Days of Prayer
and Remembrance, September 5, 2006.

America is a nation of prayer. It's impossible to tell the story of our nation without telling the story of people who pray. The first pilgrims came to this land with a yearning for freedom. They stepped boldly onto the shores of a new world, and many of them fell to their knees to give thanks.

—GEORGE W. BUSH, 43rd U.S. president.
"President Bush Commemorates National Day of Prayer,"
May 4, 2006.

Through prayer, our faith is strengthened, our hearts are humbled, and our lives are transformed. May our Nation always have the humility to trust in the goodness of God's plans.

—GEORGE W. BUSH, 43rd U.S. president.
Proclamation, National Day of Prayer,
May 3, 2006.

Through prayer we look for ways to understand the arbitrary harm left by this storm, and the mystery of undeserved suffering. And in our search we're reminded that God's purposes are sometimes impossible to know here on Earth. Yet even as we're humbled by forces we cannot explain, we take comfort in the knowledge that no one is ever stranded beyond God's care. The

Creator of wind and water is also the source of even a greater
power—a love that can redeem the worst tragedy, a love that is
stronger than death.

—GEORGE W. BUSH, 43rd U.S. president. President's
remarks at the National Prayer Day and Remembrance Service,
September 15, 2006.

Think about a country where millions of people of all faiths,
people whom I'll never have a chance to look face-to-face with
and say, thank you, take time to pray. It really is the strength of
America, isn't it? Through prayer we ask that our hearts be
aligned with God's. Through prayer we ask that we may be
given the strength to do what's right and to help those in need.

—GEORGE W. BUSH, 43rd U.S. president.
National Hispanic Prayer Breakfast, June 16, 2005.

Prayer has been an important part of American public life, as
well. Many of our forefathers came to these shores seeking the
freedom to worship. The first Continental Congress began by
asking the Almighty for the wisdom that would enable them to
settle things on the best and surest foundation. And when our
Founders provided that sure foundation in the Declaration of
Independence, they declared it a self-evident truth that our
right to liberty comes from God.

—GEORGE W. BUSH, 43rd U.S. president.
"President Commemorates National Day of Prayer at the
White House, May 5, 2005."

Since our Nation's earliest days, prayer has given strength and
comfort to Americans of all faiths. Our Founding Fathers relied

on their faith to guide them as they built our democracy. Today, we continue to be inspired by God's blessings, mercy, and boundless love.

> —GEORGE W. BUSH, 43rd U.S. president. Proclamation
> by the president, National Day of Prayer, May 3, 2005.

Through prayer, we recognize the limits of earthly power and acknowledge the sovereignty of God. According to Scripture, "the Lord is near to all who call upon him . . . he also will hear their cry, and save them." Prayer leads to humility and a grateful heart, and it turns our minds to the needs of others.

> —GEORGE W. BUSH, 43rd U.S. president. Proclamation
> by the president, National Day of Prayer, April 30, 2004.

In prayer, we ask for wisdom and guidance. And the answers seldom come in blinding revelations. Yet prayer can bring good things: grace for the moment, and faith in the future.

> —GEORGE W. BUSH, 43rd U.S. president. "President's
> Remarks at the 52nd Annual National Prayer Breakfast,
> February 5, 2004."

It is important, and it is good to begin the day with prayer and fellowship. Prayer is an opportunity to praise God for his works and to thank him for his blessings. Prayer turns our minds to the needs of others, and prayer changes our hearts as we seek God's will.

> —GEORGE W. BUSH, 43rd U.S. president. Hispanic Prayer
> Breakfast, May 15, 2003.

Millions of Americans seek guidance every day in prayer to the Almighty God. I am one of them.

—GEORGE W. BUSH, 43rd U.S. president.
Remarks on the National Day of Prayer, May 1, 2003.

There are prayers that help us last through the day, or endure the night. There are prayers of friends and strangers, that give us strength for the journey. And there are prayers that yield our will to a will greater than our own.

—GEORGE W. BUSH, 43rd U.S. president. Remarks at the
National Day of Prayer and Remembrance, September 14, 2001.

Our country was founded by great and wise people who were fluent in the language of humility, praise and petition. Throughout our history, in danger and division, we have always turned to prayer. And our country has been delivered from many serious evils and wrongs because of that prayer.

—GEORGE W. BUSH, 43rd U.S. president. Remarks during
the National Day of Prayer Reception, May 3, 2001.

Turning to prayer in times of joy and celebration, strife and tragedy is an integral part of our national heritage.

—GEORGE W. BUSH, 43rd U.S. president.
National Day of Prayer, April 30, 2001.

No matter what our background, in prayer we share something universal—a desire to speak and listen to our Maker, and to know his plan for our lives.

—GEORGE W. BUSH, 43rd U.S. president. Remarks
at the National Prayer Breakfast, February 1, 2001.

In our home there was always prayer—aloud, proud and unapologetic.

—LYNDON B. JOHNSON, 36th U.S. president.
Lyndon B. Johnson: Containing the Public Messages, Speeches,
and Statements of the president Office of the Federal Register,
1970, p. 262.

The men who have guided the destiny of the United States have found the strength for their tasks by going to their knees. This private unity of public men and their God is an enduring source of reassurance for the people of America.

—LYNDON B. JOHNSON, 36th U.S. president.
Ron DiCianni, *The Faith of the presidents,*
Charisma House, 2004.

RELIGION

Statesman, my dear Sir, may plan and speculate for liberty, but it is Religion and Morality alone, which can establish the Principles upon which Freedom can securely stand.

The only foundation of a free Constitution is pure Virtue, and if this cannot be inspired into our People in a greater Measure, than they have it now, they may change their Rulers and the forms of Government, but they will not obtain a lasting liberty.

—JOHN ADAMS, 2nd U.S. president.
June 21, 1776. Charles Francis Adams, ed.,
The Works of John Adams—Second president of the United States
(Boston: Little, Brown & Co., 1854), vol. IX, p. 401.

I have well fixed it in my Mind as a Principle, that every Nation has a Right to that Religion and Government which it chooses, and as long as any People please themselves in these great Points, I am determined they shall not displease me.

—JOHN ADAMS, 2nd U.S. president. To Abigail Adams,
June 3, 1778. Butterfield, *Adams Family Correspondence*, vol. 3, p. 32.

I assert the divine right and sacred duty of private individual judgment and deny all human authority in matters of faith. . . .

Now I know of no divine authority for Lords Parsons, Lords Brethren, Lords Councils, Lords Synods, Lords Associations, Lords Consociations or Lords General Assemblies, any more than in Lords Bishops, Lords Cardinals or Lords Kings or Gods Popes, to deliver a man over to Satan to be buffeted than there is in a Quincy Braintree or a Randolph Town Meeting.

—JOHN ADAMS, 2nd U.S. president.
To Francis van der Kemp, January 23, 1813. Adams Papers
(microfilm), reel 121, Library of Congress.

I will not condescend to employ the word Toleration. I assert that unlimited freedom of religion, consistent with morals and property, is essential to the progress of society and the amelioration of the condition of mankind.

—JOHN ADAMS, 2nd U.S. president.
To Francis van der Kemp, October 2, 1818. Ibid., reel 123.

To obtain religious and civil liberty I entered zealously into the Revolution, and observing the Christian religion divided into many sects, I founded the hope that no one would be so predominant as to become the religion of the state. That hope was thus early entertained, because all of them joined in the same cause, with few exceptions of individuals. God grant that this religious liberty may be preserved in these states, to the end of time, and that all believing in the religion of Christ may practice the leading principle of charity the basis of every virtue.

—CHARLES CARROLL, member of the Continental Congress.
To John Stanford, October 9, 1827. Kate Rowland, *The Life of
Charles Carroll of Carrollton*, 1737-1832 (New York: G.E Putnam's
Sons, 1898), vol. 2, p. 358.

Adequate security is also given to the rights of conscience and private judgment. They are by nature subject to no control but that of the Deity and in that free situation they are now left. Every man is permitted to consider, to adore, to worship his Creator in the manner most agreeable to his conscience. No opinions are dictated, no rules of faith prescribed, no preference given to one sect to the prejudice of others. The constitution, however, has wisely declared, that the "liberty of conscience thereby granted shall not be so construed as to excuse acts of licentiousness, or justify practices inconsistent with the peace or safety of the State." In a word, the convention by whom that constitution was formed were of the opinion that the gospel of Christ, like the ark of God, would not fall, though unsupported by the arm of flesh; and happy would it be for mankind if that opinion prevailed more generally.

—JOHN JAY, president of the Continental Congress, 1778–1779;
and 1st chief justice of the U.S. Supreme Court, 1789-1795.
"Charge to the Ulster County Grand Jury," September 9, 1777.
Johnston, *Correspondence of Jay*, vol. 1, pp. 162-163.

... Almighty God hath created the mind free, and manifested his supreme will that free it shall remain by making it altogether insusceptible of restraint; that all attempts to influence it by temporal punishments, or burthens, or by civil incapacitations, tend only to beget habits of hypocrisy and meanness, and are a departure from the plan of the holy author of our religion, who being lord both of body and mind, yet chose not to propagate it by coercions on either, as was in his Almighty power to do, but to extend it by the influence of reason alone.

—THOMAS JEFFERSON, 2nd U.S. President.
"A Bill for Establishing Religious Freedom," 1777. Boyd,
Papers of Thomas Jefferson, vol. 2, p. 545.

The clergy [had] a very favorable hope of obtaining an establishment of a particular form of Christianity thro' the United States And as every sect believes its own form the true one, every one perhaps hoped for its own: but especially the Episcopalians and the Congregationalists. The returning good sense of our country threatens abortion to their hopes, and they believe that any portion of power confided to me will be exerted in opposition to their schemes. And they believe truly. For I have sworn upon the altar of god eternal hostility against every form of tyranny over the mind of man.

—THOMAS JEFFERSON, 2nd U.S. president.
To Benjamin Rush, September 23, 1800.
Adams, *Jefferson's Extracts*, p. 320.

I never will, by any word or act bow to the shrine of intolerance, or admit a right of enquiry into the religious opinions of others. On the contrary we are bound, you, I, and every one, to make common cause, even with error itself, to maintain the common right of freedom of conscience.

—THOMAS JEFFERSON, 2nd U.S. president.
To Edward Dowse, April 19, 1803. Ibid., p. 330.

Our country has been the first to prove to the world two truths, the most salutary to human society, that man can govern himself, and that religious freedom is the most effective anodyne against religious dissension: the maxims of civil government being reversed in that of religion, where it's true form is "divided we stand, united we fall."

—THOMAS JEFFERSON, 2nd U.S. president.
To Jacob Delamotta, September 1, 1820. Jefferson Papers,
Library of Congress.

I am for freedom of religion and against all maneuvers to bring about a legal ascendancy of one sect over another.

> —THOMAS JEFFERSON, 2nd U.S. President,
> in a letter to Elbridge Gerry, January 26, 1799.

That religion, or the duty which we owe to our Creator, and the manner of discharging it, can be directed only by reason and conviction, not by force or violence; and therefore all men are equally entitled to the free exercise of religion, according to the dictates of conscience; and that it is the mutual duty of all to practice Christian forbearance, love, and charity towards each other.

> —PATRICK HENRY, American patriot and governor of
> Virginia. Virginia Bill of Rights, Section 16, June 12, 1776.

As piety, religion and morality have a happy influence on the minds of men, in their public as well as private transactions, you will not think it unseasonable, although I have frequently done it, to bring to your remembrance the great importance of encouraging our University, town schools, and other seminaries of education, that our children and youth while they are engaged in the pursuit of useful science, may have their minds impressed with a strong sense of the duties they owe to their God.

> —SAMUEL ADAMS, Massachusetts delegate to the Continental
> Congress, 1775-1781. To the Legislature of Massachusetts,
> January 27, 1797. Harry Alonzo Cushing,
> *The Writings of Samuel Adams*, vol. IV, p. 401.

The only foundation for a useful education in a republic is to be laid in religion. Without this there can be no virtue, and

without virtue there can be no liberty, and liberty is the object
and life of all republican governments.

> —BENJAMIN RUSH, member of the Continental Congress,
> 1776-1777. "On the Mode of Education in the Republic,"
> *Essays, Literary, Moral and Philosophical*, vol. 8. Retrieved from
> www.generationjoshua.org.

The importance of piety and religion; of industry and frugality; of prudence, economy, regularity and an even government;
all . . . are essential to the well-being of a family.

> —SAMUEL ADAMS, Massachusetts delegate
> to the Continental Congress, 1775-1781.
> Letter to Thomas Wells. November 22, 1780. Retrieved from
> http://www.marksquotes.com/Founding-Fathers/index8.htm.

That these united colonies are, and of right ought to be, free
and independent states; that they are absolved from all allegiance to the British crown; and that all political connection
between them and the State of Great Britain is, and ought to be,
totally dissolved.

> —RICHARD HENRY LEE, member of the Continental
> Congress (1774-1779, 1784-1785, 1787). Resolution moved at the
> Continental Congress, June 7, 1776; adopted July 4, 1776.

The Religion then of every man must be left to the conviction and
conscience of every man; and it is the right of every man to exercise it as these may dictate. This right is in its nature an unalienable
right. It is unalienable, because the opinions of men, depending
only on the evidence contemplated by their own minds cannot
follow the dictates of other men; It is unalienable also, because

what is here a right towards men, is a duty towards the Creator. It is the duty of every man to render to the Creator such homage and such only as he believes to be acceptable to him.

—JAMES MADISON, 4th U.S. president.
"Memorial and Remonstrance," June 20, 1785.
Rakove, *Madison Writings*, p. 30.

The founders did not intend to weaken religion by separating it from civil authority. They believed that the real test of faith was whether it is strong enough to tolerate other faiths. They were right.

—RICHARD NIXON, 37th U.S. president.
Richard Nixon, *Beyond Peace*, Random House, 1994, p. 238.

I know that we share a belief that all people, no matter where they live, have the right to freedom of religion. This is not a right that is any government's to give or to take away. It's our right from birth, because we're all children of God.

—RONALD REAGAN, 40th U.S. president.
Remarks at the annual convention of the Anti-Defamation League of B'nai B'rith, June 10, 1983.

If I could have entertained the slightest apprehension that the Constitution framed in the Convention, where I had the honor to preside, might possibly endanger the religious rights of any ecclesiastical Society; certainly I would never have placed my signature to it; and if I could now conceive that the general Government might ever be so administered as to render the liberty of conscience insecure, I beg you will be persuaded that no one would be more zealous than myself to establish effectual barriers against the horrors of spiritual tyranny, and every species of religious persecution—For you, doubtless, remember that I have often expressed my sentiments, that every man, conducting himself as a good citizen, and being accountable to God alone for his religious opinions, ought to be protected in worshipping the Deity according to the dictates of his own conscience.

—GEORGE WASHINGTON, 1st U.S. president.
To the General Committee representing the United Baptist
Churches in Virginia. May 1789. Bolter, *Washington*, p. 170.

The Citizens of the United States of America have a right to applaud themselves for having given to Mankind examples of an enlarged and liberal policy, a policy worthy of imitation. All possess alike liberty of conscience and immunities of citizenship. It is now no more that toleration is spoken of, as if it was by the indulgence of one class of people, that another enjoyed their inherent natural rights. For happily the Government of the United States, which gives to bigotry no sanction, to persecution no assistance, requires only that they who live under its protection should demean themselves as good citizens, in giving it on all occasions their effectual support.

—GEORGE WASHINGTON, 1st U.S. president.
To the Hebrew Congregation of Newport, Rhode Island,
August 17, 1790, Ibid., p. 186.

There is not a single instance in history in which civil liberty was lost, and religious liberty preserved entire.

—JOHN WITHERSPOON, member of the Continental
Congress. "The Dominion of Providence over the Passions of
Man," May 17, 1776. *Works of Witherspoon*, vol. 3, p. 37.

I have often expressed my sentiments, that every man, conducting himself as a good citizen, and being accountable to God alone for his religious opinions, ought to be protected in worshipping the Deity according to the dictates of his own conscience.

—GEORGE WASHINGTON, 1st U.S. president. In a letter to the United Baptist Churches in Virginia, May 10, 1789.

Congress shall make no law respecting an establishment of religion, or prohibiting the free exercise thereof.

—CONSTITUTION OF THE UNITED STATES. Bill of Rights, First Amendment, December 15, 1791.

I have always acted consistent with my own ideas of religion which were that there was no necessity to become a member of any particular sect as the intent of each sect is the same and I suppose that in less than a century there will be no such distinctions but that, people thinking on a larger scale, all religions will unite under one head.

—JOHN DICKINSON, member of the First Continental Congress. To Richard Penn Hicks, September 13, 1788. Logan Papers, Historical Society of Pennsylvania.

I have often lamented the squeamishness of my . . . mind upon the subject of religious creeds and modes of worship. But accustomed to think for myself in my profession . . . I have ventured to transfer the same spirit of inquiry to religion, in which, if I have no followers in my opinions (for I hold most of them secretly), I enjoy the satisfaction of living in peace with my conscience, and, what will surprise you not a little, in peace with all denominations of Christians, for while I refuse to be the slave of any sect, I am the friend of them all. In a future letter I may perhaps give you my creed.... It is a compound of the orthodoxy and heterodoxy of most of our Christian churches.

> —BENJAMIN RUSH, member of the Continental Congress,
> 1776-1777. To John Adams, April 5, 1808. Butterfield,
> *Letters of Rush*, vol. 2, pp. 962-963.

I never told my own religion, nor scrutinized that of another. I never attempted to make a convert, nor wished to change another's creed. I have ever judged of the religion of others by their lives.... For it is in our lives, and not from our words, that our religion must be read.

> —THOMAS JEFFERSON, 2nd U.S. president.
> To Margaret Bayard Smith, August 6, 1816.
> Adams, *Jefferson's Extracts*, p. 376.

I put down from time to time on Pieces of paper such Thoughts as occur'd to me.... Most of these are lost; but I find one purporting to be the Substance of an intended Creed, containing as I thought the Essentials of every known Religion, and being free of every thing that might shock the Professors of any Religion. It is express'd in these Words. viz That there is one God who made all things. That he governs the World by his Providence. That he ought to be worshipped by Adoration, Prayer and Thanksgiving. But that the most acceptable Service of God is doing Good to Man. That the Soul is immortal. And that God will certainly reward Virtue and punish Vice either here or hereafter.

> —BENJAMIN FRANKLIN, member of the Second
> Continental Congress. *Autobiography*, post-1758.
> Labaree, *Autobiography of Franklin*, p. 162.

There is in human Nature a solid, unchangeable and eternal
Foundation of Religion. There is also a germ of superstition,
seemingly a fungous growth or a spurious sprout, which the
grossest Blockheads and most atrocious Villains are able to cultivate into Systems and Sects to deceive millions and cheat and
pillage hundreds and thousands of their fellow Creatures.

—JOHN ADAMS, 2nd U.S. president.
To John Quincy Adams, May 10, 1816. Adams Papers
(microfilm), reel 431, Library of Congress.

Religion always has and always will govern mankind. Man is
constitutionally, essentially and unchangeably a religious animal. Neither philosophers or politicians can ever govern him in
any other way.

—JOHN ADAMS, 2nd U.S. president.
To Francis van der Kemp, October 2, 1818. Ibid., reel 123.

There is in all Men something like a natural Principle which
enclines them to DEVOTION or the Worship of some unseen
Power.

—BENJAMIN FRANKLIN, member of the Second
Continental Congress. "Articles of Belief and Acts of Religion,"
November 20, 1728. Labaree, *Papers of Benjamin Franklin*,
vol. 1, p. 101.

I must ever believe that religion substantially good which pro-
duces an honest life, and we have been authorized by One
whom you and I equally respect, to judge of the tree by its fruit.
Our particular principles of religion are a subject of account-
ability to our God alone. I inquire after no man's and trouble

none with mine; nor is it given to us in this life to know whether yours or mine, our friends or our foes, are exactly the right. Nay, we have heard it said that there is not a Quaker or a Baptist a Presbyterian or an Episcopalian, a Catholic or Protestant in heaven; that, on entering that gate we leave those badges of schism behind, and ourselves united in those principles only in what God has united us all. Let us not be uneasy about the different roads we may pursue. . . to our last abode.

—THOMAS JEFFERSON, 2nd U.S. president.
In a letter to Miles King, September 26, 1814.

There appears to be in the nature of man, what ensures his belief in an invisible cause of his present existence, & an anticipation of his future existence. Hence the propensities & susceptibilities, in the case of religion which with a few doubtful or individual exceptions, have prevailed throughout the world.

—JAMES MADISON, 4th U.S. president. To Jasper Adams,
September 1832. Dreisbach, *Religion and Politics*, p. 117.

In the course of time I hope that Washington may become architecturally an inspiration to the nation. This hope will be achieved when there is beautiful architectural expression of the fundamental aspects of our democracy. Certainly one of these aspects, because it is the deepest spring of our national life, is religion. Therefore, as a wonderfully beautiful expression of religion, I watch with sympathetic interest the growth of the great Cathedral on the heights overlooking Washington.

—HERBERT HOOVER, 31st U.S. president. Message
contributed to a symposium on the Washington Cathedral,
November 12, 1929 (released December 27, 1929).

The past and present show faith and hope and courage fully justified. Here stands our country, an example of tranquillity at home, a patron of tranquillity abroad. Here stands its Government, aware of its might but obedient to its conscience. Here it will continue to stand, seeking peace and prosperity, solicitous for the welfare of the wage earner, promoting enterprise, developing waterways and natural resources, attentive to the intuitive counsel of womanhood, encouraging education, *desiring the advancement of religion*, supporting the cause of justice and honor among the nations. America seeks no earthly empire built on blood and force. No ambition, no temptation, lures her to thought of foreign dominions. The legions which she sends forth are armed, not with the sword, but with the cross. The higher state to which she seeks the allegiance of all mankind is not of human, but of divine origin. She cherishes no purpose save to merit the favor of Almighty God.

—CALVIN COOLIDGE, 30th U.S. president.
Inaugural Address, March 4, 1925.

The strength of our country is the strength of its religious convictions.

—CALVIN COOLIDGE, 30th U.S. president. In a letter to Rev. James E. Freeman, Bishop of Washington, September 1923.

. . . the design of Christianity was not to make men good Riddle Solvers or good mystery mongers, but good men, good magestrates and good Subjects.

—JOHN ADAMS, 2nd U.S. president. Diary, February 18, 1756.
Butterfield, *Diary and Autobiography of John Adams*, vol. 1, p. 8.

Without morals a republic cannot subsist any length of time; they therefore, who are decrying the Christian religion, whose morality is so sublime and pure, which denounces against the wicked, the eternal misery, and insures to the good eternal happiness, are undermining the solid foundation of morals, the best security for the duration of free governments.

—CHARLES CARROLL, member of the Continental Congress.
To Charles Carroll, Jr. November 4, 1800.
Alt J. Mapp, Jr., *The Faiths of Our Fathers*
(Lanham, MD: Rowman & Littlefield, 2003), pp. 140-141.

The government of a country never gets ahead of the religion of a country. There is no way by which we can substitute the authority of the law for the virtues of men.

—CALVIN COOLIDGE, 30th U.S. president. Address at the unveiling of the equestrian statue of Bishop Francis Asbury, Washington, D.C., October 15, 1924.

Our government rests upon religion. It is from that source that we derive our reverence for truth and justice, for equality and liberty, and for the rights of mankind. Unless the people believe in these principles they cannot believe in our government. There are only two main theories of government in the world. One rests on righteousness, the other rests on force. One appeals to reason, the other appeals to the sword. One is exemplified in a republic, the other is represented by a despotism.

—CALVIN COOLIDGE, 30th U.S. president. Address at the unveiling of the equestrian statue of Bishop Francis Asbury, Washington, D.C., October 15, 1924.

In this way we are reaffirming the transcendence of religious faith in America's heritage and future; in this way we shall constantly strengthen those spiritual weapons which forever will be our country's most powerful resource in peace and war.

—DWIGHT D. EISENHOWER, 34th U.S. president.
Flag Day speech, signing bill authorizing addition of the words
"under God" to the Pledge of Allegiance, June 14, 1954.

The purpose of a devout and united people was set forth in the pages of the Bible . . . (1) to live in freedom (2) to work in a prosperous land . . . and (3) to obey the commandments of God. . . . This biblical story of the Promised land inspired the founders of America. It continues to inspire us.

—DWIGHT D. EISENHOWER, 34th U.S. president.
1954, "Our Christian Heritage," *Letter from Plymouth Rock*
(Marlborough, NH: The Plymouth Rock Foundation), p. 7.

History will also afford frequent Opportunities of showing the Necessity of a *Publick Religion*, from its Usefulness to the Publick.

—BENJAMIN FRANKLIN, member of the Second
Continental Congress. "Proposals Relating to the
Education of Youth in Pennsylvania," 1749.
Labaree, *Papers of Benjamin Franklin*, vol. 3, p. 413.

The politician who loves liberty sees . . . a gulph that may swallow up the liberty to which he is devoted. He knows that morality overthrown (and morality *must* fall without religion) the terrors of despotism can alone curb the impetuous passions of man, and confine him within the bounds of social duty.

—ALEXANDER HAMILTON, member of the Continental

Congress and 1st secretary of the treasury. *The Stand*, no. 3
(April 7, 1798). Syrett, *Papers of Alexander Hamilton*, vol. 21, p. 405.

It is my conviction that the fundamental trouble with the people of the United States is that they have gotten too far away from Almighty God.

—WARREN G. HARDING, 29th U.S. president. 1920.

The great pillars of all government and social life (are) virtue, morality, and religion. This is the armor, my friend and this alone, that renders us invincible.

—PATRICK HENRY, American patriot and governor of
Virginia. Letter to Archibald Blair, January 8, 1789. Moses Coit
Tyler, *Patrick Henry*, (Houghton Mifflin, 1897), p. 409.

The profound influence of religion on American politics is vital, but it is best when indirect: on the morals, habits, and souls of individual Americans; on the political climate and the principles that should guide policy, rather than on specific policies themselves.

Government cannot reach into people's hearts. Religion can.

—RICHARD NIXON, 37th U.S. president. Richard Milhous
Nixon, *Beyond Peace*, (Random House, 1994), pp. 238-239.

It is foreign to my purpose to hint at the arguments which establish the truth of Christian revelation. Business is to declare, that all its doctrines and precepts are calculated to promote the happiness of society, and the safety and well being of civil government.

—BENJAMIN RUSH, member of the Continental Congress,
1776-1777. "Of the Mode of Education Proper in a Republic."
Rush, *Essays: Literary, Moral, and Philosophical*, p. 6.

... While just government protects all in their religious rights, true religion affords to government its surest support.

—GEORGE WASHINGTON, 1st U.S. president. Letter to the
Synod of the Reformed Dutch Church of North America,
October 9, 1789.

Of all the dispositions and habits which lead to political prosperity, Religion and morality are indispensable supports. In vain would that man claim the tribute of Patriotism, who should labour to subvert these great Pillars of human happiness, these firmest props of the duties of Men and citizens. The mere Politician, equally with the pious man ought to respect and to cherish them. A volume could not trace all their connections with private and public felicity

—GEORGE WASHINGTON, 1st U.S. president.
Farewell Address, September 19, 1796. Rare Book and
Special Collections Division, Library of Congress.

And let us with caution indulge the supposition that morality can be maintained without religion. Whatever may be conceded to the influence of refined education on minds of peculiar structure, reason and experience both forbid us to expect that national morality can prevail in exclusion of religious principle.

—GEORGE WASHINGTON, 1st U.S. president.
In his Farewell Address, September 19, 1796.

Religion is as necessary to reason as reason is to religion. The one cannot exist without the other.

—GEORGE WASHINGTON, 1st U.S. president. In James K.
Paulding, *The Life of Washington*, (Harper & Bros., 1835), p. 209.

The United States in Congress assembled First Secretary of the Treasury... do further recommend to all ranks, to testify their gratitude to God for his goodness, by a cheerful obedience to his laws, and by promoting, each in his station, and by his influence, the practice of true and undefiled religion, which is the great foundation of public prosperity and national happiness.

—JOHN WITHERSPOON, member of the Continental Congress. "Thanksgiving Day Proclamation," October 11, 1782. *Journals of the Continental Congress* (Washington, D.C.: Government Printing Office, 1904), vol. 23, p. 647.

Religion, by teaching man his relationship to God, gives the individual a sense of his own dignity and teaches him to respect himself by respecting his neighbors.

—FRANKLIN D. ROOSEVELT, 32nd U.S. president. Annual message to Congress, January 4, 1939.

What place has religion which preaches the dignity of the human being, the majesty of the human soul, in a world where moral standards are measured by treachery and bribery and fifth columnists? Will our children, too, wander off, goosestepping in search of new gods?

—FRANKLIN D. ROOSEVELT, 32nd U.S. president. Radio address announcing an unlimited national emergency, May 27, 1941.

The sum of the whole matter is this, that our civilization cannot survive materially unless it is redeemed spiritually.

—WOODROW WILSON, 28th U.S. president. "The Road Away from Revolution." *Atlantic Monthly,* August 1923.

It is gratifying, not only to those who consider the commercial interests of nations, but also to all who favor the progress of knowledge and the diffusion of religion, to see a community emerge from a savage state and attain such a degree of civilization in those distant seas.

—MILLARD FILLMORE, 13th U.S. president.
Second Annual message, December 2, 1851.

Under the benignant *providence of Almighty God* the representatives of the States and of the people are again brought together to deliberate for the public good. The *gratitude of the nation to the Sovereign Arbiter of All Human Events* should be commensurate with the boundless blessings which we enjoy.

—JAMES K. POLK, 11th U.S. president.
Fourth Annual message to Congress, December 5, 1848.

It is painful to observe, that in prosecuting the benevolent and sole object of the American Bible Society, less opposition is experienced from avowed infidels than from those who claim to constitute the only true church of God.

—JOHN COTTON SMITH, Connecticut governor, member of
Congress, and ABS president. Letter to the delegates at the Semi-
Annual Meeting of the ABS, November 1, 1843. Corresponding
Secretary Files, ABS Archives

A community composed of elements so diverse, must resort to a higher cause than worldly policy and the schemes of individual ambition, if they would secure the permanent enjoyment of rational liberty and the favour of heaven. Nothing but the unobstructed and universal circulation of the pure word of

God, and its momentous truths impressed by Divine power on the consciences of men and on the hearts of the rising generation, can furnish an effectual guaranty to our freedom, or shield us from the worst species of tyranny or spiritual despotism.

—JOHN COTTON SMITH, Connecticut governor, member of Congress, and ABS president. Ibid.

Think . . . how many inconsiderate and inexperienced youth of both sexes there are who have need of the motives of religion to restrain them from vice, to support their virtue, and retain them in the practice of it till it becomes habitual.

—BENJAMIN FRANKLIN, member of the Second Continental Congress. In a letter to Thomas Paine, possibly quoted from Key and Mielke's *Life of Franklin*, p. 76 or 77. William Temple Franklin, ed., *Private Correspondence of Benjamin Franklin,* (H. Colburn, 1833), p. 265.

The righteous authority of the law depends for its sanction upon its harmony with the righteous authority of the Almighty. If this faith is set aside, the foundations of our institutions fail, the citizen is deposed from the high estate which he holds as amenable to a universal conscience, society reverts to a system of class and caste, and the Government instead of being imposed by reason from within is imposed by force from without. Freedom and democracy would give way to despotism and slavery. I do not know of any adequate support for our form of government except that which comes from religion.

—CALVIN COOLIDGE, 30th U.S. president. Address before the annual council on the Congregational Churches, Washington, D.C., October 20, 1925.

In closing, may I say one word: The problems which we all face—the problems of so-called economics, the problems that are called monetary problems, the problems of unemployment, the problems of industry and agriculture—we shall not succeed in solving unless the people of this country hold the spiritual values of the country just as high as they do the economic values. I am very sure that the spirit in which we are approaching those difficult tasks and the splendid cooperation which has been shown, are going to be exemplified in the lives of all the people calling themselves Christians who believe in God and uphold the works of the Church.

—FRANKLIN D. ROOSEVELT, 32nd U.S. president.
Extemporaneous address at the Hyde Park Methodist
Episcopal Church, September 29, 1933.

I have said, and I desire to reiterate it to this body of Christians gathered from many lands, that what this weary world most needs is a revival of the spirit of religion. Would that such a revival could sweep the nations today and stir the hearts of men and women of all faiths to a reassertion of their belief in the Providence of God and the brotherhood of man. I doubt if there is in the world a single problem, whether social, political, or economic, which would not find ready solution if men and nations would rule their lives according to the plain teaching of the Sermon on the Mount.

—FRANKLIN D. ROOSEVELT, 32nd U.S. president.
Greeting to the World's Christian Endeavor Convention in
Melbourne, Australia, June 15, 1938.

Those people in other lands, and I say this advisedly, those in other lands who have sought by edict or by law to eliminate the right of mankind to believe in God and to practice that belief, have, in every known case, discovered sooner or later that they are tilting in vain against an inherent, essential, undying quality, indeed necessity, of the human race—a quality and a necessity which in every century have proved an essential to permanent progress—and I speak of religion.

—FRANKLIN D. ROOSEVELT, 32nd U.S. president.
Address to the National Conference of Catholic Charities,
October 4, 1933.

In teaching this democratic faith to American children, we need the sustaining, buttressing aid of those great ethical religious teachings which are the heritage of our modern civilization. For "not upon strength nor upon power, but upon the spirit of God" shall our democracy be founded.

—FRANKLIN D. ROOSEVELT, 32nd U.S. president.
Letter on religion in democracy, December 16, 1940.

Let us determine to carry on in that same spirit—in a spirit of tolerance, and understanding for all men and for all nations—in the spirit of God and religious unity.

—HARRY S. TRUMAN, 33rd U.S. president.
Address in Columbus at a conference of the Federal Council
of Churches, March 6, 1946.

Written around the crown of this bell are the words, "Proclaim liberty throughout the land and to all the inhabitants thereof." Those words are 2,500 years old. I learned the first line over there in that Presbyterian Church. They come from the Bible. They reflect a deep belief in freedom under God and justice among men—a belief which is at the heart of what the Bible teaches us.

—HARRY S. TRUMAN, 33rd U.S. president.
Address in Independence, Missouri at the dedication of the
Liberty Bell, November 6, 1950.

The early history of our country was written by men who valued the freedom of religion and who had in common a deep faith in God. I believe it is no accident of history, no coincidence that this Nation, which declared its dependence on God even while declaring its independence from foreign domination, has become the most richly blessed nation in the history of mankind and the world.

—GERALD FORD, 38th U.S. president.
Remarks at the Southern Baptist Convention in
Norfolk, Virginia, June 15, 1976.

The road that leads away from revolution is clearly marked, for it is defined by the nature of men and of organized society. It therefore behooves us to study very carefully and very candidly the exact nature of the task and the means of its accomplishment. The sum of the whole matter is this, that our civilization cannot survive materially unless it be redeemed spiritually.

—WOODROW WILSON, 28th U.S. president. In "The Road
Away From Revolution," *The Atlantic Monthly*, August, 1923.
Woodrow Wilson, *The Politics of Woodrow Wilson: Selections from
His Speeches and Writings*, Ayer Publishing, 1970, p. 385.

Religion is not an easy thing. It is not simply a comfort to those
in trouble or a means of escaping from present difficulties, as
some people today would have us believe. Religion is not a negative thing. It is not merely a series of prohibitions against certain actions because they are wicked. Our religion includes
these elements. But it also includes much more. It is a positive
force that impels us to affirmative action. We are under divine
orders—not only to refrain from doing evil, but also to do good
and to make this world a better place in which to live. Every one
of us should measure the actions of his daily life against this
moral code which our religion gives us. Every one of us, according to the strength and wisdom God gives to him, should try
his best every day to live up to these religious teachings.

—HARRY S. TRUMAN, 33rd U.S. president.
Address at the cornerstone laying of the New York Avenue
Presbyterian Church, April 3, 1951.

My attitude toward one of the functions of the church in promoting peace is one of appreciation of the great service it can
perform in uniting better the free nations of the world.

—DWIGHT D. EISENHOWER, 34th U.S. president.
Remarks to a delegation from the National Council of Churches,
September 9, 1959.

Throughout our Nation's history Americans of all faiths have
turned to Divine Providence for the strength and wisdom to
meet whatever challenges were put before them with honor
and dignity.

—JIMMY CARTER, 39th U.S. president.
Proclamation 4532, National Day of Prayer, October 13, 1977.

Our Nation is one of great strength. God has blessed us in many ways—with a form of government now more than 200 years old, when individual human beings, no matter how different they might be from one another, could stand and speak as they choose, develop those qualities of individuality and difference that, put together, give us a strong America.

—JIMMY CARTER, 39th U.S. president.
Remarks at Growers Cooperative Warehouse, Inc.,
Wilson, North Carolina, August 5, 1978.

And let me also confess that, as I was looking forward to tonight, I got to thinking and wondering, thinking about how Pope John XXIII said, "Religion makes mankind special"—and wondering what is it about Catholic University and these six men of God which makes them, in their special way, so extraordinary. The first reason, I think, is fundamental faith, belief in the Almighty. For you accept the eternal teachings of the Sermon on the Mount. You believe that political values without moral values cannot sustain a people. And you know that there is no state religion, nor should there ever be, but spiritual principles were rooted in our nation's origins, and always must be.

—GEORGE H.W. BUSH, 41st U.S. president.
Remarks at the Catholic University of America
anniversary dinner, December 12, 1989.

First I say that this prayer breakfast is an important time to reaffirm that in this nation where we have freedom of religion, we need not seek freedom from religion. The genius of the book which I have . . . promoted almost shamelessly for the last several months—*The Culture of Disbelief*, by Professor Stephen

Carter is that very point—that we should all seek to know and to do God's will, even when we differ.

—WILLIAM CLINTON, 42nd U.S. president.
Remarks by the president at the National Prayer Breakfast,
February 3, 1994.

All across this country, there is a deep understanding rooted in our religious heritage and renewed in the spirit of this time that the bounty of nature is not ours to waste. It is a gift from God that we hold in trust for future generations.

—WILLIAM CLINTON, 42nd U.S. president.
Remarks by the president in Earth Day Speech, April 21, 1993.

Our nation is chosen by God and commissioned by history to be a model to the world of justice and inclusion and diversity without division. Jews and Christians and Muslims speak as one in their commitment to a kind, just tolerant society.

—GEORGE W. BUSH, 43rd U.S. president.
Speech to B'nai B'rith, August 28, 2000.

THANKSGIVING DAY

Whereas it is the duty of all Nations to acknowledge the providence of almighty God, to obey his will, to be grateful for his benefits, and humbly to implore his protection and favor—and Whereas both houses of Congress have by their joint Committee requested me "to recommend to the People of the United States a day of public thanksgiving and prayer to be observed by acknowledging with grateful hearts the many signal favors of Almighty God, especially by affording them an opportunity peaceably to establish a form of government for their safety and happiness.

—GEORGE WASHINGTON, 1st U.S. president,
Thanksgiving Day Proclamation, October 3, 1789.

In such a state of things it is in an especial manner our duty as a people, with devout reverence and affectionate gratitude, to acknowledge our many and great obligations to Almighty God and to implore him to continue and confirm the blessings we experience.

—GEORGE WASHINGTON, 1st U.S. president.
Thanksgiving Day Proclamation, January 1, 1795.

And finally, I recommend that on the said day the duties of humiliation and prayer be accompanied by fervent thanksgiving to the Bestower of Every Good Gift, not only for his having hitherto protected and preserved the people of these United States in the independent enjoyment of their religious and civil freedom, but also for having prospered them in a wonderful progress of population, and for conferring on them many and great favors conducive to the happiness and prosperity of a nation.

—JOHN ADAMS, 2nd U.S. president.
Thanksgiving Day Proclamation, March 23, 1798.

The National Fast, recommended by me turned me out of office. It was connected with the general assembly of the Presbyterian Church, which I had no concern in. That assembly has allarmed and alienated Quakers, Anabaptists, Mennonists, Moravians, Swedenborgians, Methodists, Catholicks, protestant Episcopalians, Arians, Socinians, Armenians, & & &, Atheists and Deists might be added. A general Suspicion prevailed that the Presbyterian Church was ambitious and aimed at an Establishment of a National Church. I was represented as a Presbyterian and at the head of this political and ecclesiastical Project. The secret whisper ran through them "Let us have Jefferson, Madison, Burr, any body, whether they be Philosophers, Deists, or even Atheists, rather than a Presbyterian President." This principle is at the bottom of the unpopularity of national Fasts and Thanksgivings. Nothing is more dreaded than the National Government meddling with Religion.

—JOHN ADAMS, 2nd U.S. president.
Letter to Benjamin Rush, *Old Family Letters*, pp. 392-393.

For these reasons I have thought proper to recommend, and I do hereby recommend accordingly, that Thursday, the 25th day of April next, be observed throughout the United States of America as a day of solemn humiliation, fasting, and prayer; that the citizens on that day abstain as far as may be from their secular occupations, devote the time to the sacred duties of religion in public and in private; that they call to mind our numerous offenses against the Most high God, confess them before him with the sincerest penitence, implore his pardoning mercy, through the Great Mediator and Redeemer, for our past transgressions, and that through the grace of his holy Spirit we may be disposed and enabled to yield a more suitable obedience to his righteous requisitions in time to come; . . . And I do also recommend that with these acts of humiliation, penitence, and prayer, fervent thanksgiving to the Author of All Good be united for the countless favors which he is still continuing to the people of the United States, and which render their condition as a nation eminently happy when compared with the lot of others.

—JOHN QUINCY ADAMS, 6th U.S. president.
Thanksgiving Day Proclamation, April 25, 1799.

The two houses of the National Legislature having by a joint resolution expressed their desire that in the present time of public calamity and war a day may be recommended to be observed by the people of the United States as a day of public humiliation and fasting and of prayer to Almighty God for the safety and welfare of these States, his blessing on their arms, and a speedy restoration of peace, I have deemed it proper by this proclamation to recommend that Thursday, the 12th of January next, be set apart as a day on which all may have an opportunity of voluntarily offering at the same time in their respective religious assemblies their humble adoration to the Great Sovereign of the Universe, of confessing their sins and transgressions, and of strengthening their vows of repentance and amendment.

—JAMES MADISON, 4th U.S. president.
Thanksgiving Day Proclamation, November 16, 1814.

No people ought to feel greater obligations to celebrate the goodness of the Great Disposer of Events of the Destiny of Nations than the people of the United States. His kind providence originally conducted them to one of the best portions of the dwelling place allotted for the great family of the human race. He protected and cherished them under all the difficulties and trials to which they were exposed in their early days. Under his fostering care their habits, their sentiments, and their pursuits prepared them for a transition in due time to a state of independence and self-government.

—JAMES MADISON, 4th U.S. president.
Thanksgiving Day Proclamation, March 4, 1815.

I consider the government of the U.S. as interdicted by the constitution from intermedling with religious institutions, their doctrines, discipline, or exercises. This results not only from the provision that no law shall be made respecting the establishment, or free exercise of religion, but from that also which reserves to the states the powers not delegated to the U.S. Certainly no power to prescribe any religious exercise, or to assume authority in religious discipline, has been delegated to the general government. It must then rest with the states, as far as it can be in any human authority. But it is only proposed that I should *recommend*, not prescribe a day of fasting & prayer.

That is, that I should indirectly assume to the U.S. an authority over religious exercises which the constitution has directly precluded them from. . . . I do not believe it is for the interest of religion to invite the civil magistrate to direct it's exercises, it's discipline or it's doctrine: nor of the religious societies that the general government should be invested with the power of effecting uniformity of time or matter among them. Fasting & prayer are religious exercises: the enjoining them an act of discipline. Every religious society has a right to determine for itself the times for these exercises, & the objects proper for them, according to their own particular tenets: and this right can never be safer than in their own hands, where the constitution has deposited it.

> —THOMAS JEFFERSON, 2nd U.S. president.
> Letter to Samuel Miller, January 23, 1808.
> Jefferson Papers, Library of Congress

It has pleased Almighty God to vouchsafe signal victories to the land and naval forces engaged in suppressing an internal rebellion, and at the same time to avert from our country the dangers of foreign intervention and invasion.

> —ABRAHAM LINCOLN, 16th U.S. president.
> Proclamation, April 10, 1862.

It has pleased Almighty God to hearken to the supplications and prayers of an afflicted people and to vouchsafe to the Army and the Navy of the United States victories on land and on the sea so signal and so effective as to furnish reasonable grounds for augmented confidence that the Union of these States will be maintained, their Constitution preserved, and their peace and prosperity permanently restored. But these victories have been accorded not without sacrifices of life, limb, health, and liberty, incurred by brave, loyal, and patriotic citizens. Domestic affliction in every part of the country follows in the train of these fearful bereavements. It is meet and right to recognize and confess the presence of the Almighty Father and the power of his hand equally in these triumphs and in these sorrows.

—ABRAHAM LINCOLN, 16th U.S. president.
Thanksgiving Day Proclamation, July 15, 1863.

The year that is drawing toward its close has been filled with the blessings of fruitful fields and healthful skies. To these bounties, which are so constantly enjoyed that we are prone to forget the source from which they come, others have been added which are of so extraordinary a nature that they can not fail to penetrate and soften even the heart which is habitually insensible to the ever-watchful providence of Almighty God.

—ABRAHAM LINCOLN, 16th U.S. president.
Thanksgiving Day Proclamation, October 3, 1863.

Now, therefore, I, Abraham Lincoln, president of the United States, do hereby appoint and set apart the last Thursday in November next as a day which I desire to be observed by all my fellow-citizens, wherever they may then be, as a day of thanksgiving and praise to Almighty God, the beneficent Creator and Ruler of the Universe. And I do further recommend to my fellow-citizens aforesaid that on that occasion they do reverently humble themselves in the dust and from thence offer up penitent and fervent prayers and supplications to the Great Disposer of Events for a return of the inestimable blessings of peace, union, and harmony throughout the land which it has pleased him to assign as a dwelling place for ourselves and for our posterity throughout all generations.

—ABRAHAM LINCOLN, 16th U.S. president.
Thanksgiving Day Proclamation, October 20, 1864.

Whereas it has pleased Almighty God during the year which is now coming to an end to relieve our beloved country from the fearful scourge of civil war and to permit us to secure the blessings of peace, unity, and harmony, with a great enlargement of civil liberty; and Whereas our heavenly Father has also during the year graciously averted from us the calamities of foreign war, pestilence, and famine, while our granaries are full of the fruits of an abundant season; and Whereas righteousness exalteth a nation, while sin is a reproach to any people. . . .

—ANDREW JOHNSON, 17th U.S. president.
Thanksgiving Day Proclamation, October 28, 1865.

In offering these national thanksgivings, praises, and supplications we have the divine assurance that "the Lord remaineth a king forever; them that are meek shall he guide in judgment and such as are gentle shall he learn his way; the Lord shall give strength to his people, and the Lord shall give to his people the blessing of peace.

—ANDREW JOHNSON, 17th U.S. president.
Thanksgiving Day Proclamation, October 8, 1866.

While thus rendering the unanimous and heartfelt tribute of national praise and thanksgiving which is so justly due to Almighty God, let us not fail to implore him that the same divine protection and care which we have hitherto so undeservedly and yet so constantly enjoyed may be continued to our country and our people throughout all their generations forever.

—ANDREW JOHNSON, 17th U.S. president.
Thanksgiving Day Proclamation, October 26, 1867.

I therefore recommend that Thursday, the 26th day of November next, be set apart and observed by all the people of the United States as a day for public praise, thanksgiving, and prayer to the almighty Creator and Divine Ruler of the Universe, by whose everwatchful, merciful, and gracious providence alone states and nations, no less than families and individual men, do live and move and have their being.

—ANDREW JOHNSON, 17th U.S. president.
Thanksgiving Day Proclamation, October 12, 1868.

Therefore, I, Ulysses S. Grant, president of the United States, do recommend that Thursday, the 18th day of November next, be observed as a day of thanksgiving and of praise and of prayer to almighty God, the creator and the ruler of the universe; and I do further recommend to all the people of the United States to assemble on that day in their accustomed places of public worship and to unite in the homage and praise due to the bountiful Father of All Mercies and in fervent prayer for the continuance of the manifold blessings he has vouchsafed to us as a people.

—ULYSSES S. GRANT, 18th U.S. president.
Thanksgiving Day Proclamation, October 5, 1869.

Whereas it behooves a people sensible of their dependence on the Almighty publicly and collectively to acknowledge their gratitude for his favors and mercies and humbly to beseech for their continuance. . . .

—ULYSSES S. GRANT, 18th U.S. president.
Thanksgiving Day Proclamation, October 21, 1870.

Within the past year we have in the main been free from ills which elsewhere have afflicted our kind. If some of us have had calamities, these should be an occasion for sympathy with the sufferers, of resignation on their part to the will of the Most high, and of rejoicing to the many who have been more favored.

—ULYSSES S. GRANT, 18th U.S. president.
Thanksgiving Day Proclamation, October 28, 1871.

Whereas the revolution of another year has again brought the time when it is usual to look back upon the past and publicly to thank the Almighty for his mercies and his blessings.

—ULYSSES S. GRANT, 18th U.S. president.
Thanksgiving Day Proclamation, October 11, 1872.

For these and all the other mercies vouchsafed it becomes us as a people to return heartfelt and grateful acknowledgments, and with our thanksgiving for blessings we may unite prayers for the cessation of local and temporary sufferings. I therefore recommend that on Thursday, the 27th day of November next, the people meet in their respective places of worship to make their acknowledgments to Almighty God for his bounties and his protection, and to offer to him prayers for their continuance.

—ULYSSES S. GRANT, 18th U.S. president.
Thanksgiving Day Proclamation, October 14, 1873.

We are reminded by the changing seasons that it is time to pause in our daily avocations and offer thanks to Almighty God for the mercies and abundance of the year which is drawing to a close.

—ULYSSES S. GRANT, 18th U.S. president.
Thanksgiving Day Proclamation, October 27, 1874.

Amid the rich and free enjoyment of all our advantages, we should not forget the source from whence they are derived and the extent of our obligation to the Father of All Mercies. We have full reason to renew our thanks to Almighty God for favors bestowed upon us during the past year.

—ULYSSES S. GRANT, 18th U.S. president.
Thanksgiving Day Proclamation, October 27, 1875.

In addition to these favors accorded to us as individuals, we have especial occasion to express our hearty thanks to Almighty God that by his providence and guidance our Government, established a century ago, has been enabled to fulfill the purpose of its founders in offering an asylum to the people of every race, securing civil and religious liberty to all within its borders, and meting out to every individual alike justice and equality before the law.

—ULYSSES S. GRANT, 18th U.S. president.
Thanksgiving Day Proclamation, October 26, 1876.

The completed circle of summer and winter, seedtime and harvest, has brought us to the accustomed season at which a religious people celebrates with praise and thanksgiving the enduring mercy of Almighty God. This devout and public confession of the constant dependence of man upon the divine favor for all the good gifts of life and health and peace and happiness, so early in our history made the habit of our people, finds in the survey of the past year new grounds for its joyful and grateful manifestation.

> —RUTHERFORD B. HAYES, 19th U.S. president
> and ABS vice president 1880 until his death in 1893.
> Thanksgiving Day Proclamation, October 29, 1877.

Now, therefore, I, Rutherford B. Hayes, president of the United States, do appoint Thursday, the 28th day of November next, as a day of national thanksgiving and prayer; and I earnestly recommend that, withdrawing themselves from secular cares and labors, the people of the United States do meet together on that day in their respective places of worship, there to give thanks and praise to Almighty God for his mercies and to devoutly beseech their continuance.

> —RUTHERFORD B. HAYES, 19th U.S. president
> and ABS vice president 1880 until his death in 1893.
> Thanksgiving Day Proclamation, October 30, 1878.

At no recurrence of the season which the devout habit of a religious people has made the occasion for giving thanks to Almighty God and humbly invoking his continued favor has the material prosperity enjoyed by our whole country been more conspicuous, more manifold, or more universal.

> —RUTHERFORD B. HAYES, 19th U.S. president
> and ABS vice president 1880 until his death in 1893.
> Thanksgiving Day Proclamation, November 3, 1879.

At no period in their history since the United States became a nation has this people had so abundant and so universal reasons for joy and gratitude at the favor of Almighty God or been subject to so profound an obligation to give thanks for his loving kindness and humbly to implore his continued care and protection.

—RUTHERFORD B. HAYES, 19th U.S. president
and ABS vice president 1880 until his death in 1893.
Thanksgiving Day Proclamation, November 1, 1880.

It has long been the pious custom of our people, with the closing of the year, to look back upon the blessings brought to them in the changing course of the seasons and to return solemn thanks to the all-giving source from whom they flow. And although at this period, when the falling leaf admonishes us that the time of our sacred duty is at hand, our nation still lies in the shadow of a great bereavement, and the mourning which has filled our hearts still finds its sorrowful expression toward the God before whom we but lately bowed in grief and supplication, yet the countless benefits which have showered upon us during the past twelvemonth call for our fervent gratitude and make it fitting that we should rejoice with thankfulness that the Lord in his infinite mercy has most signally favored our country and our people.

—CHESTER A. ARTHUR, 21st U.S. president.
Thanksgiving Day Proclamation, November 4, 1881.

Wherefore I do recommend that the day above designated be observed throughout the country as a day of national thanksgiving and prayer, and that the people, ceasing from their daily labors and meeting in accordance with their several forms of worship, draw near to the throne of Almighty God, offering to him praise and gratitude for the manifold goodness which he has vouchsafed to us and praying that his blessings and his mercies may continue.

—CHESTER A. ARTHUR, 21st U.S. president.
Thanksgiving Day Proclamation, October 25, 1882.

I do therefore recommend that on the day above appointed the people rest from their accustomed labors and, meeting in their several places of worship, express their devout gratitude to God that he hath dealt so bountifully with this nation and pray that his grace and favor abide with it forever.

CHESTER A. ARTHUR, 21st U.S. president.
Thanksgiving Day Proclamation, October 26, 1883.

The season is nigh when it is the yearly wont of this people to observe a day appointed for that purpose by the president as an especial occasion for thanksgiving unto God.

—CHESTER A. ARTHUR, 21st U.S. president.
Thanksgiving Day Proclamation, November 7, 1884.

It is fitting and proper that a nation thus favored should on one day in every year, for that purpose especially appointed, publicly acknowledge the goodness of God and return thanks to him for all his gracious gifts.

—GROVER CLEVELAND, 22nd & 24th U.S. president.
Thanksgiving Day Proclamation, November 2, 1885.

And while we contemplate the infinite power of God in earthquake, flood, and storm let the grateful hearts of those who have been shielded from harm through his mercy be turned in sympathy and kindness toward those who have suffered through his visitations.

—GROVER CLEVELAND, 22nd & 24th U.S. president.
Thanksgiving Day Proclamation, November 1, 1886.

The goodness and the mercy of God, which have followed the American people during all the days of the past year, claim their grateful recognition and humble acknowledgment. By his omnipotent power he has protected us from war and pestilence and from every national calamity; by his gracious favor the earth has yielded a generous return to the labor of the husbandman, and every path of honest toil has led to comfort and contentment; by his loving kindness the hearts of our people have been replenished with fraternal sentiment and patriotic endeavor, and by his unerring guidance we have been directed in the way of national prosperity.

—GROVER CLEVELAND, 22nd & 24th U.S. president.
Thanksgiving Day Proclamation, October 25, 1887.

In acknowledgment of all that God has done for us as a nation, and to the end that on an appointed day the united prayers and praise of a grateful country may reach the throne of grace, I, Grover Cleveland, president of the United States, do hereby designate and set apart Thursday, the 29th day of November instant, as a day of thanksgiving and prayer, to be kept and observed throughout the land.

—GROVER CLEVELAND, 22nd & 24th U.S. president.
Thanksgiving Day Proclamation, November 1, 1888.

A highly favored people, mindful of their dependence on the bounty of Divine Providence, should seek fitting occasion to testify gratitude and ascribe praise to him who is the author of their many blessings. It behooves us, then, to look back with thankful hearts over the past year and bless God for his infinite mercy in vouchsafing to our land enduring peace, to our people freedom from pestilence and famine, to our husbandmen abundant harvests, and to them that labor a recompense of their toil.

—BENJAMIN HARRISON, 23rd U.S. president and ABS vice president. Thanksgiving Day Proclamation, November 1, 1889.

By the grace and favor of Almighty God, the people of this nation have been led to the closing days of the passing year, which has been full of the blessings of peace and the comforts of plenty. Bountiful compensation has come to us for the work of our minds and of our hands in every department of human industry.

—BENJAMIN HARRISON, 23rd U.S. president and ABS vice president. Thanksgiving Day Proclamation, November 8, 1890.

To God, the beneficent and the all-wise, who makes the labors of men to be fruitful, redeems their losses by his grace, and the measure of whose giving is as much beyond the thoughts of man as it is beyond his deserts, the praise and gratitude of the people of this favored nation are justly due.

—BENJAMIN HARRISON, 23rd U.S. president and ABS vice president. Thanksgiving Day Proclamation, November 13, 1891.

The gifts of God to our people during the past year have been so abundant and so special that the spirit of devout thanksgiving awaits not a call, but only the appointment of a day when it may have a common expression. He has stayed the pestilence at our door; he has given us more love for the free civil institutions in the creation of which his directing providence was so conspicuous; he has awakened a deeper reverence for law; he has widened our philanthropy by a call to succor the distress in other lands; he has blessed our schools and is bringing forward a patriotic and God-fearing generation to execute his great and benevolent designs for our country; he has given us great increase in material wealth and a wide diffusion of contentment and comfort in the homes of our people; he has given his grace to the sorrowing.

—BENJAMIN HARRISON, 23rd U.S. president and ABS vice president. Thanksgiving Day Proclamation, November 4, 1892.

While the American people should every day remember with praise and thanksgiving the divine goodness and mercy which have followed them since their beginning as a nation, it is fitting that one day in each year should be especially devoted to the contemplation of the blessings we have received from the hand of God and to the grateful acknowledgment of his loving kindness.

—GROVER CLEVELAND, 22nd & 24th U.S. president. Thanksgiving Day Proclamation, November 3, 1893.

And with our thanksgiving let us pray that these blessings may be multiplied unto us, that our national conscience may be quickened to a better recognition of the power and goodness of God, and that in our national life we may clearer see and closer follow the path of righteousness.

—GROVER CLEVELAND, 22nd & 24th U.S. president. Thanksgiving Day Proclamation, November 1, 1894.

And with our thanksgiving let us humbly beseech the Lord to so incline the hearts of our people unto him that he will not leave us nor forsake us as a nation, but will continue to us his mercy and protecting care, guiding us in the path of national prosperity and happiness, enduing us with rectitude and virtue, and keeping alive within us a patriotic love for the free institutions which have been given to us as our national heritage.

> —GROVER CLEVELAND, 22nd & 24th U.S. president.
> Thanksgiving Day Proclamation, November 4, 1895.

And let us, through the mediation of him who has taught us how to pray, implore the forgiveness of our sins and a continuation of heavenly favor.

> —GROVER CLEVELAND, 22nd & 24th U.S. president.
> Thanksgiving Day Proclamation, November 4, 1896.

For these great benefits it is our duty to praise the Lord in a spirit of humility and gratitude, and to offer up to him our most earnest supplications. That we may acknowledge our obligation as a people to him who has so graciously granted us the blessings of free government and material prosperity, I, William McKinley, president of the United States, do hereby designate and set apart Thursday, the twenty-fifth day of November, for national thanksgiving and prayer, which all of the people are invited to observe with appropriate religious services in their respective places of worship.

> —WILLIAM MCKINLEY, 25th U.S. president.
> Thanksgiving Day Proclamation, October 29, 1897.

And above all, let us pray with earnest fervor that he, the Dispenser of All good, may speedily remove from us the untold afflictions of war and bring to our dear land the blessings of restored peace and to all the domain now ravaged by the cruel strife the priceless boon of security and tranquillity.

—WILLIAM MCKINLEY, 25th U.S. president.
Address to the People for Thanksgiving and Prayer, July 6, 1898.

I do therefore invite all my fellow-citizens, as well as those who may be at sea or sojourning in foreign lands as those at home, to set apart and observe Thursday, the 24th day of November, as a day of national thanksgiving, to come together in their several places of worship for a service of praise and thanks to almighty God for all the blessings of the year, for the mildness of the seasons and the fruitfulness of the soil, for the continued prosperity of the people, for the devotion and valor of our countrymen, for the glory of our victory and the hope of a righteous peace, and to pray that the Divine guidance which has brought us heretofore to safety and honor may be graciously continued in the years to come.

—WILLIAM MCKINLEY, 25th U.S. president.
Thanksgiving Day Proclamation, October 28, 1898.

For these reasons and countless others, I, William McKinley, president of the United States, do hereby name Thursday, the thirtieth day of November next, as a day of general thanksgiving and prayer, to be observed as such by all people on this continent and in our newly acquired islands, as well as by those who may be at sea or sojourning in foreign lands; and I advise that on this day religious exercises shall be conducted in the churches or meeting places of all denominations, in order that in the social features of the day its real significance may not be lost sight of, but prayers may be offered to the Most high for a continuance of the Divine Guidance without which man's efforts are vain, and for Divine consolation to those whose kindred and friends have sacrificed their lives for country.

WILLIAM MCKINLEY, 25th U.S. president.
Thanksgiving Day Proclamation, October 25, 1899.

It has pleased Almighty God to bring our nation in safety and honor through another year. The works of religion and charity have everywhere been manifest. Our country through all its extent has been blessed with abundant harvests.

—WILLIAM MCKINLEY, 25th U.S. president.
Thanksgiving Day Proclamation, October 29, 1900.

We can best prove our thankfulness to the Almighty by the way in which on this earth and at this time each of us does his duty to his fellowmen.

—THEODORE ROOSEVELT, 26th U.S. president.
Thanksgiving Day Proclamation, November 2, 1901.

The year that has just closed has been one of peace and of overflowing plenty. Rarely has any people enjoyed greater prosperity than we are now enjoying. For this we render heartfelt thanks to the Giver of Good; and we will seek to praise him, not by words only, but by deeds, by the way in which we do our duty to ourselves and to our fellowmen.

—THEODORE ROOSEVELT, 26th U.S. president.
Thanksgiving Day Proclamation, October 29, 1902.

Therefore, in thanking God for the mercies extended to us in the past, we beseech him that he may not withhold them in the future, and that our hearts may be roused to war steadfastly for good and against all the forces of evil, public and private. We pray for strength and light, so that in the coming years we may with cleanliness, fearlessness, and wisdom, do our allotted work on the earth in such manner as to show that we are not altogether unworthy of the blessings we have received.

—THEODORE ROOSEVELT, 26th U.S. president.
Thanksgiving Day Proclamation, October 31, 1903.

It has pleased Almighty God to bring the American people in safety and honor through another year, and, in accordance with the long unbroken custom handed down to us by our forefathers, the time has come when a special day shall be set apart in which to thank him, who holds all nations in the hollow of his hand, for the mercies thus vouchsafed to us.

—THEODORE ROOSEVELT, 26th U.S. president.
Thanksgiving Day Proclamation, November 1, 1904.

It is eminently fitting that once a year our people should set apart a day for praise and thanksgiving to the Giver of Good, and at the same time that they express their thankfulness for the abundant mercies received, should manfully acknowledge their shortcomings and pledge themselves solemnly and in good faith to strive to overcome them.

—THEODORE ROOSEVELT, 26th U.S. president.
Thanksgiving Day Proclamation, November 2, 1905.

The time of year has come when, in accordance with the wise custom of our forefathers, it becomes my duty to set aside a special day of thanksgiving and praise to the Almighty because of the blessings we have received, and of prayer that these blessings may be continued.

—THEODORE ROOSEVELT, 26th U.S. president.
Thanksgiving Day Proclamation, October 22, 1906.

Accordingly, I hereby set apart Thursday, the 29th day of November next, as a day of Thanksgiving and supplication, on which the people shall meet in their home or their churches, devoutly to acknowledge all that has been given them, and to pray that they may in addition receive the power to use these gifts aright.

—THEODORE ROOSEVELT, 26th U.S. president.
Thanksgiving Day Proclamation, October 22, 1906.

Ever throughout the ages, at all times and among all peoples, prosperity has been fraught with danger, and it behooves us to beseech the Giver of all things that we may not fall into love of ease and luxury; that we may not lose our sense of moral responsibility; that we may not forget our duty to God, and to our neighbor.

—THEODORE ROOSEVELT, 26th U.S. president.
Thanksgiving Day Proclamation, October 26, 1907.

For the very reason that in material well-being we have thus abounded, we owe it to the Almighty to show equal progress in moral and spiritual things.

—THEODORE ROOSEVELT, 26th U.S. president.
Thanksgiving Day Proclamation, October 31, 1908.

Therefore, I hereby appoint Thursday, the 25th day of November, as a day of general Thanksgiving, and I call upon the people on that day, laying aside their usual vocations, to repair to their churches and unite in appropriate services of praise and thanks to Almighty God.

—WILLIAM TAFT, 27th U.S. president.
Thanksgiving Day Proclamation, November 15, 1909.

These blessings have not descended upon us in restricted measure, but overflow and abound. They are the blessings and bounty of God.

—WILLIAM TAFT, 27th U.S. president.
Thanksgiving Day Proclamation, November 5, 1910.

Rich in the priceless possessions and abundant resources wherewith the unstinted bounty of God has endowed us, we are unselfishly glad when other peoples pass onward to prosperity and peace. That the great privileges we enjoy may continue and that each coming year may see our country more firmly established in the regard and esteem of our fellow nations is the prayer that should arise in every thankful heart.

—WILLIAM TAFT, 27th U.S. president.
Thanksgiving Day Proclamation, October 30, 1911.

A God-fearing nation, like ours, owes it to its inborn and sincere sense of moral duty to testify its devout gratitude to the All-giver for the countless benefits it has enjoyed.

—WILLIAM TAFT, 27th U.S. president.
Thanksgiving Day Proclamation, November 7, 1912.

Now, therefore I, Woodrow Wilson, president of the United States of America, do hereby designate Thursday the twenty-seventh of November next as a day of thanksgiving and prayer, and invite the people throughout the land to cease from their wonted occupations and in their several homes and places of worship render thanks to almighty God.

—WOODROW WILSON, 28th U.S. president.
Thanksgiving Day Proclamation, 1913.

It has long been the honoured custom of our people to turn in the fruitful autumn of the year in praise and thanksgiving to Almighty God for his many blessings and mercies to us as a nation.

WOODROW WILSON, 28th U.S. president.
Thanksgiving Day Proclamation, October 28, 1914.

Now, therefore, I, Woodrow Wilson, president of the United States of America, do hereby designate Thursday the twenty-fifth of November next as a day of thanksgiving and prayer, and invite the people throughout the land to cease from their wonted occupations and in their several homes and places of worship render thanks to Almighty God.

—WOODROW WILSON, 28th U.S. president.
Thanksgiving Day Proclamation, October 20, 1915.

Now, therefore, I, Woodrow Wilson, president of the United States of America, do appoint Thursday, the thirtieth of November, as a day of National Thanksgiving and Prayer, and urge and advise the people to resort to their several places of worship on that day to render thanks to Almighty

God for the blessings of peace and unbroken prosperity which he has bestowed upon our beloved country in such unstinted measure.

—WOODROW WILSON, 28th U.S. president.
Thanksgiving Day Proclamation, November 17, 1916.

And while we render thanks for these things, let us pray Almighty God that in all humbleness of spirit we may look always to him for guidance; that we may be kept constant in the spirit and purpose of service; that by his grace our minds may be directed and our hands strengthened; and that in his good time liberty and security and peace and the comradeship of a common justice may be vouchsafed all the nations of the earth.

—WOODROW WILSON, 28th U.S. president.
Thanksgiving Day Proclamation, November 7, 1917.

While we render thanks for these things, let us not forget to seek the Divine guidance in the performance of those duties, and divine mercy and forgiveness for all errors of act or purpose, and pray that in all that we do we shall strengthen the ties of friendship and mutual respect upon which we must assist to build the new structure of peace and good will among the nations.

—WOODROW WILSON, 28th U.S. president.
Thanksgiving Day Proclamation, November 16, 1918.

The season of the year has again arrived when the people of the United States are accustomed to unite in giving thanks to Almighty God for the blessings which he has conferred upon our country during the twelve months that have passed. A year ago our people poured out their hearts in praise and thanksgiving that through divine aid the right was victorious and peace had come to the nations which had so courageously struggled in defense of human liberty and justice.

—WOODROW WILSON, 28th U.S. president.
Thanksgiving Day Proclamation, November 5, 1919.

In a spirit, then, of devotion and stewardship we should give thanks in our hearts, and dedicate ourselves to the service of God's merciful and loving purposes to his children.

—WOODROW WILSON, 28th U.S. president.
Thanksgiving Day Proclamation, November 12, 1920.

Let our prayers be raised, for direction in the right paths. Under God, our responsibility is great; to our own first, to all men afterward; to all mankind in God's own justice.

—WARREN G. HARDING, 29th U.S. president.
Thanksgiving Day Proclamation, October 31, 1921.

I recommend that the people gather at their family altars and in their houses of worship to render thanks to God for the bounties they have enjoyed and to petition that these may be continued in the year before us.

—WARREN G. HARDING, 29th U.S. president.
Thanksgiving Day Proclamation, November 2, 1922.

It is urged that the people, gathering in their homes and their usual places of worship, give expression to their gratitude for the benefits and blessings that a gracious Providence has bestowed upon them, and seek the guidance of Almighty God, that they may deserve a continuance of his favor.

—CALVIN COOLIDGE, 30th U.S. president.
Thanksgiving Day Proclamation, November 5, 1923.

An abundant prosperity has overspread the land. We shall do well to accept all these favors and bounties with a becoming humility, and dedicate them to the service of the righteous cause of the Giver of all good and perfect gifts. As the nation has prospered let all the people show that they are worthy to prosper by rededicating America to the service of God and man.

—CALVIN COOLIDGE, 30th U.S. president.
Thanksgiving Day Proclamation, November 5, 1924.

As we have grown and prospered in material things, so also should we progress in moral and spiritual things. We are a God-fearing people who should set ourselves against evil and strive for righteousness in living, and observing the Golden Rule we should from our abundance help and serve those less fortunately placed. We should bow in gratitude to God for his many favors.

—CALVIN COOLIDGE, 30th U.S. president.
Thanksgiving Day Proclamation, October 26, 1925.

We are not unmindful of the gratitude we owe to God for his watchful care which has pointed out to us the ways of peace and happiness; we should not fail in our acknowledgment of his divine favor which has bestowed upon us so many blessings.

—CALVIN COOLIDGE, 30th U.S. president.
Thanksgiving Day Proclamation, October 30, 1926.

While in gratitude we rejoice, we should humbly pray that we may be worthy of a continuation of Divine favor.

—CALVIN COOLIDGE, 30th U.S. president.
Thanksgiving Day Proclamation, October 26, 1927.

Through his Divine favor, peace and tranquillity have reigned throughout the land; he has protected our country as a whole against pestilence and disaster and has directed us in the ways of National prosperity.

—CALVIN COOLIDGE, 30th U.S. president.
Thanksgiving Day Proclamation, October 23, 1928.

We should accept these blessings with resolution to devote them to service of Almighty God.

—HERBERT HOOVER, 31st U.S. president.
Thanksgiving Day Proclamation, November 5, 1929.

Notwithstanding that our forefathers endured the hardships and privations of a primitive life, surrounded by dangers and solaced only with meager comforts, they nevertheless bequeathed to us a custom of devoting one day of every year to universal thanksgiving to Almighty God, for the blessing of life itself and the means to sustain it, for the sanctuary of home and the joys that pervade it, and for the mercies of his protection from accident, sickness, or death.

—HERBERT HOOVER, 31st U.S. president.
Thanksgiving Day Proclamation, November 6, 1930.

We approach the season when, according to custom dating from the garnering of the first harvest by our forefathers in the New

World, a day is set apart to give thanks even amid hardships to Almighty God for our temporal and spiritual blessings.

—HERBERT HOOVER, 31st U.S. president.
Thanksgiving Day Proclamation, November 3, 1931.

Whereas at this season of the year our people for generations past have always turned their thoughts to thankfulness for the blessings of Almighty God. . . .

—HERBERT HOOVER, 31st U.S. president.
Thanksgiving Day Proclamation, November 3, 1932.

May we on that day in our churches and in our homes give humble thanks for the blessings bestowed upon us during the year past by Almighty God.

—FRANKLIN D. ROOSEVELT, 32nd U.S. president.
Thanksgiving Day Proclamation, November 21, 1933.

We can truly say, "What profiteth it a nation if it gain the whole world and lose its own soul." With gratitude in our hearts for what has already been achieved, may we, with the help of God, dedicate ourselves anew to work for the betterment of mankind.

—FRANKLIN D. ROOSEVELT, 32nd U.S. president.
Thanksgiving Day Proclamation, November 15, 1934.

Let us then on the day appointed offer our devotions and our humble thanks to Almighty God and pray that the people of America will be guided by him in helping their fellow men.

—FRANKLIN D. ROOSEVELT, 32nd U.S. president.
Thanksgiving Day Proclamation, November 12, 1935.

Let us, therefore, on the day appointed, each in his own way, but together as a whole people, make due expression of our thanksgiving and humbly endeavor to follow in the footsteps of Almighty God.

—FRANKLIN D. ROOSEVELT, 32nd U.S. president.
Thanksgiving Day Proclamation, November 12, 1936.

Let us, therefore, on the day appointed forego our usual occupations and, in our accustomed places of worship, each in his own way, humbly acknowledge the mercy of God, from whom comes every good and perfect gift.

—FRANKLIN D. ROOSEVELT, 32nd U.S. president.
Thanksgiving Day Proclamation, November 9, 1937.

In our deepest natures, in our very souls, we, like all mankind since the earliest origin of mankind, turn to God in time of trouble and in time of happiness. "In God We Trust."

—FRANKLIN D. ROOSEVELT, 32nd U.S. president.
Thanksgiving Day Proclamation, November 19, 1938.

Let us, on the day set aside for this purpose, give thanks to the Ruler of the Universe for the strength which he has vouchsafed us to carry on our daily labors and for the hope that lives within us of the coming of a day when peace and the productive activities of peace shall reign on every continent.

—FRANKLIN D. ROOSEVELT, 32nd U.S. president.
Thanksgiving Day Proclamation, October 31, 1939.

On the same day, in the same hour, let us pray: Almighty God, who hast given us this good land for our heritage; We humbly beseech Thee that we may always prove ourselves a people mindful of Thy favor and glad to do Thy will. Bless our land with honourable industry, sound learning, and pure manners.

—FRANKLIN D. ROOSEVELT, 32nd U.S. president.
Thanksgiving Day Proclamation, November 9, 1940.

Let us ask the Divine Blessing on our decision and determination to protect our way of life against the forces of evil and slavery which seek in these days to encompass us. On the day appointed for this purpose, let us reflect at our homes or places of worship on the goodness of God and, in giving thanks, let us pray for a speedy end to strife and the establishment on earth of freedom, brotherhood, and justice for enduring time.

—FRANKLIN D. ROOSEVELT, 32nd U.S. president.
Thanksgiving Day Proclamation, November 8, 1941.

It is fitting that we recall now the reverent words of George Washington, "Almighty God, we make our earnest prayer that Thou wilt keep the United States in Thy holy protection," and that every American in his own way lift his voice to heaven.

—FRANKLIN D. ROOSEVELT, 32nd U.S. president.
Proclamation 2571 on Thanksgiving Day, November 26, 1942.

God's help to us has been great in this year of march towards world-wide liberty.

—FRANKLIN D. ROOSEVELT, 32nd U.S. president.
Thanksgiving Day Proclamation, November 11, 1943.

To the end that we may bear more earnest witness to our gratitude to Almighty God, I suggest a nationwide reading of the holy Scriptures during the period from Thanksgiving Day to Christmas.

Let every man of every creed go to his own version of the Scriptures for a renewed and strengthening contact with those eternal truths and majestic principles which have inspired such measure of true greatness as this nation has achieved.

—FRANKLIN D. ROOSEVELT, 32nd U.S. president.
Thanksgiving Day Proclamation, November 1, 1944.

May we on that day, in our homes and in our places of worship, individually and as groups, express our humble thanks to Almighty God for the abundance of our blessings and may we on that occasion rededicate ourselves to those high principles of citizenship for which so many splendid Americans have recently given all.

—HARRY TRUMAN, 33rd U.S. president.
Proclamation 2673 on Thanksgiving Day, November 12, 1945.

At this season, when the year is drawing to a close, tradition suggests and our hearts require that we render humble devotion to Almighty God for the mercies bestowed upon us by his goodness.

—HARRY TRUMAN, 33rd U.S. president.
Thanksgiving Day Proclamation, October 28, 1946.

Older than our nation itself is the hallowed custom of resting from our labors for one day at harvest time and of dedicating that day to expressions of gratitude to Almighty God for the many blessings which he has heaped upon us. Now, as the cycle of the year nears completion, it is fitting that we should lift up our hearts again in special prayers.

—HARRY TRUMAN, 33rd U.S. president.
Thanksgiving Day Proclamation, November 10, 1947.

We pray this year not only in the spirit of thanksgiving but also as suppliants for wisdom in our approach to the problems confronting this Nation. Believing in the dignity of man and his right to live in freedom and peace, we ask divine guidance in helping to safeguard these gifts for ourselves and other peoples of the earth.

—HARRY TRUMAN, 33rd U.S. president.
Thanksgiving Day Proclamation, November 12, 1948.

There should be in the hearts of all good men and true a realization that as the Psalmist said: "There is no king saved by the multitude of an host; a mighty man is not delivered by much strength." Humbly grateful for these benefactions, may we add to our prayers of thanksgiving a plea for divine guidance of the leaders of our Nation and the leaders of all other nations in their efforts to promote peace and freedom for all men.

—HARRY TRUMAN, 33rd U.S. president.
Thanksgiving Day Proclamation, November 10, 1949.

Contemplating these blessings with humility, we have a deepened sense of our responsibility to serve unselfishly, and we pray to Almighty God for wisdom in our relations with our fellow men.

—HARRY TRUMAN, 33rd U.S. president.
Thanksgiving Day Proclamation, October 19, 1950.

Let us all on that day, in our homes and in our places of worship, individually and in groups, render homage to Almighty God. Let us recall the words of the Psalmist, "O give thanks unto the Lord; for he is good: for his mercy endureth forever." Let us also, on the appointed day, seek divine aid in the quest for peace.

—HARRY TRUMAN, 33rd U.S. president.
Thanksgiving Day Proclamation, November 1, 1951.

On that day let us, with a full awareness of our privileges and a deepening sense of the obligations which they entail, each in his own way, but together as a whole people, give due expression to our thanks, and let us humbly endeavor to follow the paths of righteousness in obedience to the will of Almighty God.

—HARRY TRUMAN, 33rd U.S. president.
Thanksgiving Day Proclamation, November 8, 1952.

For the courage and vision of our forebears who settled a wilderness and founded a Nation; for the "blessings of liberty" which the framers of our Constitution sought to secure for themselves and for their posterity, and which are so abundantly realized in our land today; for the unity of spirit which has made our country strong; and for the continuing faith under his guidance that has kept us a religious people with freedom of worship for all, we should kneel in humble thanksgiving.

—DWIGHT EISENHOWER, 34th U.S. president.
Thanksgiving Day Proclamation, November 7, 1953.

We are grateful for the innumerable daily manifestations of Divine goodness in affairs both public and private, for equal

opportunities for all to labor and to serve, and for the continuance of those homely joys and satisfactions which enrich
our lives.

—DWIGHT EISENHOWER, 34th U.S. president.
Thanksgiving Day Proclamation, November 6, 1954.

Let us, on the appointed day, in our homes and our accustomed
places of worship, each according to his own faith, bow before
God and give him humble thanks.

—DWIGHT EISENHOWER, 34th U.S. president.
Thanksgiving Day Proclamation, October 11, 1955.

Humbly aware that we are a people greatly blessed, both materially and spiritually, let us pray this year not only in the spirit
of thanksgiving but also as suppliants for God's guidance, to
the end that we may follow the course of righteousness and be
worthy of his favor.

—DWIGHT EISENHOWER, 34th U.S. president.
Thanksgiving Day Proclamation, November 12, 1956.

It behooves us to dwell upon the deep religious convictions of
those who formed our Nation out of a wilderness, and to recall
that our leaders throughout the succeeding generations have
relied upon Almighty God for vision and strength of purpose.

—DWIGHT EISENHOWER, 34th U.S. president.
Thanksgiving Day Proclamation, November 8, 1957.

Let us be especially grateful for the religious heritage bequeathed
us by our forebears as exemplified by the Pilgrims, who, after

the gathering of their first harvest, set apart a special day for rendering thanks to God for the bounties vouchsafed to them.

> —DWIGHT EISENHOWER, 34th U.S. president.
> Thanksgiving Day Proclamation, October 31, 1958.

On that day let us gather in sanctuaries dedicated to worship and in homes devoted to family sharing and community service to express our gratitude for the inestimable blessings of God; and let us earnestly pray that he continue to guide and sustain us in the great unfinished task of achieving peace among men and nations.

> —DWIGHT EISENHOWER, 34th U.S. president.
> Thanksgiving Day Proclamation, November 5, 1959.

President Lincoln wisely knew that a man's declaration of his gratitude to God is, in itself, an act which strengthens the thanksgiver because it renews his own realization of his relationship to his God.

> —RICHARD NIXON, 37th U.S. president.
> Thanksgiving Day Proclamation, November 5, 1970

Yet, because mankind was not created merely to survive, in the fact of all hardship and suffering, these men and women—and those of the other early settlements—prevailed. And the settlers gathered to give thanks for God's bounty, for the blessings of life itself, and for the freedom which they so cherished that no hardship could quench it. And now their heritage is ours.

> —RICHARD NIXON, 37th U.S. president.
> Thanksgiving Day Proclamation, November 5, 1971.

From Moses at the Red Sea to Jesus preparing to feed the multitudes, the Scriptures summon us to words and deeds of gratitude, even before divine blessings are fully perceived. From Washington kneeling at Valley Forge to the prayer of an astronaut circling the moon, our own history repeats that summons and proves its practicality.

—RICHARD NIXON, 37th U.S. president.
Thanksgiving Day Proclamation, November 17, 1972.

Throughout our history, each generation has endured hardship and loss, but our faith and trust in God's providence has remained undiminished. At this first thanksgiving in twelve years in which the United States will have been at peace, we see that God's grace also remain undiminished. For this we give thanks.

—RICHARD NIXON, 37th U.S. president.
Thanksgiving Day Proclamation, November 16, 1973.

But the fundamental meaning of Thanksgiving still remains the same. It is a time when the differences of a diverse people are forgotten and all Americans join in giving thanks to God for the blessings we share—the blessings of freedom, opportunity and abundance that make America so unique.

—GERALD FORD, 38th U.S. president.
Thanksgiving Day Proclamation, November 11, 1974.

Let each of us, in his own way, join in expressing personal gratitude for the blessings of liberty and peace we enjoy today. In so doing, let us reaffirm our belief in a dynamic spirit that will continue to nurture and guide us as we prepare to meet the challenge of our third century.

—GERALD FORD, 38th U.S. president.
Thanksgiving Day Proclamation, November 4, 1975.

The early settlers of this land possessed an unconquerable spirit and a reliance on Divine Providence that remains a part of the American character. That reliance, coupled with a belief in ourselves and a love of individual freedom, has brought this nation through two centuries of progress and kept us strong.

—GERALD FORD, 38th U.S. president.
Thanksgiving Day Proclamation, October 25, 1976.

Although the first years of America's struggle for independence were often disheartening, our forebears never lost faith in the Creator, in their cause, or in themselves.

—JIMMY CARTER, 39th U.S. president.
Thanksgiving Day Proclamation, November 11, 1977.

Two hundred years ago the Continental Congress proclaimed a day of thanks, and asked for deliverance from war. This year, let us observe Thanksgiving in the spirit of peace and sharing, by declaring it a day of Thankful Giving, a day upon which the American people share their plenty with the hungry of other lands.

—JIMMY CARTER, 39th U.S. president.
Thanksgiving Day Proclamation, October 20, 1978.

Thanksgiving Day was first celebrated in this land not in a moment of unbridled triumph, but in times of great adversity. The colonies of Massachusetts and Virginia had few material possessions to help them face the dangers of the wilderness. They had no certainty that the harvests for which they gave thanks would be sufficient to carry them through a long winter. Yet they gave thanks to God for what they had and for the hope of this new land.

—JIMMY CARTER, 39th U.S. president.
Thanksgiving Day Proclamation, September 28, 1979.

As we pause on Thanksgiving to offer thanks to God, we should not forget that we also owe thanks to this country's forefathers who had the vision to join together in Thanksgiving, and who gave us so much of the vision of brotherhood that is ours today.

—JIMMY CARTER, 39th U.S. president.
Thanksgiving Day Proclamation, November 13, 1980.

Let us recommit ourselves to that devotion to God and family that has played such an important role in making this a great Nation, and which will be needed as a source of strength if we are to remain a great people.

—RONALD REAGAN, 40th U.S. president.
Thanksgiving Day Proclamation, November 12, 1981.

I have always believed that this anointed land was set apart in an uncommon way, that a divine plan placed this great continent here between the oceans to be found by people from every corner of the Earth who had a special love of faith and freedom. Our pioneers asked that he would work his will in our daily lives so America would be a land of morality, fairness, and freedom.

—RONALD REAGAN, 40th U.S. president.
Thanksgiving Day Proclamation, September 27, 1982.

As was written in the first Thanksgiving Proclamation 120 years ago, "No human counsel hath devised nor hath any mortal hand worked out these great things. They are the gracious gifts of the Most high God." God has blessed America and her people, and it is appropriate we recognize this bounty.

—RONALD REAGAN, 40th U.S. president.
Thanksgiving Day Proclamation, September 15, 1983.

This year we can be especially thankful that real gratitude to God is inscribed, not in proclamations of government, but in the hearts of all our people who come from every race, culture, and creed on the face of the Earth. And as we pause to give thanks for our many gifts, let us be tempered by humility and by compassion for those in need, and let us reaffirm through prayer and action our determination to share our bounty with those less fortunate.

—RONALD REAGAN, 40th U.S. president.
Thanksgiving Day Proclamation, October 19, 1984.

Although the time and date of the first American thanksgiving observance may be uncertain, there is no question but that this treasured custom derives from our Judeo-Christian heritage.

"Unto Thee, O God, do we give thanks," the Psalmist sang, praising God not only for the "wondrous works" of his creation, but for loving guidance and deliverance from dangers.

—RONALD REAGAN, 40th U.S. president.
Thanksgiving Day Proclamation, November 15, 1985.

Perhaps no custom reveals our character as a Nation so clearly as our celebration of Thanksgiving Day. Rooted deeply in our Judeo-Christian heritage, the practice of offering thanksgiving underscores our unshakable belief in God as the foundation of our Nation and our firm reliance upon him from Whom all blessings flow. Both as individuals and as a people, we join with the Psalmist in song and praise: "Give thanks unto the Lord, for he is good."

—RONALD REAGAN, 40th U.S. president.
Thanksgiving Day Proclamation, October 13, 1986.

Thanksgiving Day is one of our most beloved holidays, an occasion set aside by Americans from earliest times to thank our Maker prayerfully and humbly for the blessings and the care he bestows on us and on our beautiful, bountiful land. Through the decades, through the centuries, in log cabins, country churches, cathedrals, homes, and halls, the American people have paused to give thanks to God, in time of peace and plenty or of danger and distress.

—RONALD REAGAN, 40th U.S. president.
Thanksgiving Day Proclamation, July 28, 1987.

Today, cognizant of our American heritage of freedom and opportunity, we are again called to gratitude, thanksgiving, and contrition. Thanksgiving Day summons every American to pause in the midst of activity, however necessary and valuable, to give simple and humble thanks to God. This gracious gratitude is the "service" of which Washington spoke. It is a service that opens our hearts to one another as members of a single family gathered around the bounteous table of God's Creation.

—RONALD REAGAN, 40th U.S. president.
Thanksgiving Day Proclamation, August 4, 1988.

Through the eloquent words of president Washington's initial Thanksgiving proclamation—the first under the Constitution—we are reminded of our dependence upon our heavenly Father and of the debt of gratitude we owe to him. "It is the Duty of all Nations," wrote Washington, "to acknowledge the Providence of almighty God, to obey his Will, to be grateful for his Benefits, and humbly to implore his Protection and Favor." Two hundred years later, we continue to offer thanks to the Almighty —not only for the material prosperity that our Nation enjoys, but also for the blessings of peace and freedom. Our Nation has no greater treasures than these.

—GEORGE H.W. BUSH, 41st U.S. president.
Thanksgiving Day Proclamation, November 17, 1989.

Acknowledging our dependence on the Almighty, obeying his Commandments, and reaching out to help those who do not share fully in this Nation's bounty is the most heartfelt and meaningful answer we can give to the timeless appeal of the Psalmist: "O give thanks to the Lord for he is good: for his steadfast love endures forever."

—GEORGE H.W. BUSH, 41st U.S. president.
Thanksgiving Day Proclamation, November 14, 1990.

Finally, as we gather with family and friends on Thanksgiving, we know that our greatest blessings are not necessarily material ones. Indeed, perhaps the best thing about this occasion is that it reminds us that God loves each and every one of us. Like a faithful and loving parent, he always stands ready to comfort, guide, and forgive. That is our real cause for Thanksgiving, today and every day of our lives.

—GEORGE H.W. BUSH, 41st U.S. president.
Thanksgiving Day Proclamation, November 25, 1991.

Since the earliest days of our Republic, Americans have been deeply aware of our indebtedness to the Almighty and our obligations as a people he has blessed. Even in the course of long, difficult journeys to these shores, our ancestors gratefully acknowledged the sustaining power of God—and the faithfulness they owed in return.

—GEORGE H.W. BUSH, 41st U.S. president.
Thanksgiving Day Proclamation, November 20, 1992.

This is the true spirit of Thanksgiving: acknowledging God's graciousness, and in response, reaching out in service to others. This spirit was apparent in Plymouth, Massachusetts, in 1621, when Pilgrim immigrants sat down with native Americans and celebrated their common harvest.

—WILLIAM CLINTON, 42nd U.S. president.
Thanksgiving Day Proclamation, November 17, 1993.

It is our great fortune to live in a country of abundance and promise—a land of freedom for all. Still only a few generations removed from our Nation's founders, we continue to blaze a trail toward stability and justice. Aspiring to lift ourselves closer to God's grace, we remain determined to ease the pain of the many people who know only poverty and despair. Clearly, ours is an unfinished journey.

—WILLIAM CLINTON, 42nd U.S. president.
Thanksgiving Day Proclamation, October 27, 1994.

This cherished season also calls us to look forward to the challenges that lie before us as individuals and as a country. With God's help, we can shoulder our responsibilities so that future generations will inherit the wealth of opportunities we now enjoy. In everything we do, we must plan for the Thanksgivings to come and continue our efforts to build an America where everyone has a place at the table and a fair share in our Nation's harvest.

—WILLIAM CLINTON, 42nd U.S. president.
Thanksgiving Day Proclamation, November 9, 1995.

Let us now, this Thanksgiving Day, reawaken ourselves and our neighbors and our communities to the genius of our founders in daring to build the world's first constitutional democracy on the foundation of trust and thanks to God. Out of our right and proper rejoicing on Thanksgiving Day, let us give our own thanks to God and reaffirm our love of family, neighbor, and community. Each of us can be an instrument of blessing to those we touch this Thanksgiving Day—and every day of the year.

—WILLIAM CLINTON, 42nd U.S. president.
Thanksgiving Day Proclamation, November 11, 1996.

And, like the Pilgrims who celebrated Thanksgiving more than 300 years ago, we thank God for bringing us safely to the threshold of a new world, full of exhilarating challenge and promise.

—WILLIAM CLINTON, 42nd U.S. president.
Thanksgiving Day Proclamation, November 21, 1997.

I encourage all the people of the United States to assemble in their homes, places of worship, or community centers to share the spirit of goodwill and prayer; to express heartfelt thanks to God for the many blessings he has bestowed upon us; and to reach out in true gratitude and friendship to our brothers and sisters across this land who, together, comprise our great American family.

—WILLIAM CLINTON, 42nd U.S. president.
Thanksgiving Day Proclamation, November 17, 1998.

As we acknowledge the past, we do so knowing that the individual blessings for which we give thanks may have changed, but our gratitude to God and our commitment to our fellow Americans remain constant.

—WILLIAM CLINTON, 42nd U.S. president.
Thanksgiving Day Proclamation, November 20, 1999.

I encourage all the people of the United States to assemble in their homes, places of worship, and community centers to share the spirit of fellowship and prayer and to reinforce the ties of family and community; to express heartfelt thanks to God for our many blessings; and to reach out in gratitude and friendship to our brothers and sisters across this land who, together, comprise our great American family.

—WILLIAM CLINTON, 42nd U.S. president.
Thanksgiving Day Proclamation, November 17, 2000.

President Lincoln asked God to "heal the wounds of the nation and to restore it as soon as may be consistent with the Divine purposes to the full enjoyment of peace, harmony, tranquillity, and Union." As we recover from the terrible tragedies of September 11, Americans of every belief and heritage give thanks to God for the many blessings we enjoy as a free, faithful, and fair-minded land.

—GEORGE W. BUSH, 43rd U.S. president.
Thanksgiving Day Proclamation, November 16, 2001.

As the Pilgrims did almost four centuries ago, we gratefully give thanks this year for the beauty, abundance, and opportunity this great land offers. We also thank God for the blessings of freedom and prosperity; and, with gratitude and humility, we acknowledge the importance of faith in our lives.

—GEORGE W. BUSH, 43rd U.S. president.
Thanksgiving Day Proclamation, November 21, 2002.

This Thanksgiving, we again give thanks for all of our blessings and for the freedoms we enjoy every day. Our Founders thanked the Almighty and humbly sought his wisdom and blessing. May we always live by that same trust, and may God continue to watch over and bless the United States of America.

—GEORGE W. BUSH, 43rd U.S. president.
Thanksgiving Day Proclamation, November 21, 2003.

All across America, we gather this week with the people we love to give thanks to God for the blessings in our lives. We are grateful for our freedom, grateful for our families and friends, and grateful for the many gifts of America. On Thanksgiving Day, we acknowledge that all of these things, and life itself, come from the Almighty God. . . . On this Thanksgiving Day, we thank God for his blessings and ask him to continue to guide and watch over our Nation.

—GEORGE W. BUSH, 43rd U.S. president.
Thanksgiving Day Proclamation, November 23, 2004.

We give thanks to live in a country where freedom reigns, justice prevails, and hope prospers. We recognize that America is a better place when we answer the universal call to love a neighbor and help those in need. May God bless and guide the United States of America as we move forward.

—GEORGE W. BUSH, 43rd U.S. president.
Thanksgiving Day Proclamation, November 18, 2005.

Brad O'Leary serves as chairman of The PM Group and Publisher of *The O'Leary Report* (www.OLearyReport.com).

He is the executive producer or producer of numerous television specials and films, including *The Planet is Alive*, an ecumenical movie chronicling the life of Pope John Paul II. This groundbreaking film aired on Russian television on December 24, 1991—the first time a religious program was ever aired there.

O'Leary also conducts numerous charity projects in Vietnam, where he has worked closely with Vietnam's Catholic Cardinal Jean Baptiste Pham Minh Man on a number of projects, including the construction of a new seminary in Saigon, the sponsorship of two orphanages, and a school program for the Sisters of St. Vincent DePaul. His charity work in Vietnam first began when he collaborated with the U.S. Conference of Catholic Bishops and Bob Hope on a benefit for the boat people.

More recently, he brought a mission to Vietnam that resulted in 2,000 Vietnamese children receiving hearing aids that allowed them to hear for the first time. It later became a television special titled *The Gift of Hearing*.

O'Leary is also a bestselling author of 15 books, including: *The Audacity of Deceit: Barack Obama's War on American Values*; *Shut Up, America! The End of Free Speech*; and most recently, *America's War on Christianity* and *God and America's Leaders*.

Yes, the truth is out there. It just seems a lot harder to find these days.
In reality, it's only harder to *tell*.

The vaulted Information Age has warped into the Misinformation Age, plagued by
political correctness, pandemic propaganda and a compromised establishment press.

For many, intimidation, censorship ridicule and blackballing make truth too risky an investment.

At WND Books, we believe that silent submission amid raging deception carries
crushingly high costs. And truth is the only thing worth investing in.

WND BOOKS

Because the world has a right to know.

WND Books • A WorldNetDaily Company • Washington, DC • www.wndbooks.com

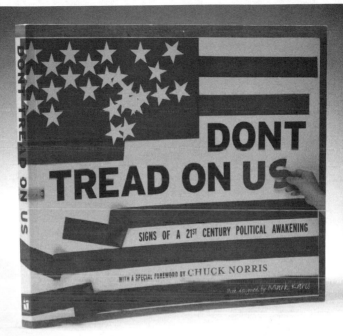

They come from the fields, and towns, and cities.

Sophisticates and the common.

They come to the power centers, exactly like their ancestors two centuries ago,

When American intuition tells the citizens that government by the people

and for the people is being threatened... they come to make their voices heard!

———

In this tribute to that spirit of America, *Don't Tread on US!* offers a pictorial record

of the new tea parties and their participants: classic signs that communicate most effectively

with our brethren all across the land who oppose what's going on in Washington today.

With a radical health-care agenda being marched across open territory,

those citizens — tens of millions of them — are rallying, and will make their voices heard.

The colonial heart still beats today, and the people have spoken: ***Don't Tread on US!***

WND Books

WND Books • A WorldNetDaily Company • Washington, DC • www.DontTreadOnUS.com

What does the tea party movement really stand for? And where does it go from here? Joseph Farah, founder, editor, and CEO of WorldNetDaily, was a tea partier before there was even a tea party movement. In his new book, Farah fleshes out the origins and evolution of the movement.

Defining the terms of the debate, the true meaning of independence, the danger in waiting for political messiahs, and the vital need for a spiritual core, Farah provides an inspired road map for this country's citizens to extricate themselves from the overreaching grip of government and reclaim the beliefs of the Founding Fathers.

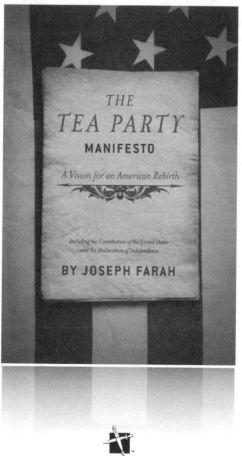

WND BOOKS

WND Books • A WorldNetDaily Company • Washington, DC • www.wndbooks.com

Intrigue cloaks the identity of the Antichrist, sparking copious interpretations of the prophecies
—and some consensus.

Joel Richardson shatters that consensus by illustrating a connection between the Biblical Antichrist
and a mysterious Islamic messiah figure called the Mahdi.

Charismatic, deceptive and rising up in the promise of peace, myriad eerie similarities exist between
Christian end-time prophesy and Islamic expectations of world domination.

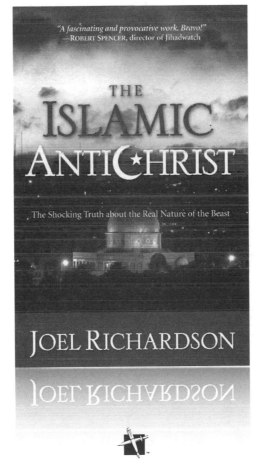

"A fascinating and provocative work. Bravo!"
—ROBERT SPENCER, director of Jihadwatch

THE
ISLAMIC
ANTIC★HRIST

The Shocking Truth about the Real Nature of the Beast

JOEL RICHARDSON

WND BOOKS

WND Books • A WorldNetDaily Company • Washington, DC • www.wndbooks.com

Not fit enough to survive.

That's what best-selling author Ray Comfort exposes after putting the evidence for evolution under the microscope.

If they dare to challenge their own hypothesis, even the most faithful of atheists will find the still-absent "missing link" a heavy cross to bear, and hunger for real Truth before meeting their Maker.